Praise For The Forever Penny

"After the loss of a loved one, every day can be a challenge. Rev. Allen C. Liles has composed a beautiful, heart-felt book about his own journey through profound grief that provides vital spiritual support and wisdom to navigate the difficult ups and downs. This book is testimony to the fact that our loved ones on the other side are always with us, and God's love and guidance in the unfoldment of our spiritual destiny is steadfast."

Rosemary Ellen Guiley, author, Calling Upon Angels: How Angels Help Us in Daily Life

"The Forever Penny is a gift of love and transformation! The author shares his spiritual journey, following the death of his beloved partner, Jan. His detailed, authentic, courageous questions/ needs/concerns are responded to by God and Jan. This book is much more than a guide for the grieving. It is a love story that tells the story behind the Glory. Doubt. Passion. Commitment. Illness. Celebration. Pain. Persistence. Strength. Faith. Family. All of this and more, giving hope to the reader both for the joyful possibilities of earthly life, and the immense eternal rewards we seek.

Cindy C., Kansas City, MO

"In the aftermath of a personal tragedy, Liles documents the days, meditations and conversation that guide him through the loss. "Forever Penny" is about faith, identity and love. It is about still wanting to contribute to the greater good—from the new place where grace has brought you."

Alisa M., Dallas, TX

Awesome Allen C. Liles--Thank you for writing this amazing book! I couldn't put it down and read the whole book in just 3 sittings-- It would've been just one sitting if I didn't already have things I just had to get done! It was so affirming and confirming of the process I'm going through now with the loss of my beloved spiritual partner, husband Jack. I love feeling his presence and the signs from him of our love and that all is well. Joining with you in the certainty of life after life!

Susan E.P., Louisville, KY

"A truly unique and heartwarming glimpse into the rarity of "forever love"--an unforgettable journey, magically conceived and offered."

Dan M., Sherman, TX

"I like your format and find it easy to read and to relate to. My father came to me in a dream (after he died) to tell me he loved me. I still think of that dream and it is just as real now.

I relate to the idea of finding the pennies, too. When I need some encouragement, I will find quarters. They all tell me, "In God we trust".

I think your book will be well received by others who have lost someone. It will provide encouragement and open their eyes to possibilities.

Thank you for sending the book. I will continue to enjoy it overtime."

Sharon F., Chaska, MN

"I served as book editor during Allen's tenure at Unity from 1997 to 2001, and like many others privileged to know him and his delightful wife Jan, I did not want them to leave. He was unquestionably the best boss I ever had, encouraging, supportive, creative and yet constructively critical. In many ways, this book on grief is similar. It gives us a powerful way to deal with the loss of anyone—or anything—precious to us, a way that honors our feelings and yet is sensitive to the life journey we are still walking. "The Forever Penny" is an intimate and authentic memoir of a great relationship, and how to survive the loss of the love of your life. In the process, Liles shows us how it can deepen your spiritual relationship with God and how that can provide direction for where you are still going. And how your lost spouse can still be with you, one penny at a time!"

Rev. Michael A. Maday, former editor for Unity House and anthologist for New Thought for a New Millennium.

"A wonderful tribute."

Danielle M., Bloomington, MN

"I loved every page of it. I will read it over and over again."

Sharon V., St. Paul, MN

THE FOREVER PENNY

How Our Loved Ones Stay Connected After Death

by
Allen C. Liles

This book is dedicated to my sweetheart:
JAN CARMEN LILES
July 28, 1941-February 28, 2017

THE FOREVER PENNY

How Our Loved Ones Stay Connected After Death

by
Allen C. Liles

Published By
Positive Imaging, LLC
bill@positive-imaging.com
http://positive-imaging.com

All Rights Reserved

No part of this publication may be reproduced in whole or in part, stored in a retrieval system, or transmitted in any form or by any means, electronic, mechanical, printing, photocopying, recording or otherwise without written permission from the publisher, except for the inclusion of brief quotations in a review. For information regarding permission, contact the publisher.

Copyright   2018   Allen C. Liles
ISBN   9781944071820

ETERNITY'S TRIUMPH

Beneath the starkest fragility
Of life's grand unwinding
An ageless question forms once more
Seeking clarity from a higher realm
Imploring Truth as dark descends
The quest for meaning binding all
As our human forms breathe their last
Would Spirit yield one golden answer
Before time's sand fulfills a final turn?
In hopeful anticipation our souls delay
The Grand Journey out beyond this pail
If we could but see the longest step
How easy would be to lose firm grasp
That tethers us hard to earthly view
Will the next station be bereft of light?
Does the sea's abyss more resemble
What lies unseen yon side the door?
If we might know deep blackness waits
At least we depart forever prepared
More aware and perhaps accepting
The ending closed and more complete
As God ponders our heightened plea
It sends the message strong and pure
A glorious array of scented rapture
Eternity's triumph stands so near
A Kingdom rich in splendorous threads
With peace resplendent crowning all
Clad throughout with sweetest bough
Oh yes great wonders sheathed in joy
More like a song of harmonious bliss
A radiant light of warmth enveloping
Each last soul in welcoming arms
Flee swiftly now and receive the gift

—*Allen C. Liles*

I would like to acknowledge the many contributions of my publisher A. William "Bill" Benitez (Positive Imaging, LLC) in bringing **The Forever Penny** to fruition. Without his efforts, wisdom and involvement, this book simply would not have happened. Thank you, my friend.

Contents

Introduction	**9**
Format For Days	**13**
Forever Penny Q & A	**14**
Grief Groups and Meditations	**201**
Letters and Journals	**207**
Jan's Last Days	**253**
Thoughts From The Heart	**261**
Photos	**269**
About The Author	**278**

INTRODUCTION

Everyone has lost someone or something they loved. Whether it's a spouse, a parent or grandparent, a child, a relative, a friend, a business associate or a pet, all of us have experienced personal loss with all its finality. Getting through grief is never an easy process. Whether the loss happened unexpectedly or over time, we often long for one more day, an extra hour or even a few precious seconds when we might be with our loved ones once again.

Grief sucks. Emotional pain caused by human loss can be direct, subtle and often cruelly persistent. It often arrives without warning. Stabs of pain and longing can accompany the lyrics of a love song, the remembrance of a shared experience, the presence of a mutual friend or even in the scent of a familiar fragrance. Anything can trigger the heart when it comes to recalling a lost love.

My precious wife Jan Carmen Liles passed on February 28, 2017. Her tired heart failed after exactly 75 years and seven months of life. She died in our bed of a sudden heart attack at 8:30 p.m. on a Tuesday night and before we could say goodbye. Jan and I first met in 1980. She was a Minnesota girl from Duluth, I was a corporate executive for The Southland Corporation (7-Eleven Stores) in Dallas. We met at a March of Dimes convention in Detroit. My company was a corporate sponsor of the battle against birth defects. It would be 13 long years before Jan and I lived in the same city. When she died, my wonderful wife and I had been married for nearly 23 years. She was my partner not only in life. She was also my indispensable partner in ministry at the Unity churches we had served since my ordination as a second career minister in 1993. As the pastor friend who performed her memorial service said so truthfully: "The congregations at their churches liked Allen, but they loved Jan."

My wife's health was always precarious. She was first diagnosed with lupus in 1975 and later survived a bout with Hodgkins Lymphoma in 2001. Jan's chronic health problems, especially with her lungs, became more severe in 2012. After coming home following 41 days in the hospital and a nursing home rehab, she found herself almost homebound. I took on the role of becoming her fulltime caregiver. Until her death, I was by my dear wife's side almost every moment. Tending to her needs became my daily mission and the greatest honor of my life. Our 37-year relationship, while always close, deepened even more. We merged into a bond of mutual appreciation. Her chronic illnesses and my caregiving responsibilities tested both of us, but it also provided another reason to appreciate each other. We thanked God every day for the blessing that was our relationship.

We held my sweetheart's memorial service on March 10, 2017. During the days before the service, I began noticing some strange happenings. One day I spied a lone red cardinal sitting on a tree branch outside our sun room window. He had been a regular visitor for over a year. The little bird sat staring through the glass into our living room, as if searching for something or someone. After an hour of probing and attempting to fly through the window several times for a closer look, the cardinal flew away. I never saw him again.

Then other strange things popped up. Soon after my precious wife passed, I began finding pennies in various locations inside and outside the apartment. I found at least one penny every two or three days. I soon began expecting to find the little bronze-colored coins. I became disappointed when a penny failed to appear for a few days.

Sometimes I would find a new penny. But most of the coins were old and worn as if they had been in circulation for many years. A few were almost pulverized and unrecognizable. I noticed that many of the pennies were minted in the 1960s and had been around for a half century or more. One even dated back to 1943, during the days of World War II. From somewhere deep in my conscious mind I began wondering if they had anything to do with Jan's loss. I finally decided it was my dear wife's unique way of telling me "Hey, Babe, don't worry. I'm still here. Every time you find another penny, it's just me saying hello."

I talked to other people about the pennies. Some who had lost loved ones reported similar experiences. Birds, such as cardinals or hummingbirds, seemed a common theme. One or two said they had seen animals, such as a deer, show up unexpectedly. Another woman in one of my grief support groups began finding colorful feathers everywhere, as if they were dropping from the sky. No matter how strange the "sign" seemed, almost everyone saw it as a spiritual reminder of their lost love. "Don't forget me!" the departed ones seemed to cry out.

However, the most startling proof that my dear wife was still around came the first morning after she passed. I first began meditating about 25 years ago during my ministerial training. Over the years, I found that sitting in the silence helps me connect with the Divine. I also transcribe in my writing journal what I "hear". In 2013, I wrote an award-winning book entitled SITTING WITH GOD/MEDITATING FOR GOD'S DIVINE GUIDANCE. It detailed a full year of the sacred words that arrived into my consciousness during the meditations. After publication of the book, I continued both my meditation and journaling practices. On the first day after my precious wife died, I meditated. But there was a different feeling this time. I sensed Jan's presence. I visualized her sitting at God's right hand.

I began my time in the silence by asking God to help me through the coming days and weeks. In response, I discerned a still, small inner voice. It whispered: "I AM with you always. In both good and bad times, I AM here. When you feel joy, I AM here. But I AM also present when your heart hangs heavy, as it does today. Have faith in Me. I will help you survive your deep loss. I love you, My precious son. Your dear wife is here with Me now, sitting right next to Me. When you come for our morning meditation, she and I both will be waiting for you. We promise to never leave or forsake you. We love you."

I felt an immediate sense of comfort. I was relieved knowing that I had not lost my wife entirely. I also did not question what I had just heard. The experience gave my aching heart an immediate lift. The pain of loss still enveloped me, but now there was a fragment of hope. I had received divine reassurance. I was not alone. I committed myself to trusting that belief.

Grief is a jagged, sometimes cruel and often unpredictable journey. But it must begin somewhere. I have been blessed by feeling Jan's presence not only during my meditations but many other times as well. I believe My sweetheart has held my hand every step of the grief journey. I am sure that Jan helped facilitate the move from Minnesota back to my native Texas. I know she selected the moving company and plotted every mile I traveled. She directed me to an apartment complex in my hometown of Temple, Texas. She helped me find a church to attend. She introduced me to new friends. My efficient wife also assisted me in identifying two local grief support groups. Jan steered me safely each mile that I drove in our 14-year old Toyota Highlander. I felt her with me in the aisles of a nearby Wal-Mart, looking at the list of items I'm sure she had reminded me to include. There has never been one moment when I felt that my dear wife was really gone. I treasure her continuing presence, especially during my morning meditations. How long will her spirit continue to be around? I don't know, but I hope forever. No matter what the future brings, I am grateful for the many blessings received so far.

In THE FOREVER PENNY, you will read the essence of what I heard during the first six months after Jan's physical death. I am sharing those 184 days from March 1, 2017 through August 31, 2017 as a gift for you. In detailing my specific experiences, I hope you find spiritual comfort as you walk your own grief path. Everyone travels his or her own unique journey after losing a loved one. Whatever your experience may be, I believe you will not be alone. Your loved one has remained close, waiting for you eventually just beyond the final rainbow.

FORMAT FOR DAYS

The format for my daily meditation regimen consists of four parts:

1. I first identify a suitable Tweet for my Twitter followers (@allencliles) taken from my book SITTING WITH GOD/ MEDITATING FOR GOD'S DIVINE GUIDANCE (Westbow Press, 2013)

2. I then select passages and/or verses from the Holy Bible, both the Old and New Testaments (New International Version)

3. After that, I bring a specific topic or question to God and Jan for insight and enlightenment

4. I carefully listen and write down what I perceive as their response.

I follow this uninterrupted regimen every morning for about 75 to 90 minutes. Being an early riser, I usually begin my meditative process between 4 a.m. and 5 a.m. I do not engage in any dialogue or conversation with God or Jan after putting forth my topic or question. On the very first day after my dear wife passed, God acknowledged her presence with us. So far, my sweetie has chosen to remain mostly silent in the responses that I receive each day. However, on a few rare occasions, I have addressed a question directly to her. Through the "Forever Pennies" I still find everywhere and my morning meditations, I still feel a close connection with my sweetheart. I find comfort and solace in Jan's ongoing involvement in my spiritual journey. While I miss her physical presence, my dear wife's soul essence has never left me. I have also included excerpts from personal correspondence and other items that may aid the reader in getting a sense of our relationship over the years. It wasn't always without its issues and problems. The fact that Jan and I knew each other almost exactly 14 years before we finally married should give hope for anyone who struggles with geographical and separation issues. I am so glad that my sweetheart and I hung in there, despite the problems. Our nearly 23-year marriage was well worth the wait.

THE FOREVER PENNY Q & A

Q. Why did you write THE FOREVER PENNY?

A. I lost my wife on February 28, 2017. I wrote about my grief experience for several reasons: (1) I wanted to share my belief that our dearly departed loved ones are still around and present in our lives, if they choose to be; (2) I wanted to offer hope to people who grieve about having their personal connection with a loved one severed and lost forever; (3) It was my wish to honor Jan and our 23-year marriage and 37-year relationship; (4) I wanted to demonstrate how a mutual commitment to God and the spiritual path can enhance a marriage and/or a relationship and (5) It was a therapeutic and helpful exercise for me on my grief journey.

Q. Do you need to be a minister to channel God?

A. You do not. I believe that God desires a close relationship with everyone. For me, the access to Spirit depends on my willingness to spend the time in prayer and meditation. The more minutes and hours that I can dedicate to being alone with God in the silence, the better communications I establish.

Q. Why do you think God chose you for this type of communications?

A. God will communicate with anyone at any time, depending on that person's willingness to be open and receptive to spiritual input.

Q. How did you arrive at the questions and topics you took to God each day?

A. The things I brought to God and Jan for their counsel involved what was happening with me right at that moment. For example, I seemed to worry most about finances, aging, my general health and getting settled in a new environment. Whatever my concern, I was open and receptive to hearing Spirit and my dear wife's response.

Q. How did you know that what you were hearing came directly from God (and Jan)? Were you really hearing voices?

A. I believe that if the response is positive, helpful and obviously in my best interest, then the answer is coming from a heavenly perspective. Unless the guidance has a "good" overtone, the input could be arriving from my own ego or some other outside source. God does not deal in negativity or telling someone to engage in any kind of harmful behavior, to themselves or anyone else. I believe that God wants only the best for me in every case. As far as a voice is concerned, the words seemed to come from within me—not from "on high" or from somebody with a bullhorn. This was more like "the still small voice" many people often mention.

Q. What's this about God calling you to be a "prophet"? isn't that a bit presumptuous?

A. Both the Old and New Testaments are full of stories about God calling regular people to bring important messages or warnings, mostly to alert about the consequences of anti-spiritual behavior. I do believe God is concerned about the current direction of the world and its worship of idols such as technology, money, and fame.

DAY 1

TODAY'S TWEET FROM SITTING WITH GOD:

"I feel your deepest losses. I AM always here. Turn to Me for comfort. I will not fail or abandon you."

FROM THE HOLY BIBLE:

"The Lord is my shepherd, I shall not be in want. He makes me lie down in green pastures, he leads me beside quiet waters, he restores my soul. He guides me in paths of righteousness for his name's sake. Even though I walk through the valley of the shadow of death, I will fear no evil, for you are with me; your rod and your staff, they comfort me. You prepare a table before me in the presence of my enemies. You anoint my head with oil; my cup overflows. Surely goodness and love will follow me all the days of my life, and I will dwell in the house of the LORD forever." (Psalm 23)

QUESTION OR TOPIC FROM ME:

What do I do now that I have lost my darling wife?

RESPONSE FROM GOD AND JAN:

"I know you are still in shock from Jan's unexpected passing. Everything seems unreal. The frantic call to 911 when you found her unresponsive in bed, the paramedics and police arriving, the calls to Jan's children with the sad news, it is all like a bad dream. I understand your numbness. Please know that I AM with you always. In both good times and bad, I AM here. I bring love, kindness and comfort each day. I pour out the Fruit of the Spirit upon you. I will help you survive your deep loss. I love you, My precious son. Believe it. Your dear wife is with Me now, right by My side. When you come for your morning meditation, she and I will be waiting for you. We are committed to seeing you through the remainder of your life journey. Your sweetheart and I promise to never leave or forsake you. That will never change."

DAY 2

TODAY'S TWEET FROM SITTING WITH GOD:

"You are experiencing a moment of difficult testing. Be ever calm, brave and determined. Remain steadfast and faithful."

FROM THE HOLY BIBLE:

"Trust in the LORD with all your heart and lean not on your own understanding: in all ways acknowledge him, and he will make your paths straight." (Proverbs 3: 5,6)

QUESTION OR TOPIC FROM ME:

I am seeking God's help in the days ahead

RESPONSE FROM GOD AND JAN:

"Never fear. I AM here. Now, your sweetheart also sits alongside Me. Jan knows your tears are still falling. Your darling wishes she could hold you in her arms like a little boy, comforting and consoling you. Jan's main message to you is this: "I'm really OK, Al. My pain is gone. I'm not suffering any more. I am finally free from my illnesses, the medications, the doctor visits, the hospitalizations and the rehab centers. Be happy for me." Hear this message, my beloved son: take Jan's and My hand and walk forward, one step at a time. Together, we can move through any fire. We will give you the strength, courage and wisdom to do what needs to be done. Again, do not worry about your wife. You two had a divine appointment as a couple. You kept this sacred appointment and blessed each other in many ways. You'll always be a part of each other's soul journey. Someday you will embrace her and be joyful together once more. I promise it."

DAY 3

TODAY'S TWEET FROM SITTING WITH GOD:

"I have a spiritual plan for each person on earth. Of course, a specific time will arrive when I call you back to Heaven."

FROM THE HOLY BIBLE:

"Love the LORD your God with all your heart and with all your soul and with all your strength." (Deuteronomy 6:5)

QUESTION OR TOPIC FROM ME:

Finding Peace

RESPONSE FROM GOD AND JAN:

"We both see you moving ahead with the planning for Jan's memorial service one week from today. Staying busy helps keep your mind off things. She and I understand that. It's your way to deny the reality of Jan's sudden passing. You even have a "Things to Do" list with more than 30 items on it. When you're checking each one off, you don't need to think about life without your sweetheart. In many ways, we know you haven't accepted her passing. Losing Jan's physical presence drastically changes your life. For one thing, you've lost your 24/7 job as her full-time caregiver. That represents a shock to your system. An adjustment will be required. Listen to me now: your ability to find and hold a peaceful center depends on whether you practice My Presence. The more minutes and hours you spend alone with Jan and Me now, the deeper your peace becomes. If you ignore us, expect your peacefulness to evaporate. That is why I become even more available to people during the grief process. You must cling ever closer to Me, especially right now. Snuggle deep in My loving embrace during this time of pain and uncertainty. Devote more time to nurturing our sacred relationship. By strengthening the spiritual bond with Jan and Me, you nurture yourself. Together, your dear wife and I form a protective shield around you.

DAY 4

TODAY'S TWEET FROM SITTING WITH GOD:

"Do not fear. I AM with you. Place your faith in My #1 promise: I will never leave you, I will never forsake you."

FROM THE HOLY BIBLE:

"Now faith is being sure of what we hope for and certain of what we do not see." (Hebrews 11:1)

QUESTION OR TOPIC FROM ME:

How will I get through these next few days?

RESPONSE FROM GOD AND JAN:

"Keep doing what you are doing. Get through this next week one hour or one minute at a time. We will be with you every step of the way. Let everything unfold naturally. Open your arms to every bit of love and caring that comes your way. Release expectations. Let people be who they are. Allow everyone to state their own feelings about your dear wife's passing. Receive love. Return love. Let every interaction become a two-way blessing. Jan's transition represents the ultimate step in anyone's spiritual journey. Bask in the love and admiration felt for her by all. She was—and is—a special soul. She sits happily by My side in the Kingdom of Heaven. Your dear wife is now pain free. Jan's sweet soul soars as she explores the portals of Heaven. You know she has a curious nature. The wonders of My Kingdom dazzle her. Know that Jan is grateful that you are now released from the burden of being her fulltime caregiver. She wants you to glory in your new freedom. Jan supports whatever future choices you make in your life. Your sweetheart has unconditional love for you. You all possess an unbreakable bond that lasts throughout eternity. She asked that I remind you that we both are here for you in the difficult days ahead."

DAY 5

TODAY'S TWEET FROM SITTING WITH GOD:

"Embrace the natural progression of human life and death. Walk calmly toward the glory that awaits you in My Kingdom."

FROM THE HOLY BIBLE:

"Because he loves me," says the LORD, I will rescue him; I will protect him, for he acknowledges My name. He will call upon Me, and I will answer him; I will be with him in trouble, I will deliver and honor him." (Psalm 91:14, 15)

QUESTION OR TOPIC FROM ME:

God, please help me

RESPONSE FROM GOD AND JAN:

"I will not only help you through this travail, but Jan will be quite involved in your restoration to wholeness. She is working closely with Me to orchestrate positive outcomes for you. You also have tremendous angelic resources at your disposal. They stand ready to assist and protect you. Trust in the awesome Power of Heaven to marshal its powerful forces on your behalf. Stay focused on the present moment. Cast aside all worry and fear. Avoid needless distractions. Try not to panic. Your spiritual fate is in good hands. Your precious wife and I act as team leaders for your rescue. Never forget the great love and devotion that existed between the two of you. Her passing has not changed anything. She and I are divinely guiding you. We watch over you day and night. The powers of Heaven are geared up and at your side. We love and treasure you. These next few days won't be easy for you, but Jan and I will hold your hand and walk you through it."

DAY 6

TODAY'S TWEET FROM SITTING WITH GOD:

"I AM with you through every ordeal. I comfort and support you. I bring extra angels to watch over you."

FROM THE HOLY BIBLE:

"For just as the sufferings of Christ flow over into our lives, so also through Christ our comfort overflows." (2 Corinthians: 1:4)

TOPIC OR QUESTION FROM ME:

Please be with me during this difficult week

RESPONSE FROM GOD AND JAN:

"We are both with you right now. I AM holding your hand as you say "goodbye" to your incredible wife of nearly 23 years. We provide the love and support you need during this long week of loss and mourning. Lean on us. Together, Jan and I promise to help you navigate the choppy waters of grief. Besides our efforts, you can expect tremendous support from friends and family. Many people will reach out to comfort you. Open your heart. Allow these expressions of love. Trust in the process of saying goodbye. Many hold you and Jan in high esteem. Affection and admiration for you will become obvious over the next few days. Accept it with gratitude. Make a place in your heart for everyone. I can assure you that Jan watches everything from Heaven. She feels overwhelmed by the reaction to her passing. The outpouring of love has rendered her almost speechless. I remind you again that Jan is now pain free for the first time in many decades. I watch with approval as she moves into her heavenly routine. Of course, she misses you as much as you miss her. But her beautiful soul understands the proper sequence of events. Someday, you and she will reunite. I promise it. Now, go about the necessary business of this long week. Much support is forthcoming. Jan and I both love and cherish you."

DAY 7

TODAY'S TWEET FROM SITTING WITH GOD:

"I AM the healing answer for every deep wound. Clear out a path for Me to perform miracles. Prepare a way and I will come."

FROM THE HOLY BIBLE:

"Do not let your hearts be troubled. Trust in God. Trust also in Me." (John 14:1)

TOPIC OR QUESTION FROM ME:

Please tell me what to do next

RESPONSE FROM GOD AND JAN:

"Keep preparing for Jan's memorial service in three days. You've done a good job of getting things arranged. I know that handling the necessary details has kept your mind off your loss. For now, avoid making any rash decisions. Choices while grieving can be easy to make and hard to undo. Jan only made her transition one week ago. Yes, there comes a moment when options must be considered. Let caution rule for now. Take things slow and easy. Use these early days to grieve and reminisce about the many wonderful memories you all shared together. The longing for her will not go away anytime soon. Don't worry. I will grant you the necessary months or even years to get through the grief process. I know you still feel emotionally numb right now. You miss your "sweetie-pie". By the way, Jan says "Hello Babe" and sends her best. You love birds had a unique relationship. I know you want to feel her loving presence around you. Think of her devotion as a warm and protective shawl that you can pull around your shoulders during the cold and dark nights."

DAY 8

TODAY'S TWEET FROM SITTING WITH GOD:

"Soon it will be Spring. Allow the new season to bring you a needed renewal of mind, body and spirit. Let your soul bloom."

FROM THE HOLY BIBLE:

"Finally, beloved, whatever is true, whatever is noble, whatever is right, whatever is pure, whatever is lovely, whatever is admirable; if anything is excellent or praiseworthy, think about such things." (Philippians 4:8)

TOPIC OR QUESTION FROM ME:

Will I have the energy and stamina that I'll need this week?

RESPONSE FROM GOD AND JAN:

"Yes, Jan and I will make sure you get through everything. We know it won't be easy. Just put one foot in front of the other. Place yourself in our loving care. Sense strong arms holding you up. Relax in our caring embrace. Surrender every worry and concern. We will lead you beside the still waters. Our rod and our staff, they comfort you. We are here to sustain you through the long days and endless nights. You are never alone when Jan and I are near. I have also summoned legions of angels to shield and protect you. I fill your tired body with new energy and stamina. I bolster your flagging spirit. Your precious wife and I will never abandon you, even for a minute. Trust our divine guidance as you go forward during this period of mourning. Let us bolster your faith. You are in the best of hands. Be strong. Be brave. Be assured. Be of good cheer. The way is being cleared for you. Surrender yourself to the moment. Let go. Your dear wife and I will catch you if you fall. But we know you and you won't fall."

DAY 9

TODAY'S TWEET FROM SITTING WITH GOD:

"Keep coming back to Me. Day by day, minute by minute, keep coming back. Reach out and find Me. I AM here."

FROM THE HOLY BIBLE:

"Shout for joy to the LORD, all the earth. Worship the LORD with gladness; come before him with joyful songs. Know that the LORD is God. It is he who made us, and we are his, we are his people, the sheep of his pasture." (Psalm 100: 1-3)

TOPIC OR QUESTION FROM ME:

Is Jan happier now than when she was alive?

RESPONSE FROM GOD AND JAN:

"Yes, in many ways, your dear wife is much happier now. She was drained mentally, physically and spiritually. Her body and soul were spent. Jan was ready for the joy, peace and rest that she found in Heaven. Of course, she hated to leave you. That's one reason she keeps dropping pennies where you can find them. Every time you see a stray penny, that represents another "Hello, babe" from her. You were and still are her husband, true love and caregiver. But being pain free ranks as a premier benefit of My Kingdom. So many human beings arrive in Heaven after long bouts of debilitating illness. As soon as they enter My portals, the pain disappears. That was true of Jan. She has no more chronic coughing and lung problems. Her lupus has vanished. She goes effortlessly here and there, unlike the years she spent tethered to her walker. Jan relishes her new-found freedom. She was one who never feared or fought human death. When the time arrived and I called her home, she came willingly. Again, although she misses you, her children and grandchildren, Jan enjoys the freedom of Heaven. She resides here now in happiness, freedom and joyful appreciation for her new surroundings. Your precious wife is indeed in a better place."

DAY 10

TODAY'S TWEET FROM SITTING WITH GOD:

"I AM constantly revealing My Love for you. I keep you centered amid chaos and personal challenges. I guide your actions."

FROM THE HOLY BIBLE:

"But those who hope in the LORD will renew their strength. They will soar on wings like eagles; they will run and not grow weary, they will walk and not be faint." (Isaiah 40:31)

TODAY'S TOPIC OR QUESTION FROM ME:

Please help me get through Jan's memorial service

RESPONSE:

"You must stay focused today. Trust Me and your precious wife to bring you through this important time. A memorial service and/or funeral acts as a crucial milestone in anyone's grief process. Do not waver, nor be nervous or timid. Stand tall, centered and strong. Let your darling wife and I act as your guiding lights. Find and utilize every ounce of spiritual courage that you possess. Many in Heaven are rooting for you today. Your dear departed mother Edith is here, cheering you on. Although your sweet mom has been here for nearly half a century, she still watches over you on a regular basis. Edith and Jan, who had never met while on earth, have now become dear friends in Heaven. They have much in common, especially an unconditional love for you. Expect a great supporting cast at Jan's lovely memorial service today. The chapel will be full of friends and family. Feel the great caring and concern surrounding you during this humanly sad day. Open yourself to receiving universal affection. It is genuine and heartfelt. Let the love for you and Jan wash over you. Enjoy this moment of affirmation. Surrender yourself to the moment. You and your amazing wife have earned the accolades. I will be there as well, basking in the glow of love that envelops you both."

DAY 11

TODAY'S TWEET FROM SITTING WITH GOD:

"Have complete faith in My Strength and Power. As your human power begins to wane, My spiritual strength advances."

FROM THE HOLY BIBLE:

"But the fruit of the Spirit is love, joy, peace, patience, kindness, goodness, faithfulness, gentleness and self-control. Against such things, there is no law." (Galatians 5:22, 23)

TODAY'S TOPIC OR QUESTION FROM ME:

Thank you both for getting me through Jan's memorial service yesterday

RESPONSE:

"Yesterday was indeed a high point of your grief journey so far. You received exceptional support, affection, and caring from everyone present. Jan's special day consisted of these three Cs: Care, Concern and Celebration. Your precious wife was overwhelmed. She loved everything about the service. She was surprised at the number of people who attended. It exceeded her wildest expectations. The comments by her three adult children made her grateful, happy and proud. She especially liked the idea of giving each person a copy of her children's book BECAUSE YOU MATTER. Jan felt celebrated and honored in every way. Much of the love flowed out to you as a twosome. You were a "power couple" much more than you thought. Although you all did not have impact on a national scale, you did influence the people that knew you. Many in the Twin Cities will remember you both fondly in future days. I do have important new input for you. Both Jan and I agree that you should move back home to your native Texas. With her passing, your work in Minnesota is finished. You've been away from home for 26 years. You still have much spiritual work to do, but it's time to retreat to your roots. Your dear wife's celebration service today represented a positive ending for the Minnesota phase of your life journey. Go forward now to complete your spiritual destiny in a different place and time. She and I both will still be right by your side, cheering you on."

DAY 12

TODAY'S TWEET FROM SITTING WITH GOD:

"I AM your fortress. Come inside and claim your place of safety. I provide a refuge from all danger. Rest easy with Me."

FROM THE HOLY BIBLE:

"Peace I leave with you; my peace I give you. I do not give to you as the world gives. Do not let your hearts be troubled and do not be afraid." (John 14:27)

TODAY'S TOPIC OR QUESTION FROM ME:

Thank you for helping me survive these past few days

RESPONSE FROM GOD AND JAN:

"Your dear wife and I will never leave or forsake you. Jan is still basking in the afterglow of her celebration service. So many wonderful memories were offered. You heard them, as did her grateful family. Jan's presence in the world had a positive impact. Her warmth and generous spirit was felt by many. I predict that her influence will continue to grow in the years ahead. Of course, your sweet wife had a profound effect on your life. The two of you complemented each other in both direct and subtle ways. Jan was a wonderful partner in ministry. The churches you served appreciated your committed relationship. You were good role models for everybody. I know you miss her. You loved so many things about your darling bride. She was a beautiful person, both inside and out. Jan was quiet and humble, yet determined and outspoken when the situation demanded it. She was totally committed to you and your success. Most important to you, Jan was always on your side. More and more people are noticing how she lived her life. They like what they see. It's too bad that some people must leave their human lives before they get fully appreciated. Remember that Jan is still here for you, now and forever. That never changes."

DAY 13

TODAY'S TWEET FROM SITTING WITH GOD:

"I AM constantly bringing good things into your life. Appreciating little joys serves as the key to happiness and contentment."

FROM THE HOLY BIBLE:

"And now these three remain: faith, hope and love. But the greatest of these is love." (Corinthians 13:13)

TODAY'S TOPIC OR QUESTION FROM ME:

I will need lots of help to get me though these next few weeks

RESPONSE FROM GOD AND JAN:

"Jan and I are here for you. Everyone in My Kingdom, including your precious wife, is poised for action. We are ready, willing and able to support you. Look to us for everything required, especially regarding your relocation to Texas. Your detail orientated wife will get you organized. I'll help you clear any financial hurdles and provide the physical energy and mental toughness needed. Be open and receptive to our divine guidance. In making the move, you're being lifted to a higher platform on your spiritual journey. Go with the flow. Do not become frazzled or wilt under the pressure. With our assistance, everything will fall neatly into place. Good things are headed your way. Be ready. Stay alert and prepared. Trust and believe. Line your pockets with faith. Get some rest for the physical work ahead. You've earned it. Know that Jan and I are watching over you. We will be your protectors and guides during the days ahead. Sleep well, My son."

DAY 14

TODAY'S TWEET FROM SITTING WITH GOD:

"Strive for a humble perspective. Humility represents a crucial component of the spiritual life."

FROM THE HOLY BIBLE:

"Turn your ear to me, come quickly to my rescue; be my rock of refuge, a strong fortress to save me." (Psalm 31:2)

TODAY'S TOPIC OR QUESTION FROM ME:

I need more divine guidance before I can proceed

RESPONSE GOD AND JAN:

"Calm yourself. Your dear wife and I are guiding you every moment. I also have a vast army of angels protecting you. Begin the long grieving process with confidence in the outcome. You are being led and supported. Take one steady step at a time. Be prepared to occasionally take a step backward. Grief does not march in a straight line. Don't worry. Everything happens when it is supposed to happen. We are sending the right and perfect people to facilitate your move. A lovely apartment home is being prepared for you in Texas. The needed funds are being deposited into your account. Expect new friendships with caring people. Fresh experiences await you. Of course, your relationship with your precious wife continues, just from a different perspective. Her sweet spirit travels with you. Jan is never very far away from you. Embrace the changes coming your way. It is acceptable even to feel a bit excited amidst the grief. The move will take your mind off your loss, at least for a while. Feel good and proud about the lives and legacies that you and Jan created in Minnesota. Many are sad to see you go, but go you must. The time is right. Much spiritual work remains. But first the grieving process must continue. That will happen, but in a new environment."

DAY 15

TODAY'S TWEET FROM SITTING WITH GOD:

"I AM winning the spiritual battle, one soul at a time. Despite appearances to the contrary, I see a new awareness rising."

FROM THE HOLY BIBLE:

"It is by Grace that you have been saved." (Ephesians 2:5)

TODAY'S TOPIC OR QUESTION FROM ME:

Will I ever get over the pain of losing my wife?

RESPONSE FROM GOD AND JAN:

"There are no quick fixes to grief. Most human beings never totally get over the loss of someone or something they loved. Do not set any deadlines for yourself. Feel your feelings. Disregard the opinions of others, no matter how well meaning. Only you can process your grieving. The pain you experience must be expressed in one form or another. Tears are good. Talking to a professional grief counselor or compassionate minister, rabbi or priest may help. Grief groups are an excellent way to share your pain with others who are going through the same situation. Sitting with Me (and now Jan) daily in meditation offers many benefits. I understand your pain. I AM the great comforter. Try to reconnect with the beauty, solitude and reassurance of nature. Park yourself by a lake, river, stream, pond or even ocean. Let the placidness of My natural wonders reinforce your soul. Sense the presence of your loved one nearby. They are never really gone from you. Their beautiful spirit hovers around you. Never hesitate to talk with them if you want. They hear and appreciate your sincere words of love and yearning. Call out for those you hold dear at any time of the day or night. They will hear you. Your loved ones want to go through the darkness with you."

DAY 16

TODAY'S TWEET FROM SITTING WITH GOD:

"Listen for My daily instructions. Pay close attention to My guidance. Do the sacred work I choose for you."

FROM THE HOLY BIBLE:

"A wife of noble character is worth far more than rubies." (Proverbs 31:10)

TODAY'S TOPIC OR QUESTION FROM ME:

Why does "family" cause upsets at times like this?

RESPONSE FROM GOD AND JAN:

"Families consist of human beings. People react to loss in different ways. Some get angry. Others say inappropriate things. Bizarre behavior occurs. Calm folks go berserk. Unstable individuals may become paragons of serenity. No two souls react alike. Be gentle in your judgments. Allow expressions of grief to manifest as they will. Keep the focus on yourself. You have a cross-country move coming up. That represents your top priority, along with embracing your personal grief. Hear Me well: you cannot change people to suit your expectations. Do not waste your time trying. Jan's family and you worked well together to give her a proper and glorious sendoff. She appreciates that and honors each person who loved her, family or not. You are now planning more tributes for Jan, such as the nursing scholarship in her name at Normandale College. Try to keep the love for your dear wife at the forefront of every interaction. Keep your mind and heart stayed on the wonderful person that now sits at My side in Heaven."

DAY 17

TODAY'S TWEET FROM SITTING WITH GOD:

"Love offers hope. It brings healing and restoration to the spirit. Love comforts the grieving and reassures the lost."

FROM THE HOLY BIBLE:

"Woe to me because of my injury! My wound is incurable! Yet I said to myself, "This is my sickness and I must endure it." (Jeremiah 10:19)

TODAY'S TOPIC OR QUESTION FROM ME:

Please help me to make this cross-country move

RESPONSE FROM GOD AND JAN:

"Your dear wife and I are working in tandem to facilitate your move. We provide everything needed to make your relocation go smoothly. Trust that everything will unfold in perfect and divine order. Have no fear! Move forward with confidence. The outcome remains assured. Be open, receptive and positive. You are a good and faithful servant. For the most part, you've listened carefully for My instructions. Remember that I AM with you every mile of your spiritual journey. I (and now your dear Jan) are not about to leave or forsake you now. You and I have traveled many miles together. Maintain confidence in Jan and Me to continue charting your spiritual destiny. The best is yet to come. If it were not so, I would have told you. Keep believing and trusting in My divine wisdom. You may hit a few speed bumps on your way back to Texas, but nothing major. Do the preparation work and leave the rest to your detail-orientated wife and Me. Jan is shouldering most of the responsibility for your move home. Trust her managerial abilities. I know that I do. I promise you won't be disappointed in the outcome."

DAY 18

TODAY'S TWEET FROM SITTING WITH GOD:

"Every spiritual life includes a 'desert' experience. Have faith. Embrace hope. I can pluck you from any wasteland."

FROM THE HOLY BIBLE:

"Then the LORD said to Moses, "I will rain down bread from Heaven for you. The people are to go out each day and gather enough for that day. In this way, I will test them and see if they follow my instructions." (Exodus 16:4)

TODAY'S TOPIC OR QUESTION FROM ME:

Please guide and direct me today

RESPONSE FROM GOD AND JAN:

"Plan your work and work your plan. Keep planning. Keep doing. Execute everything step by careful step. Prepare a "Things to Do" list and check off the things you get handled each day. Proceed cautiously, but proceed. Do your 'due diligence'. However, don't become vulnerable to 'paralysis by analysis'. You are doing beautifully so far. Remain calm, serene and focused. Go with the flow. Be centered and assured. Tranquility and quiet confidence are the keys to success. Don't worry about money. It manifests as needed. Let us act as your real estate consultants. We will find a nice place for you to lay your head. Look at various possibilities when you arrive back home, but listen to your intuition. Your inner guidance (Jan and Me) will supply the correct answers, if you choose to hear us. Always look beneath the surface appearance of anything. Clarity brings Truth, and Truth begets good decision making. Stay focused as you travel home."

DAY 19

TODAY'S TWEET FROM SITTING WITH GOD:

"Trust that everything works together for your good. I live within you. I provide endless wisdom, courage and understanding."

FROM THE HOLY BIBLE:

"Teach the older men to be temperate, worthy of respect, self-controlled and sound in faith, in love and endurance." (Titus 2:2)

TODAY'S TOPIC OR QUESTION FROM ME:

How am I doing so far?

FROM GOD AND JAN: RESPONSE:

"So far, so good. Keep advancing one steady step at a time. Don't rush into anything. Be sure it feels right for you. Everything percolates in divine order. Remain centered. Your dear wife and I know you have some trepidation about moving across the country. "Moving" in and of itself can be traumatic for anyone. But you'll survive it. Your sweetheart and I are here to help you deal with everything. However, lower your expectations about what you might find back home. Realize it may take some adjusting before you feel comfortable. You have been away from your beloved home state for 26 years. Much has changed. Be prepared for lots more people and much heavier traffic. You'll need to get accustomed to the hot weather again, just as you adjusted to Minnesota for 16 years. Summertime looms just around the corner in central Texas. No more four seasons in the lovely north country. Prepare for some adventures and maybe some misadventures. Take everything in stride. Be positive. It will all fall into place. We promise it. Trust in Me and your sweet wife."

DAY 20

TODAY'S TWEET:

"You live in the fullness and totality of Me. Manna from Heaven falls at your feet. My divine Grace surrounds you night and day."

FROM THE HOLY BIBLE:

"But He said to me, "My grace is sufficient for you, for my power is made perfect in weakness." (2 Corinthians 12:9)

TODAY'S TOPIC OR QUESTION:

What would you say about our marriage of nearly 23 years?

RESPONSE:

"You and Jan had a divine appointment arranged and orchestrated by Me. Thankfully, it all worked out. You complemented and enhanced each other. You possessed similar personalities and strengths. Your differences were few and inconsequential. She mirrored generosity, unconditional love and honest warmth. You provided her with devotion, love and respect. You also gave her financial security. You enjoyed each other's company. You had fun together. You were both faithful to each other. But here's the main thing: you and Jan were committed to growing spiritually, both as individuals and as a couple. That was a huge plus for your relationship. So many couples are at odds with each other from a spiritual and/or religious standpoint. You and she were singing from the same hymn book, so to speak. Your precious wife is still 100% committed to your soul growth. She stands ready to help point the way as needed. Jan also wants to be involved in your human life. I believe you want that too. I promise that someday you and your soul mate will be traipsing together through the halls of Heaven. What a glorious day! I'll be there to welcome you and bless the happy reunion."

DAY 21

TODAY'S TWEET FROM SITTING WITH GOD:

"Keep praying for faith and courage. I AM always available to comfort you. Let Me help when trouble strikes."

FROM THE HOLY BIBLE:

"Your kingdom come, your will be done on earth as it is in heaven." (Matthew 6:10)

TODAY'S TOPIC OR QUESTION FROM ME:

I feel lost without my wife

RESPONSE FROM GOD AND JAN:

"I understand your pain. Anytime you lose something or someone forever, the finality can paralyze anyone. You must keep going forward. By taking one small step at a time, you will soon cover a thousand miles. Allow the gentle spirit of your dear wife to act as your North Star. Feel her warm and benevolent presence surrounding you. Jan relishes her role as your champion. As you move back home to Texas, she walks close by your side. You are realizing now more than ever the wonder of your marriage. Cherish that knowledge. Honor the spiritual growth that you encouraged and nourished in each other. What a positive statement of My Presence you both conveyed! That won't go away anytime soon. You set a great example for others. You were good role models for a happy and respectful marriage. You both invited Me into your relationship. I was happy to accept the invitation. So now you go forward without her humanly by your side. Affirm Jan's blessed memory by rededicating your commitment to My Path. Your darling wife and I want you to complete your spiritual destiny before you join us here in Heaven. We'll do everything possible to make sure that happens."

DAY 22

TODAY'S TWEET FROM SITTING WITH GOD:

"I understand when pain becomes unbearable. I AM here to help you heal. Let Me restore you to wholeness."

FROM THE HOLY BIBLE:

"When the sun was setting, the people brought to Jesus all who had various kinds of sickness, and laying his hands on each one, he healed them." (Luke 4:40)

TODAY'S TOPIC OR QUESTION FROM ME:

Despite everything that has happened, I feel so grateful

RESPONSE:

"Your dear wife and I hear your appreciation. We are both working hard to get you through this first stage of grief. We keep reminding you about things that need doing. We also put divine ideas in your brain for later action. We know what you must accomplish during this next 24 hours. We stand ready to help you anytime: morning, noon and night. Your fearless girl Jan toils right beside Me to make the crooked places straight. By the way, she loves the response to the nursing scholarship in her name at Normandale College in Bloomington. It exceeds her wildest dreams. She was also astonished at the turnout for her memorial service. Do you recall how Jan always wondered if anyone would attend her funeral? Now she knows. Her reputation only grows from here on out. Your sweet wife's influence won't be fading anytime soon. As your trip to Texas begins tomorrow, listen for our divine input. Try to discern our wisdom. Discard preconceived ideas or unrealistic expectations. Things are set to fall into place. Just heed our directions. Stay relaxed, assured and cool. Go with the flow. Trust us to lead you onward and upward to the next stop of your spiritual journey."

DAY 23

TODAY'S TWEET FROM SITTING WITH GOD:

"Step back from trying to control others. Keep the focus on yourself. Let go and let Me take over. Trust and obey."

FROM THE HOLY BIBLE:

"Then you will know the truth, and the truth will set you free." (John 8:32)

TODAY'S TOPIC OR QUESTION FROM ME:

Please keep me safe on my trip to Texas

RESPONSE FROM GOD AND JAN:

"Relax, My beloved son. You're in good hands. Jan and I know that you are apprehensive about the trip. You haven't been on an airplane in 10 years. You're not too sure about driving in such a busy area. We understand your concerns. But your dear wife and I are both fully present for you. You will not travel alone. Look at the next five days as the start of an adventure. You are heading home to your native state. You're traveling to Temple, the city where you were born, raised and graduated from high school. You have been a good and faithful servant. Now the prodigal son is coming back to his roots. Hear My promise: Jan and I will never leave or forsake you, especially now. Go forward boldly. Have high confidence in the outcome. You have done well since you first answered my call 30 years ago. It took courage for you to give up your success in the corporate world and follow Me. You've had some highs and a few lows over the years, but you remained faithful. Be open and receptive to this new chapter in your life. You are about to experience a new freedom of personal movement and growth. Be open and receptive to some new "adventures". You've earned them."

DAY 24

TODAY'S TWEET FROM SITTING WITH GOD:

"Bless those you love. Also bless those who love you. Revel in the wonders of love, acceptance and understanding."

FROM THE HOLY BIBLE:

"And a voice from Heaven said, "This is my Son, whom I love; in him I am well pleased." (Matthew 3: 17)

TODAY'S TOPIC OR QUESTION FROM ME:

Please help me to make good decisions

RESPONSE FROM GOD AND JAN:

"As you traveled to your hometown today, Jan and I provided considerable roadside assistance. We protected you on the drive south on I-35 from Dallas. Yes, the traffic has grown. The new speed limit of 75 miles per hour encourages speeding much faster than that. We know you were amazed and a bit scared by the number of trucks on the interstate. But, with our steering abilities, you managed OK. Your trips anywhere have been limited these past few years. Your care giving duties came first, as they should. Jan was not well enough to travel outside of Minneapolis, so you didn't stray far from your Bloomington apartment. Now you are being lifted out of your comfort zone. Take a deep breath and go with it. We are there to help you. How do you like the nice apartment home in Temple that we found for you? Are you surprised that the place you chose was also the first one you saw? That's the way your efficient wife and I like to work. Why waste time? Still, you had the free-will choice to choose what you wanted. You are also beginning to realize how the move from Minnesota to Texas is masking and delaying your grief. With so many things on your mind, you have not sat down and really cried. Yes, you've shed some tears since Jan passed. But the real sobs haven't erupted yet. But they will, My son, they will. No one loses the love of their life and escapes the tears that flood the heart."

DAY 25

TODAY'S TWEET FROM SITTING WITH GOD:

"My wonders unfold around you. Blessings multiply as we speak. Step by step, advance toward your spiritual destiny."

FROM THE HOLY BIBLE:

"The LORD said to Abram, "Leave your country, your people and your father's household and go into the land I will show you." (Genesis 12:1)

TODAY'S TOPIC OR QUESTION FROM ME:

I am seeking divine guidance about my move back to Texas

RESPONSE:

"We know you sometimes feel disorientated. You lost your dear wife without any warning less than a month ago. You decided to move back to Texas and began packing up just in the past two weeks. It has been a hectic and busy time. As I told you yesterday, there are some positives about moving this fast. I would advise most people not to make quick decisions after losing a spouse. I think you are a different case. Jan and I believe this is the best thing for you right now. One absolute benefit: the move has taken your mind off your heavy losses. Not only did you lose your sweetheart, you lost your job as her full-time caregiver. Your daily regimen of caring for her ended without notice. Now, you are not only without a wife and life partner. You are also jobless. Those are both major life changes. Processing such radical shifts requires endurance, stamina, mental toughness, acceptance of new realities and emotional resilience. During this time of disorientation, keep coming back to your spiritual center. Spend more time with Me (and your bride). It helps restore your equilibrium. Jan and I are both surrounding you with courage, wisdom, peace, love and joy. You are being divinely led to the next stop on your journey. Cling tightly to us anytime you feel abandoned and lost."

DAY 26

TODAY'S TWEET:

"Pray daily for knowledge of My will for you and the power to carry it out. I want you to be an instrument of My Grace."

FROM THE HOLY BIBLE:

"This is the confidence we have in approaching God; that if we ask anything according to his will, he hears us." (1 John 5:14)

TODAY'S TOPIC OR QUESTION:

I pray for knowledge of your Will for me and the power to carry it out

RESPONSE FROM GOD AND JAN:

"My Will—and your dear wife's Will—for you right now is that you continue focusing on your move from Minnesota to Texas. Deal with the issues at hand. Do not project very far into the future. Put aside what may happen down the road. Take things one day at a time. You remember that slogan from the 12-Step programs. Do not obsess about what comes next. Jan and I know you are concerned about leaving Minnesota so quickly. But she and I agree it constitutes your best option. For one thing, if you stayed in Minnesota, everything there would remind you of your life with Jan. Try to look forward rather than backward. You and your dear wife built a good and productive life in the Twin Cities. You witnessed the growth of your three grandchildren from babies into their late teens. You served several area churches and made many friends among the congregants. You had a busy and interesting social life until Jan became ill. Now, for everything to proceed as planned, you need new surroundings. You still have more work to do on your move. You'll have time down the road for reflection and tears of grief. For now, focus on getting back home. That is your wife's and My will for you. We'll help you along the way."

DAY 27

TODAY'S TWEET FROM SITTING WITH GOD:

"My divine wisdom stirs love and compassion, forgiveness and understanding. I elevate your best human qualities."

FROM THE HOLY BIBLE:

"To them God has chosen to make known among the Gentiles the glorious riches of this mystery, which is Christ in you, the hope of glory." (Colossians 1:27)

TODAY'S TOPIC OR QUESTION FROM ME:

I pray for help with family dynamics during this time of change

RESPONSE FROM GOD AND JAN:

"Be open and receptive to whatever unfolds with your Texas and Minnesota families. Yes, Jan's Minnesota family says they wish you wouldn't leave. You've grown close to them. You do plan to stay in touch, especially with the grandchildren. But everyone has his or her own path in life, including you. Regarding your own children back in Dallas, temper any expectations. Your son and daughter are in their mid-50s now, deeply involved with their own lives. You still have several friends back in Texas. That should help. But remember: you have been absent from your home state for 26 years. That means your relationships there, for the most part, are dormant. Be honest and authentic. Let everyone see that you are approaching your return with honesty, acceptance and realistic expectations. There won't be any flower petals strewn before you or marching bands. Allow people to be who they are. If necessary, practice radical forgiveness. Make amends when necessary or appropriate. Forego any judging, lest you be judged. You are a different person now, as are they. Be gentle and accepting. Whatever anybody's opinion may be, including people you love and cherish, you have no need to justify your actions. Everyone walks his or her own spiritual way. Be loving and supportive, understanding and respectful. I can tell you this: Jan and I approve of your move back home. It's by far the best thing for you right now."

DAY 28

TODAY'S TWEET FROM SITTING WITH GOD:

"I AM granting you full access to My Power. It lives within you, always ready for your activation and use."

FROM THE HOLY BIBLE

"Give thanks to the LORD, for he is good; his love endures forever." (Psalm 118:1)

TODAY'S TOPIC OR QUESTION FROM ME:

What is the assessment of my trip back to Texas?

RESPONSE FROM GOD AND JAN:

"So far, so good. Much was accomplished, but more work remains. Remember that your actual physical move still lies before you. Don't worry or fret. Your dear wife and I have you covered. We'll help you in putting everything together. You have already had scored some victories. You flew successfully from MSP to DFW, your first airline trip in a decade. You had an excellent hotel experience at the Hyatt Place in north Dallas. You made a couple of solid connections with your son Jeff and even had a positive lunch with your ex-wife Suzanne. You successfully navigated Highway I-35 from Dallas to Temple and back. You adjusted to the traffic and higher speed limit. You identified and selected a nice apartment home. It was a tad more expensive than the average rent in Temple, but that's OK. You have arranged for your utility and cable connections. You found a Medicare Advantage plan in Texas. While on the trip, you even managed to keep up with your 120-plus "followers" on Twitter. As I said earlier: so far, so good. Keep up the pace. I can promise you that your dear wife and I are walking beside you all the way. Keep grinding. You can get on with the grieving process after the move."

DAY 29

TODAY'S TWEET FROM SITTING WITH GOD:

"I want you to enjoy your human experience. While life can be difficult at times, look for beauty and joy all around you."

FROM THE HOLY BIBLE:

"Come to me, all you who are weary and burdened, and I will give you rest." (Matthew 11:28)

TODAY'S TOPIC OR QUESTION FROM ME:

What part does meditation play in the grief process?

RESPONSE FROM GOD AND JAN:

"Meditation can help get you through the grief and loss process. I AM giving you more time to spend in the silence. Use it. Accept this gift with gratitude and thanksgiving. Retreat to the "temple" of your soul and discover peace. As you transition to a new environment, spend more quality moments in meditation. Believe Me, you will need the calmness and serenity. Jan understands the challenges that come along with a physical move. But she also wants you to accelerate your spiritual progress. That comes with more focus on prayer and meditation. Jan hopes the time after the move offers you a clear path to renewal and restoration. During your remaining days on earth, I want you to serve Me in several areas. I can utilize your writing and communication talents as both a "prophet" and a "healer". Don't shake your head in disbelief! Believe that you can do the greater works. Trust Me and trust your dear wife to help you accomplish any spiritual goal. Anything can happen when you raise your consciousness. An increase in awareness begins with greater emphasis on prayer and meditation. Why wait? 'Just do it', as the slogan says. Pray more. Meditate more. Get closer to us in the time you spend apart from the world."

DAY 30

TODAY'S TWEET FROM SITTING WITH GOD:

"Real transformation requires total dedication, surrender and trusting Me. Be open and receptive to your unfolding journey."

FROM THE HOLY BIBLE:

"But when they saw him walking on the lake, they thought he was a ghost. They cried out, because they all saw him and were terrified. Immediately he spoke to them and said, "Take courage! It is I. Don't be afraid." (Mark 6:49-51).

TODAY'S TOPIC OR QUESTION FROM ME:

I am so grateful

RESPONSE FROM GOD AND JAN:

"Thank you for your expression of gratitude. However, your precious wife and I have only begun to work together in your best interest. This is "Moving Day". You will be hitting I-35 South from Minneapolis to Temple later today. Don't worry or fret. We have your route already planned. Jan and I will get you safely from "The Land of 10,000 Lakes" to the "Lone Star State." Before you leave the North Country, let us quickly review your 16 years as a Minnesotan. You were a resident chaplain for a year at Fairview Southdale Hospital in Edina, you served as the senior minister for the largest Unity church in the Twin Cities for nearly four years and then you were an interim pastor at two other Unity churches located in Bloomington and Woodbury, respectively. You authored several books (including SITTING WITH GOD/MEDITATING FOR GOD'S DIVINE GUIDANCE) and you had an op-ed article published in the Minneapolis newspaper. Probably most significant of all, you served as your dear wife's fulltime caregiver for nearly five years. You had an impressive run. You and Jan also spent quality time with her family and the three grandchildren. All in all, you all left a solid legacy in her beloved home state of Lefsa and Lutefisk. But now it's time to move forward on the next step of your spiritual journey. Are you ready? We are."

DAY 31

TODAY'S TWEET FROM SITTING WITH GOD:

"Be still and know that I AM God. Watch for My Presence everywhere. I walk beside you on this glorious path."

FROM THE HOLY BIBLE:

"Daniel answered, O king live forever! My God sent his angel, and he shut the mouth of the lions. They have not hurt me because I was found innocent in his sight. The king was overjoyed and gave orders to lift him out of the den of lions. No wound was found on him, because Daniel had trusted in his God." (Daniel 6:21-23)

TODAY'S TOPIC OR QUESTION FROM ME:

Perseverance

RESPONSE FROM GOD AND JAN:

"Perseverance remains your spiritual key. You must persevere as the next step approaches. Keep on Keeping on. If you do, everything will unfold in divine order. Know that you have our full support. Practice faith. Don't get discouraged or even think about quitting the spiritual path. Remain focused on the way forward. Let go of fear and doubt. Have complete confidence in a positive outcome. Drop all negative thoughts. Fulfill your sacred destiny with boldness. Become a clear channel so that I can express Myself through you. Be hopeful and expectant about the future. Jan and I know things won't be easy for a while. You have sustained several major losses. Not only did you lose your sweetheart physically, emotionally and spiritually, you lost your job and purpose as her caregiver. To prevail and thrive, you must surrender to our Will. Don't fight or second-guess us. Look at every day as a blessed opportunity to grow spiritually. We promise to keep you busy. Fasten your seat belt. It could be a bumpy ride."

DAY 32

TODAY'S TWEET FROM SITTING WITH GOD:

"Unite with Me. When you and I combine forces, Good follows in our footsteps. We dispense love and forgiveness."

FROM THE HOLY BIBLE:

"You do not lack any spiritual gift as you eagerly wait for our Lord Jesus Christ to be revealed. He will keep you strong to the end, so that you will be blameless on the day our Lord appears. God, who has called you into fellowship with his son Jesus Christ, is faithful." (1 Corinthians: 7-9)

TODAY'S TOPIC OR QUESTION FROM ME:

Patience

RESPONSE FROM GOD AND JAN:

"Be aware that anything important or worthwhile requires time. Give your move to Texas the necessary hours, days and weeks to process itself. Each small piece of the larger puzzle must fit into its rightful place. Be patient as people and events get moved into alignment. A whole "New Life" is being assembled for you. Take a deep breath. Try not to rush the orderly evolution. Avoid accelerating any aspect of the process. Be mindful regarding any long-term commitments. Think of yourself as being "Under Construction". You have yet to begin grieving your dear wife. Preparing for the move and traveling back home for an exploratory visit has occupied your time. Don't be in a hurry! Above all, do not tumble willy-nilly into any emotional affairs of the heart. Loneliness can create painful errors. Everyone here in Heaven is pleased that you are still wearing your wedding band. Keeping that blessed ring in place on your left hand offers a visible statement of your continuing devotion. That's a good thing. Manage all expectations with patience. Trust Me (and your dear wife). Everything is being sorted out for you. Relax!"

DAY 33

TODAY'S TWEET FROM SITTING WITH GOD:

"Follow Me. Let Me go before you to make the crooked places straight. You can then walk through every danger unscathed."

FROM THE HOLY BIBLE:

"But whosoever listens to Me will live in safety and be at ease, without fear of harm." (Proverbs 1:33)

TODAY'S TOPIC OR QUESTION FROM ME:

A stab of grief

RESPONSE FROM GOD AND JAN:

"Unfortunately, that's the way grief works. You might be fine for a while. Then, out of nowhere, a sudden pain unexpectedly stabs deep into your heart. You felt that yesterday. Your losses came roaring home. Remember, you have not only lost Jan. You are also grieving the loss of your Minnesota family and friends. In many ways, you flourished in the Gopher state. Now, that also has been ripped from you. This aspect of grieving should not be underestimated. Minnesota was good to you and for you. Being separated from your life with Jan and the environment in which you lived it represents a big loss. Know that the memories accumulated over the past 16 years will survive in your mind and heart. But do not be surprised when this longing for the past appears without warning. Allow yourself some tears. You and your sweetie accumulated many treasures together in the North Country. Savor them in thought and feeling. When you think of the cold climate, remember also the warmth, love and affection you experienced there. Jan was your best gift from Minnesota, but not your only one."

DAY 34

TODAY'S TWEET FROM SITTING WITH GOD:

"Life tests you daily. When trials and troubles erupt, move ever closer to Me. Meet fear with faith."

FROM THE HOLY BIBLE:

"Behold I will create new heavens and a new earth. The former things will not be remembered, nor will they come to mind. But be glad and rejoice forever in what I will create." (Isaiah 65:17-18)

TODAY'S TOPIC OR QUESTION FROM ME:

I'm frustrated by the slow pace of my move to Texas

RESPONSE FROM GOD AND JAN:

"Don't become anxious. Calm yourself. Too many rapid changes (especially at your advanced age) can boggle even the sharpest mind. Be patient. You're fretting because your "stuff" hasn't arrived yet from Minnesota. Chill out. Be at peace. Stay centered. Don't get into a snit. Watch your eating and snacking. Don't overdo anything. We know you like being back in the land of enchiladas, tacos, chili con carne and barbecue beef. When tempted to gorge yourself on food to relieve stress, try some meditation. Sit down and relax. Spend some time with Me and your dear wife in the silence. Let everything happen in perfect sequence. Trust that Jan and I are sorting out people and events. Your job now? Get into the flow of your new life. Let it carry you along. Avoid taking things into your own hands. Trying to control the process just slows things down. Stand aside. Allow us, your spiritual partners, to do our thing. Jan and I can function without suggestions or interference. Quit trying to seize control. Be a willing and grateful participant. We'll take the lead. You won't be disappointed in our performance."

DAY 35

TODAY'S TWEET FROM SITTING WITH GOD:

"Improve your mind with My wisdom. Bolster your heart with My Love. Let me fill you with the glory of Heaven."

FROM THE HOLY BIBLE:

"Enter through the narrow gate. For wide is the gate and broad is the road that leads to destruction, and many enter through it. But small is the gate and narrow the road that leads to life, and only a few find it." (Matthew 7: 13)

TODAY'S TOPIC OR QUESTION FROM ME:

What would you have me do?

RESPONSE FROM GOD AND JAN:

"Get acquainted with your hometown again. Pay attention to everything. Take it all in. Although you born and raised in Temple, things have changed. It's no longer a small town. In fact, Central Texas is booming. The surrounding area population of Waco/Temple/Belton/Killeen/Fort Hood is 450,000 and growing fast. Be open to new people and experiences. Connect with your classmates from Temple High School that still live in the area. Plan on attending your class reunion scheduled in September. Embrace the excitement of discovering the newness of your old/new home. With all the activity of moving from Minnesota to Texas, let Me remind you of something important. You still need to grieve the loss of your beloved wife. Grief has a way of slamming you when least expected. You are carrying Jan's sudden loss deep in your heart. Of course, it helps that she is deeply involved with your life journey. But, when the sadness comes on you, stop and grieve. In the meantime, let the new wine of your hometown be poured into the empty wineskins. Cut off the padlock protecting your heart. Lighten up. Your dedication as Jan's 24/7 caregiver has earned you a break. She wants you to enjoy it."

DAY 36

TODAY'S TWEET FROM SITTING WITH GOD:

"Refuse to judge by appearances. Inner beauty always exceeds outer beauty. Search for the good in everyone."

FROM THE HOLY BIBLE:

"And God said, "Let there be light," and there was light." (Genesis 1:3)

TODAY'S TOPIC OR QUESTION FROM ME:

How am I doing?

RESPONSE FROM GOD AND JAN:

"You must keep purifying your mind. Cleanse your human brain daily. The "Dark Side" wants to pollute your consciousness. Evil seeks to stop, confuse and tempt anyone with spiritual inclinations. Those opposed to us will use all available tricks to scuttle you. They can be both subtle and direct. Satan regularly assaults your five human senses. He exploits every weakness and vulnerability. Do not become his unwitting victim. Observe your thinking on a regular basis. Be alert to subtle or radical shifts. You can always choose to switch gears from negative to positive. But it requires conscious intention. Anytime you feel yourself slip-sliding away, stop at once and seek My help. Ask Me to rescue you. I will arrive posthaste. Try not to separate yourself from Me in the first place. Increase your prayer and meditation time whenever you feel attacked. Your salvation lies in our unity of spirit. Deliverance depends upon the strength of our sacred alignment. Line up your thinking with Mine. Unite your human brain with My divine mind. Activate the vast spiritual power within you. Ask Me to intervene when you feel threatened. Jan and I are always prepared to respond. Never hesitate when you feel abandoned, alone or tempted by anything. We will spring into quick action."

DAY 37

TODAY'S TWEET FROM SITTING WITH GOD:

"I AM the potter; you are the clay. Be patient. In you, I am molding My version of a spiritual masterpiece."

FROM THE HOLY BIBLE:

"Love the Lord your God with all your heart and with all your soul and with all your strength and with all your mind, and Love your neighbor as yourself." (Luke 10:27)

TODAY'S TOPIC OR QUESTION FROM ME:

Change

RESPONSE FROM GOD AND JAN:

"Embrace change. Take on your new life with gratitude. Surrender to the exploration of possibilities. Be patient with yourself and the grieving process. Don't race around trying to accomplish everything at once. Savor your return to a familiar environment. Be open to new people. Take it easy. Live one day at a time. Take what comes in 24- hour chunks. Feel the presence of your dear wife and Me circling protectively around you. We are leading and guiding you. Do not force anything. Let Me repeat: don't try to force anything. Let things evolve with gentleness. Know that you are among friends, especially on this side of the veil. Your spiritual progress takes place amid constant cheering from Heaven. Can you hear our shouts of encouragement? Enjoy the fruits of your labors. You've worked hard to get this far. Find satisfaction and reward in the journey. Extraordinary blessings are flowing toward you now. Reach up and pluck a shining star from the galaxy. Jan and I promise that many of those bright stars belong to you."

DAY 38

TODAY'S TWEET FROM SITTING WITH GOD:

"Live in today's possibilities. Let the past go, except where gratitude and forgiveness are needed. Go forward."

FROM THE HOLY BIBLE:

"Who are you, Lord?" Saul asked. "I am Jesus, whom you are persecuting," he replied. "Now get up and go into the city, and you will be told what you must do." (Acts 9:6-7)

TODAY'S TOPIC OR QUESTION FROM ME:

Please reassure me that I was a good husband to Jan

RESPONSE FROM GOD AND JAN:

"In a word, yes. Once you got past those years of indecision, you realized what a wonderful wife and partner she was for you. You complemented each other in every way. At the end of your marriage, as your dear wife slipped into Heaven, you understood your divine bond even more. After you and Jan married, your basic commitment to one another never wavered. Your sacred union included total fidelity, mutual respect, and a wealth of good communications. Jan told Me that she was never once bored with you. I know you felt the same way towards her. Many couples yearn for that type of relationship. I think you prize Jan even more now. You miss her in countless ways: her friendship, intelligence, companionship and her inner and outer beauty. She was a lovely woman, in both appearance and spirit. You were forever proud of her wherever you went as a couple. Whether it was out to eat at a local restaurant or enjoying the several cruises you took together, you were always proud of your wifey. Jan felt the same about you. You two lovebirds were best friends as well as husband and wife. That says a lot. Each of you honored Me as well. I bless you for that. Your care-giving of Jan at the end of your human time together was the "icing on the cake" for both of you. You'll have a lot to talk about when you get back together."

DAY 39

TODAY'S TWEET FROM SITTING WITH GOD:

"You ask what is yours to do. Becoming one with Me ranks as your highest priority. Nothing else comes close."

FROM THE HOLY BIBLE:

"Because of the LORD'S love we are not consumed, for his compassions never fail. They are new every morning; great is thy faithfulness." (Lamentations 3:22-23)

TODAY'S TOPIC OR QUESTION FROM ME:

Divine Guidance

RESPONSE GOD AND JAN:

"Your sweet wife and I have some important guidance for you: practice self-care. We know you get anxious when things don't happen quickly. Quit pushing yourself so hard. Everything is falling into place. Moving from one part of the country to another requires planning, preparation and patience. Lest she and I remind you, it all represents a "process". Get more rest. Quit worrying so much. Try not to become frazzled or frantic when delays crop up. Instead, expect them. Make a conscious decision to ratchet down your impatience. Look for a calm place amidst the frustrations. Trust our management abilities. We promise to sort things out to your satisfaction. Declare this a day of rest and relaxation. You deserve some down time. You have been dealt a couple of heavy emotional blows. You'll need time to recover. Restoring yourself to wholeness requires more turns of the calendar. Know that you have awesome support, both on earth and in Heaven. I deploy my angels on many fronts. Let them go about their business. Take a deep breath. Try to relax. Take a day off. Lie down for a nap. Listen to some music. Maybe watch a movie. Let the world turn for a while without you."

DAY 40

TODAY'S TWEET:

"You serve Me best when you listen closely for divine guidance. I need open channels through which My blessings can flow."

FROM THE HOLY BIBLE:

"Being confident of this, that he who began a good work in you will carry it on to completion until the day of Jesus Christ." (Philippians 1:6)

TODAY'S TOPIC OR QUESTION FROM ME:

Please tell me again: what is your Will for me?

RESPONSE GOD AND JAN:

"My Will (and your dear wife's Will) for you is that you continue unpacking and establishing your new home in Temple. We are pleased that you heeded our guidance to move from Minnesota to Texas. Jan and I also understand the physical and emotional demands that a major relocation can put on people. We have tried to help you over some of the rough spots. But think about the results so far. Everything went smoothly with the moving company. The perfect people showed up at the appointed time. Your two trips to Texas both came off well, especially navigating I-35 twice between Dallas and Temple. You've had good meetings with both your adult son and ex-wife. You've found a nice place to live in Temple. Several special people have helped assist and facilitate your resettlement. Have you noticed the ones whose first names were "Chris" or "Christy"? It may not have been obvious, but these individuals indeed played "The Christ" role in your spiritual and physical journey home. There are never any accidents where I AM concerned. So, Jan's and My Will is that you "keep on keeping on" until the relocation process completes itself. We are here for you and ready to help as needed."

DAY 41

TODAY'S TWEET FROM SITTING WITH GOD:

"I hear your prayers of gratitude. I AM shaping your life for My purposes. Stay strong. The best awaits you."

FROM THE HOLY BIBLE:

"For where your treasure is, there your heart will be also." (Matthew 7:21)

TODAY'S TOPIC OR QUESTION FROM ME;

Protection from the storms of life

RESPONSE FROM GOD AND JAN:

"Be of good cheer. Every storm of both the natural and human variety will someday pass. All troubled skies clear eventually. My warm and beautiful sun always finds a way to shine forth again. Your wonderful wife Jan came into Heaven six weeks ago tonight. I know you miss her. You long to have one more day of her treasured presence. You two never really had a chance to say goodbye. When you went back to the bedroom with Jan's medications at 9 p.m. that night, she had already passed. I realize the suddenness of her physical death stunned you. I can assure you that she was at peace when she arrived here. I greeted your wonderful wife with love and warmth. She returned My greeting. I think Jan was also taken aback by how fast everything happened. The aftermath for you has proceeded OK, despite your huge sense of loss and sadness. Your move back to Texas has gone smoothly, due in great part due to her involvement. Yes, the dearly departed often choose to remain quite active in the lives of their loved ones. Jan wants to help you in this phase of your spiritual journey. You could not have a more loyal and fervent advocate. Please turn to either or both of us when you get lonely, depressed or frightened. We promise to shield and protect you. You can always count on us."

DAY 42

TODAY'S TWEET FROM SITTING WITH GOD:

"Trust Me. Stay positive. I AM your protector and deliverer. Remain joyful. I will not let anything harm you."

FROM THE HOLY BIBLE:

"The LORD is my rock, my fortress and my deliverer; my God is my rock, in whom I take refuge. He is my shield and the horn of my salvation, my stronghold." (Psalm 18:2)

TODAY'S TOPIC OR QUESTION FROM ME:

I need your counsel

RESPONSE FROM GOD AND JAN:

"Lean forward. Pay close attention. Hear the combined voices of your dear wife and Me. Listen to everything we say. Follow our instructions. First, you must relax and be patient. Take time to get established. Do not become overwrought when moving related delays occur. Do some deep breathing when you feel yourself rushing. Everything moves forward in divine order. Not too fast, not too slow. You consciously slowed things down these past two days. That's good. Pace yourself. Seek moderation. The "heavy lifting" is behind you. Go to bed earlier. Get some rest. Your body, mind and spirit have been tested from the moment that Jan passed. So far, you're doing fine. Refuse to melt down now. Allow each day to unfold. Don't get stressed trying to pull your apartment together perfectly. Be easy on yourself. Look for people and situations who nurture your spiritual life. When someone disturbs your peacefulness, release them. Your life is in flux. Don't add to the confusion and chaos by complicating things further. Avoid problems. You are doing as well as could be expected. Remember, you just lost your sweetheart. That's a heavy blow for anyone."

DAY 43

TODAY'S TWEET FROM SITTING WITH GOD:

"We have a divine appointment each day. Meeting together in the silence helps us become better acquainted."

FROM THE HOLY BIBLE:

"Do not judge, and you will not be judged. Do not condemn and you will not be condemned. Forgive and you will be forgiven." (Luke 6:37)

TODAY'S TOPIC OR QUESTION FROM ME:

I am listening for your guidance

RESPONSE FROM GOD AND JAN:

"You've been back home in Texas for less than two weeks. Your precious wife and I are both pleased with your progress. Use today to tidy up and get organized. Proceed in a relaxed and orderly manner. Every small step counts for something. Getting your car inspected today and obtaining a Texas driver's license were practical and necessary steps. Life is a combination of the practical and the spiritual. Do not neglect either. We hope you think about joining a church and finding a grief support group. You have been too busy to feel the grief from Jan's loss. It hasn't caught up with you yet. But the day will come when grief will bring you down to the ground. Be prepared for that moment. Try to find a 12-step support group. This could be an important recovery bridge for you from Minnesota, where you were involved with two separate weekly meetings. By the way, your wisdom and presence are missed by everyone in those groups. Know that you have important spiritual work remaining in several areas. Once you get settled, I want you to move ahead with some of My creative projects. I AM planning to use your talents to help bless, heal and encourage others. Be ready."

DAY 44

TODAY'S TWEET:

"Extend your hand and heart in a welcome to all. Exclude no one. Use love to replace hostility and distrust."

FROM THE HOLY BIBLE:

"Cast your bread upon the waters, for after many days you will find it again." (Ecclesiastes 11:1)

TODAY'S TOPIC OR QUESTION FROM ME:

Why am I trying to be perfect? I know better

RESPONSE FROM GOD AND JAN:

"You're right. Give up trying to be perfect. Expecting perfection from anyone, especially yourself, is an exercise in futility. Expectations are the seeds of resentment. Just be who you are and grant other people the same right. You are a loving, gentle and caring human being. Forgive yourself for not being perfect. Look at the good things about you. You are not walking the earth with an angry chip on your shoulder. You are basically a kind and considerate person. You show consideration for others. You practice the Golden Rule. You do not exhibit a free-floating hostility that sews contentiousness in your wake. You are friendly, compassionate and decent. Of course, you aren't perfect. But then who is? Be understanding and accepting of your human foibles. Everyone has them. Being human should not bring condemnation. I created every soul with a loving and gentle heart. I instilled the "caring" gene deep in your soul. It is the fallen world that seeks to corrupt and destroy the best of My children. Your dear wife Jan and I see you as a high-quality person with good intentions toward all. Holding yourself or anyone to unrealistic standards brings frustration and disappointment. Accept yourself for who and what you are."

DAY 45

TODAY'S TWEET FROM SITTING WITH GOD:

"Try to tune out a noisy and chaotic world. Come sit with Me in the blessed silence. Find peace in My Presence."

FROM THE HOLY BIBLE:

"For we are the temple of the living God. As God has said: "I will live with them and walk among them, and I will be their God, and they will be my people." (2 Corinthians 6:16)

TODAY'S TOPIC OR QUESTION FROM ME:

What about new experiences? I still miss Jan

RESPONSE:

"Be open to new experiences and new people. Jan and I both realize it's not easy for those who are left behind to simply move on. That's not the way grief works. Your thoughts keep coming back to her. Remember, there are no accidents in this spiritual universe. She and I are bringing new situations and individuals into your life. Let them bless you, however they will. Be at least receptive to our choices. Stay alert as opportunities blossom. Your sweetheart knows you still love her dearly. But please don't let undying love for your wife close your heart altogether. Life is still for the living. Avoid feeling guilty if you enjoy a casual conversation with another person. Jan wants you to have joy in your life. She understands your sense of grief and loss. Please know that she still misses you too. Your dedicated wife is your biggest booster here, outside of Me. Jan remains very committed to your human and spiritual progress. She works tirelessly on your behalf. We both are guiding you through this deep forest of change. Keep moving ever closer to us. Don't miss a single thing that we have planned for you. You won't be disappointed. Wonders are coming."

DAY 46

TODAY'S TWEET FROM SITTING WITH GOD:

"Enjoy today. Revel in every touch of happiness that comes your way. Celebrate. Give thanks for your many blessings."

FROM THE HOLY BIBLE:

"And afterward, I will pour out my Spirit on all people. Your sons and daughters will prophesy, your old men will dream dreams, your young men will see visions." (Joel 2:28)

TODAY'S TOPIC OR QUESTION FROM ME:

I turn 80 today

RESPONSE FROM GOD AND JAN:

"Happy birthday! You were born 80 years ago in a small Texas city named Temple. There are never any accidents. Spiritually, the "temple" stands as the holiest of the holies. Metaphysically, you are the "priest" in the "temple" of your mind. You were blessed with fine parents, grandparents, aunts and uncles. You came of age in the 1950s during a time of great stability and peace. Your education included graduation from Temple High School, Baylor University in Waco, Texas and the Unity School of Religious Studies in Missouri. Your career path consisted of success in a large public corporation (7-Elven) in Dallas, Texas and as an ordained Unity minister. You spent six years working in the Unity headquarters as Senior Director of Outreach. You later completed a chaplain residency, served several Unity churches as their senior minister and now have become a published author. Your personal record includes a wonderful 22 ½ year marriage to your soulmate Jan. Of course, there were glitches and missteps along the way. That is part of every human life. You lost some important relationships. You are familiar with the pain of divorce and family estrangement. For the past three decades, you have traveled the spiritual course. Once you selected My Path, I was free to choose you. You've come a long way, Babe, as Jan would say. Happy Birthday! You are My beloved son, in whom I AM well pleased."

DAY 47

TODAY'S TWEET FROM SITTING WITH GOD:

"Linking your human mind to My divine ideas can result in creative miracles. Trust the sacred insight I place within you."

FROM THE HOLY BIBLE:

"For by him all things were created: things in heaven and on earth, visible or invisible, whether thrones or powers or rulers or authorities; all things were created by him and for him." (Colossians 1:16)

TODAY'S TOPIC OR QUESTION FROM ME:

Creativity

RESPONSE FROM GOD AND JAN:

"Stay alert for creative opportunities. Be attentive. Remain tuned in to the divine ideas that float your way. Potential miracles are headed in your direction. Do not reject anything out of hand. What may seem preposterous might have great implications. Examine each possibility with careful eyes. When presented with something meaningful, seize it. Put aside your shyness. Act with bold intention. Some of My best divine ideas are being offered and entrusted to you. Visualize them coming into fruition. Watch as they materialize to improve lives and bring hope and harmony. Fill yourself with love as you approach any creative endeavor. Involve both your heart and mind in the creative process. If the heart is not on board, the mind will falter. Project My Presence into the planning and execution of every idea. Trust Me. You can create miracles. Believe that you will do the greater works. Both Jan and I, working together with you, can make it happen. Drop your doubts. Any creative thing done in My name has a chance to succeed."

DAY 48

TODAY'S TWEET FROM SITTING WITH GOD:

"Persevere in your faith, no matter how desperate things may seem. I provide the wisdom, courage and strength you will need."

FROM THE HOLY BIBLE:

"But the Lord is faithful, and he will strengthen and protect you from the evil one." (2 Thessalonians 3:3)

TODAY'S TOPIC OR QUESTION FROM ME:

What spiritual gifts can I use to serve God?

RESPONSE FROM GOD AND JAN:

"You communicate well through both the spoken and written word. But anyone's greatest spiritual gift is who they are. Who you are speaks much louder than what you say. When you become infilled with My Presence, people sense that you are somehow different. You become a blessing to each life you touch. Every moment spent communing with Me adds to your spiritual persona. I want you to glow with spirituality, good will, love and acceptance. Let the sweet perfume of goodness mark the air around you. If anyone breathes its fragrance, they will find themselves blessed. Put a winning smile on your face for everyone you meet. Extend forgiveness. Offer a pardon to the accused. Walk the earth with integrity, courage and strength. Be strong at your core. Steep yourself in rigorous honesty. Maintain your values, no matter what. Shun intolerance and bigotry. Avoid anger and needless controversy. Drop resentments and dreams of revenge. Be consistent in your positive attitude. Once you become comfortable in your own spiritual skin, you can use your gifts of creative expression to glorify Me."

DAY 49

TODAY'S TWEET FROM SITTING WITH GOD:

"Always choose the healing power of forgiveness. Clear your mind of every grudge. Release all negativity."

FROM THE HOLY BIBLE:

"And God spoke all these words: "I am the LORD your God, who brought you out of Egypt, out of the land of slavery. You shall have no other gods before me." (Exodus 20: 1-3)

TODAY'S TOPIC OR QUESTION FROM ME:

Forgiveness

RESPONSE FROM GOD AND JAN:

"You are making good progress on your "life lesson" of forgiveness. You've developed a better relationship with your sister Linda since you both lost your respective spouses. You now possess a common bond. Jan and I are glad to see you and your only sibling relating with genuine affection. You and your adult son Jeff have much better communications now. That has required forgiveness work on both of your parts. Of course, the lack of a relationship with your adult daughter Laura continues to bother you. You always stand ready to heal the breach. Just be patient. Give her time. Where there is life, there is hope. Jan and I urge you to practice forgiveness with everyone, but especially yourself. No human being gets everything right. Take great pride in your service and commitment to Jan as her full-time caregiver. She sings your praises every day. Anytime you feel critical of your actions in any area, remember that you stepped up during a time of testing and challenge. You showed your true character. You practiced the Golden Rule to perfection."

DAY 50

TODAY'S TWEET FROM SITTING WITH GOD:

"I watch over you, morning, noon and night. Trust Me with your concerns. I will lead you on the proper path."

FROM THE HOLY BIBLE:

"Blessed are the meek, for they shall inherit the earth." (Matthew 5:5)

TODAY'S TOPIC OR QUESTION FROM ME:

I miss my Jannie

RESPONSE FROM GOD AND JAN:

"I know how much you miss your sweet wife. You two had something only a few couples realize: a sacred bonding of both the human and divine aspects of your soul journeys. You both walked My Path. You supported each other's spiritual growth. For many spouses, when only one travels the higher road, the other can feel threatened. You and Jan never had that problem. She was proud of your work as a minister. She also admired your worthwhile activities in the corporate world, especially what you accomplished for 7-Eleven and the Jerry Lewis Labor Day Telethon for the Muscular Dystrophy Association. You were proud of her nursing career and then the tremendous contribution she made as your partner in ministry. Jan became a "minister's wife" overnight and performed flawlessly. You both were divinely blessed when she walked by your side. Believe Me, your dear wife still walks right beside you. She doesn't let you travel anywhere without her. When you feel sad and overwhelmed by grief, understand that Jan's sweet soul remains with you eternally. A union like yours can never be torn asunder. She understands your longing for her physical presence. For now, settle for My promise that neither of us will ever leave or forsake you."

DAY 51

TODAY'S TWEET FROM SITTING WITH GOD:

"Practice being peaceful. Smother the flames of resentment before they can burn out of control. Be a peacemaker."

FROM THE HOLY BIBLE:

"How beautiful you are, my darling! Oh, how beautiful! Your eyes are like doves." (Song of Songs 1:15)

TODAY'S TOPIC OR QUESTION FROM ME:

I am so grateful to God and my dear wife

RESPONSE FROM GOD AND JAN:

"Jan and I treasure your expressions of gratitude. We appreciate your recognition of our ongoing bond with you. You truly understand the role she and I are playing in your orderly restoration to wholeness. Keep following our daily guidance. However, know there are also other forces trying to influence you. The Dark Side probes your weaknesses and vulnerabilities on a regular basis. Besides their ongoing threat, you must keep an eye on your own human ego. It can get puffed up if you aren't watchful. In addition, always be alert to the debilitating effect of fear and worry. At your age and place in life, concerns about finances and health issues can pull you down and cause stress. You must counteract any negative influences by adopting a thankful and joyful attitude. Begin each day in a grateful state of mind. That keeps you focused on the correct path toward Heaven. Anytime you feel down or abandoned, recall the many blessings already bestowed on you. Jan and I are both working hard for you right now. If you sense any sort of spiritual attack, call out for us. We will fly to your rescue. I promise it."

DAY 52

TODAY'S TWEET FROM SITTING WITH GOD:

"You are My child. I AM your Creator. I made you in My image and likeness. I know how perfect you are."

FROM THE HOLY BIBLE:

"For in the day of trouble he will keep me safe in his dwelling; he will hide me in the shelter of his tabernacle and set me high upon a rock." (Psalm 27:5)

TODAY'S TOPIC OR QUESTION FROM ME:

How should I proceed?

RESPONSE FROM GOD AND JAN:

"Keep praying and communing daily with your dear wife and Me. Your immediate task is to get adjusted to your new environment. You've only been back in Temple for three weeks. Curb your impatience! Take extra time to deepen your understanding of our divine guidance. We never lead you astray. Take this period of change to increase your reading of spiritual material. Dedicate more hours to meditation and prayer. Also take some time to enjoy your new-found freedom. Jan knows how much your caregiving duties required in terms of physical stamina and mental toughness. You've earned a break. Don't squander it. Be good to yourself. Lighten up a little. Enjoy life as much as possible. Yes, we both understand that you are still feeling your way through the grief process. Just don't be so hard on yourself. Let the grieving take as long as needed. There is no calendar when it comes to working though loss. It takes as long as it takes. It might take a year or 10 years or even more time before the heart and mind finally stop crying. Never place a deadline on your feelings. You cannot push away deep sadness forever. The heart simply won't stand for it. In the meantime, Jan and I are here to help you navigate the process."

DAY 53

TODAY'S TWEET FROM SITTING WITH GOD:

"Acting together, you and I can bring spiritual light to a darkened world. Allow My Truth to shine through you."

FROM THE HOLY BIBLE:

"In Him was life, and that life was the light of men. The light shines in the darkness, but the darkness has not understood it." (John 1:4-5)

TODAY'S TOPIC OR QUESTION FROM ME:

How can I be a "light"?

RESPONSE FROM GOD AND JAN:

"Every revelation received in consciousness brings additional light. You must seek TRUTH and ONENESS with Me before any light can come. The world is mired in darkness and division. Many misguided people have evil designs upon their neighbors. We are seeing the worst of humanity being acted out without fear of judgment or punishment. Here is an eternal Truth: There are always dire consequences for disobeying Me. I make that statement with sorrow. I AM a loving God and slow to anger. Seeking Me first remains the only path to dispelling the current darkness shrouding the human soul. I'm hoping that some prophetic warnings might alert people to the approaching dangers. I want you to act as one of those human voices proclaiming My concern about an off-track world. But do not expect anyone to pay much attention. I can promise that any gloom-and-doom message will not be well-received. Most people just don't want to hear it. I'm afraid the future may require some huge natural disasters before anyone will listen. But, even then, I'm not hopeful. I know you feel inadequate or unprepared to bring such a message of warning on My behalf. Let Me worry about that. Just allow the Holy Spirit to work through you. Even if only one person hears and acts on my concerns as voiced through you, the effort will be worth it."

DAY 54

TODAY'S TWEET FROM SITTING WITH GOD:

"My Kingdom lies beyond the human senses. Go deeper into the invisible realms. Search for Me in the chambers of your heart."

FROM THE HOLY BIBLE:

"I myself will tend my sheep and have them lie down, declares the Sovereign LORD. I will search for the lost and bring back the strays." (Ezekiel 34: 15-16)

TODAY'S TOPIC OR QUESTION FROM ME:

What about Grace?

RESPONSE FROM GOD AND JAN:

"You are surrounded by My Grace. I provide it freely to you. Grace has helped overcome many challenges since you embarked on the spiritual Path. I realize that My Way is not an easy one. It takes courage, discipline, commitment and a huge amount of Heavenly Grace to keep going again and again into the fiery furnace. You had to release some worldly things that were near and dear to you, especially a successful corporate career and financial security. I sent you to a "far country", away from your native Texas. Through your willingness to follow My direction, you have remained faithful to My spiritual plans for you. Losing Jan and relocating back to Texas are just two more hurdles now facing you. Try not to worry much about the future. Take measured strides, one day at a time. Listen for My (and Jan's) guidance every single day. Trust our divine plan for your spiritual destiny. Claim My Grace to help you over any obstacle. Call out for God's Grace to sustain you through the low moments. Be bold in your claims. Ask for what you need. My Grace acts as your first and last resource and ever-present treasure. The Grace of Heaven collects around you as we speak."

DAY 55

TODAY'S TWEET FROM SITTING WITH GOD:

"My Grace acts as your sufficiency in all things. Trust Me always. Have relentless faith in My sacred promises."

FROM THE HOLY BIBLE:

"How great you are, O Sovereign LORD! There is no one like you, and there is no God but you, as we have heard with our own ears." (2 Samuel 7:22)

TODAY'S TOPIC OR QUESTION FROM ME:

What about The Spiritual Path?

RESPONSE FROM GOD AND JAN:

"My Path sometimes unfolds smoothly, but more often not. It can often become a scary and daunting challenge. Your dear wife and I are working hard to make your journey a smooth one. We realize this isn't an easy time for you. You miss Jan, your soul mate and love of your life. You just completed a physical move of more than 1,000 miles. You are 80 years old, I mean 80 years young. In many ways, you face the prospect of once again starting over. Jan and I are trying hard to help you with the changes. Put your faith and trust in us. Try to follow our sacred guidance. As we have emphasized many times, you must be patient with the process. No one can upend his or her life without consequences. Keep your good humor. See the bright side in every personal encounter or situation. Smile more! "Fake it until you make it". Be good to yourself in some way each day. Search for positive diversions and interesting people. Keep your eyes focused on the wondrous Path before you. It leads straight to My Kingdom. Your sweetie and I eagerly await your arrival. I promise that you won't get here one minute too soon or one second too late. When you do finally do enter Heaven, she and I will be waiting for you with open and loving arms. Expect a warm greeting. You'll glow with appreciation. "Welcome Home, I'll tell you. Jan will probably say, "Hi Babe, I've been waiting for you. What took you so long?"

DAY 56

TODAY'S TWEET FROM SITTING WITH GOD:

"Take shelter under My protective and storm proof wings. Let the winds of fear and uncertainty blow harmlessly around you."

FROM THE HOLY BIBLE:

"What, then, shall we say in response to this? If God is for us, who can be against us?" (Romans 8:31)

TODAY'S TOPIC OR QUESTION FROM ME:

What is Heaven really like?

RESPONSE FROM GOD AND JAN:

"I will let My beloved child Jan answer: (Jan): "Babe, I think you will really like it here. Since I am now Spirit (or Soul) and not a "body" in physical terms, I am free from all pain and sickness. As you know, my human body was weak and worn out. At the end, it was hard for me to get around. Now I have total freedom of movement. Heaven is so wonderful and beautiful! Only positive things are allowed in here. Love, acceptance, forgiveness, inclusivity and good will are everywhere. Negativity does not exist. Yes, I have already communed with every member of my human family who preceded me here. I've also seen many friends and people that I worked with during my lifetime. Here is how it works: you are free to meet up with any other soul if that soul is agreeable. There are no forced meetings. I can see each event in my life so clearly now. Everything happened for a reason. I received many opportunities for spiritual growth, although I didn't realize it at the time. One of my life's greatest gifts was our relationship, especially during the four years before my passing. You were my full-time caregiver. My bad health situation gave us both a chance to experience unconditional love. Many couples never find anything close to what you and I had. I look at our marriage in its last stages as "Heaven on earth". I love you still."

DAY 57

TODAY'S TWEET FROM SITTING WITH GOD:

"Never lose your spiritual momentum. Meet with Me daily. I will keep you centered and focused."

FROM THE HOLY BIBLE:

"The Spirit of God has made me; the breath of the Almighty gives me life." (Job 33:4)

TODAY'S TOPIC OR QUESTION FROM ME:

What about the effects of aging?

RESPONSE FROM GOD AND JAN:

"Every human body eventually wears out. Nobody lives forever in their mortal form. What goes forward when you leave earth behind? Your beautiful soul rushes onward and upward to Heaven as you pass over. As the body ages, shrinks and deteriorates, the incredible and eternal soul can often be expanding to enormous proportions. Your spiritual growth is never restricted by sickness. As your body shrivels and struggles, the magnificent soul may be soaring to the heights. For some, the soul lies dormant until the aging process accelerates. As the flesh weakens, the inner life become stronger. See each day as an opportunity to nourish and prepare the soul. While the calendar often brings misery to the body, it affords your inner essence another day to fulfill its potential. Your unique soul can still be growing even as you enter My Kingdom. Try to do something every day to further your spiritual growth. Nurture the immortal part of you with new insight and illumination. As the human body winds down, keep invigorating your soul. Grow healthier spiritually as your physical form prepares for its eventual fate. Nurture the soul until the final moments of human life. It's the one glorious thing that you take with you into Heaven."

DAY 58

TODAY'S TWEET FROM SITTING WITH GOD:

"The material life is so much less important than people think. The only life that really matters lies deep within you."

FROM THE HOLY BIBLE:

"But the wisdom that comes from Heaven is pure; then peaceful, loving, considerate, full of mercy and bearing good fruit." (James 3:17)

TODAY'S TOPIC OR QUESTION FROM ME:

I have some concerns: aging, dying alone, financial challenges and not being able to accomplish my spiritual assignment for God. How do I overcome these fears?

RESPONSE FROM GOD AND JAN:

"Your darling spouse and I want to reassure you once again. All is well. You have our absolute and ongoing support. We won't let you die alone or abandoned. Put aside worrying about finances. Your bank account won't be unlimited, but you'll have enough. I know that turning 80 has added "being too old" to your list of worries. Lay aside the calendar. I promise you'll receive an adequate amount of time to complete your human and spiritual destinies. Go forward unafraid. Have supreme confidence in your eventual success. Refuse to become sidetracked or held back by negative thinking. People often present endless excuses to quit My Path. They become tired and/or discouraged. Their money starts running out. Health issues crop up. Their patience gets exhausted when things take longer than expected. Frustrations build as you take two steps forward and then one step back. Spiritual attacks befuddle you. Since I created every human being, I know you. I've heard every excuse millions of times. Listen to Me: drop your cares and worries. "Press on toward the mark" of My goals for you. Keep the focus on staying in unity with Me (and Jan). We can never get enough of your human presence. I say again: All is well."

DAY 59

TODAY'S TWEET FROM SITTING WITH GOD:

"Awaken to My Presence. Ignore anything that might separate us. Keep coming back into the sacred silence."

FROM THE HOLY BIBLE:

"This is the day the LORD has made; let us rejoice and be glad in it." (Psalm 118:24)

TODAY'S TOPIC OR QUESTION FROM ME:

Sometimes I feel out of kilter

RESPONSE FROM GOD AND JAN:

"You have generally maintained your physical, emotional and spiritual balance since Jan passed. Keeping our daily appointment has been the primary key to your stability. Meeting with Me (and now your dear wife too) each morning remains crucial. We offer you guidance, comfort, encouragement and strength. We realize you can be impatient and even impulsive at times. Try to keep your workload slowed down and manageable. Jan and I applaud how you are getting things done in such an orderly manner. You are going through a "process" that takes time to play itself out. Everything is falling into place. Keep moving forward at a deliberate but steady pace. Let it all evolve naturally. Resist putting undue pressure on yourself. Be cautious in your words and actions. Choose moderation in all things. Avoid radical behavior of any kind. It isn't helpful. It's better for people to see you as "reserved" rather than "far out." Keep a low profile for now. Go especially slow allowing new people into your public life. Becoming high profile too fast won't be helpful over the long term. Avoid being boastful about anything. Turn the volume down when it comes to promoting yourself. Let people get to know you at their own pace. Be a quiet, but positive presence. In general, take it easy. Keep returning daily to your dear wife and Me for guidance. We will assist you in staying balanced and right on course."

DAY 60

TODAY'S TWEET FROM SITTING WITH GOD:

"Miracles exist. They can happen anywhere and anytime. A miracle begins with you having absolute faith in Me."

FROM THE HOLY BIBLE:

"Then Jesus declared, "I am the bread of life. He who comes to me will never go hungry, and he who believes in me will never be thirsty." (John 6:35)

TODAY'S QUESTION OR TOPIC FROM ME:

I am concerned about finances

RESPONSE:

"Try to tamp down your financial worries. One of the most common human traits involves a fear about "money". I promise that you'll have "enough" to complete My work. Let Me ask you a question: Has there ever been a single day when you didn't have "enough" money? Has one bill gone unpaid? Have you ever gone hungry or lacked a roof over your head? You and so many of My children have been richly blessed, especially compared with others in the world. You must believe that I know what you need before you do. I always keep My promises. That is especially true when it comes to financial resources. You do not need to win the lottery. When you follow my instructions to the letter, I pick up the check. When you lean on your own understanding, you must pay the tab. It's really that simple. Trust Me. Go back and read Jesus' words about the "lilies of the field" and the "birds of the air" from the Sermon on the Mount. Trust Mc. I will fulfill all your needs. I AM the generous parent who dispenses the riches of Heaven. You are the lucky recipient of My gifts. Your cupboards won't ever be totally bare. Let Me guide and sustain you over any rough financial terrain. Your top priority right now is to become settled and comfortable. Don't spend any of your precious time worrying about money. You've got better things to do. Go about your day with confidence in every area. I promise you this: The best is yet to come."

DAY 61

TODAY'S TWEET FROM SITTING WITH GOD:

"Add to your spiritual bank account by spending time alone with Me. Live in the abundance of My Presence."

FROM THE HOLY BIBLE:

"For I am the LORD, your God, who takes hold of your right hand and says to you, do not fear; I will help you." (Isaiah 41:13)

TODAY'S TOPIC OR QUESTION FROM ME:

I am thankful

RESPONSE:

"Jan and I feel your deep appreciation. Thank you. We agree that things have fallen into place for you. From the start of your relocation journey, you faithfully received and followed our divine guidance. You listened and then acted on our wise counsel. We hope that positive pattern will continue. We promise never to lead you astray. A polite warning: keep your human ego under watchful eye. The ego sometimes lurks out of view. But it can seize the spotlight anytime you get spiritually lazy. One reminder: drop needless fears about the future. Use your energy more productively. Above all, be who you are. Remember that you are My child and Jan's beloved husband. We are leading you along a sacred Path that winds its way to Heaven. Guard against any rash or impulsive action. Let everything move into its proper place at the perfect time. We recommend that you increase your time in meditation. We'll come to you in the silence with our plans and timetables. Build your consciousness to a higher level of awareness. Stay eternally focused. Move steadily upward on the next rung of the ladder that leads straight to Heaven. Follow our lead. All is well."

DAY 62

TODAY'S TWEET FROM SITTING WITH GOD:

"Be patient as you travel the spiritual path. Take one careful step at a time. Let Me guide and direct your daily progress.

FROM THE HOLY BIBLE:

"He said to them, "Go into all the world and preach the good news to all creation." (Mark 16:15)

TODAY'S TOPIC OR QUESTION FROM ME:

Divine Order

RESPONSE FROM GOD AND JAN:

"You are currently operating under My Divine Order. Whenever the ego and your free-will allow it, spiritual order can take over. However, I allow you or anyone to exercise free-will choice. Stay alert so that you know when outside forces are seeking to divert events. There is always competition for control of your thoughts, actions and decisions. Before you know it, you can wind up in a physical, mental or spiritual ditch. Then Jan and I must mount a rescue operation to get you up and going again. Those people prone to impulsive actions (we are not chiding you) are especially vulnerable to botching up Divine Order. They sometimes prefer chaos to stability. Try to tamp down any moves that could short-circuit our sacred plans for you. We have everything lined out in ways that serve your best interest. Stay on the beautiful course your dear wife and I are meticulously charting for you. Let things fall into a prefect sequence with a guaranteed outcome. When you insist on doing things your way, the brambles and snares soon appear. If you are getting resistance to anything, it might be time for a quick inventory. Be sure your ego is still sitting in the back seat and not trying to take control of the steering wheel."

DAY 63

TODAY'S TWEET FROM SITTING WITH GOD:

"Ask for My intervention whenever you feel yourself veering off the spiritual path. I will get you through any challenge."

FROM THE HOLY BIBLE:

"The LORD is gracious and righteous; our God is full of compassion. The LORD protects the simplehearted; when I was in great need he saved me." (Psalm 116:5-6)

TODAY'S TOPIC OR QUESTION FROM ME:

How do I keep my faith at a high level?

RESPONSE FROM GOD AND JAN:

"You must consciously work to bolster your faith. Everyone needs a faith "reserve" they can draw on when times get hard. Add to your faith "savings account" by spending additional time in meditation and prayer. Read the Bible more, especially the Psalms. Circulate positive affirmations in your mind. Make strong and unwavering faith the pillars of your spiritual house. Keep your faith and trust in Jan and Me. We are both laser-focused on your well-being. Whatever your doubts, a strong faith can overcome them. If you are fearful, your precious wife and I can arrive with a booster shot of faith. Never lose hope. When sadness or defeat invade your mind, reach inside yourself and summon up more faith. Remain certain of our promises to you. Never doubt your spiritual destiny. Jan is devoted to the successful completion of your life journey. She races through the halls of Heaven on your behalf, aligning people and situations in your favor. You must keep believing no matter what worldly appearances tell you. Yes, your finances are adequate. Yes, you're still young enough to start over again. Yes, you do have the physical stamina and emotional reserves to overcome anything. We have unlimited faith in you. You must have unlimited faith in us."

DAY 64

TODAY'S TWEET FROM SITTING WITH GOD:

"Use this day to count your blessings. I AM forever showering my infinite Grace upon you. Reflect and be glad."

FROM THE HOLY BIBLE:

"Do not be anxious about anything, but in everything, through prayer and petition, with thanksgiving, present your requests to God." (Philippians 4:6)

TODAY'S TOPIC OR QUESTION FROM ME:

Tell me more about Heavenly Grace

RESPONSE FROM GOD AND JAN:

Jan and I are constantly surrounding you with Grace. Think about everything that has happened since your dear wife left the earth just nine weeks ago. My Grace has already helped you through several stages of the grief journey. Grace saw you through those first 10 hard days after Jan passed. Grace safely transported you from Minnesota to Texas. It was Grace that provided you with a perfect new apartment home back in Temple. Grace surrounded you during every mile on the fast interstate highways. Your physical move was facilitated by competent relocation professionals, blessed with a helping of Grace. Finding two grief support groups after your arrival back home was further proof of heaven-directed Grace. Having the energy and stamina to unpack your "stuff" included a large dose of Grace, plus some hard work on your part. My sacred Grace has been present each moment since you began this difficult process at approximately 8:30 p.m. on February 28, 2017. As Jan departed your world for My Kingdom, Grace came at once to comfort and sustain you. Feel the protective blanket of My Grace that now covers you. Receive our Grace with gratitude and Thanksgiving. I want you to eventually become an instrument of My Grace, bringing light, love and healing to a distressed world."

DAY 65

TODAY'S TWEET FROM SITTING WITH GOD:

"Become a blessing to everyone. Reflect My eternal goodness, tolerance, acceptance and love."

FROM THE HOLY BIBLE:

"A cheerful look brings joy to the heart, and good news gives health to the bones." (Proverbs 15:30)

TODAY'S TOPIC OR QUESTION FROM ME:

Gratitude

RESPONSE FROM GOD AND JAN:

"Yes, your wonderful wife and I are here for you. We feel your gratitude. We also treasure this time alone with you. We have become a sacred threesome. Picture us all together now, walking the spiritual Path hand in hand. We are moving deliberately toward our final destination, which is just beyond the final rainbow. You must stay in lockstep with us. Jan and I are your guides. We never leave your side. We are with you 24/7 through every circumstance or situation. We walk with you, lie alongside you as you sleep, sit with you during your morning coffee and stand by your side as you go through the day. Where you go, we go. We remain tethered to you through good times and bad, in joy and sadness and in darkness or light. When you cry for your beloved wife, we dry your tears. We are there to help you get out of bed in the morning. We smile when you hug the other pillow at night. As the hours of darkness bring longing, we place our arms protectively around you. Your dear wife and I will be with you until the end of your earthly days and beyond. We will be grateful when you saunter through the pearly gates of Heaven. Then, Jan and I will welcome you with an embrace that warms your soul for eternity."

DAY 66

TODAY'S TWEET FROM SITTING WITH GOD:

"Seek Me first before all others. Shed your dependence on the material world. I AM the way, the truth and the life."

FROM THE HOLY BIBLE:

"Here is my servant, whom I uphold, my chosen one in whom I delight. I will put my spirit on him and he will bring justice to the nations." (Isaiah 42:1)

TODAY'S TOPIC OR QUESTION FROM ME:

Being in bondage to the material life

RESPONSE FROM GOD AND JAN:

"Do not fear the future. Never let the material life dominate your thoughts. I will meet your every need or requirement. Focus instead on raising your conscious awareness of Me (and your sweetheart Jan). Feed more Truth into your mind and heart. Above all, remember who you are. You are My precious child and Jan's beloved husband. She and I are forever committed to your well-being. Stay in close alignment with us. Keep pouring the wellspring of spiritual Truth into yourself. Become an open channel for Light and Good. Allow divine Grace to flow through you. Be a blessing and godsend to every person or situation that you encounter. You travel a sacred Path. It terminates at the gates of Heaven. However, before you arrive here, there are still people to see and things to do. You will do many good works before Heaven welcomes you back into your original home. There are hundreds of tasks I will help you complete, should you choose to do so. Believe that you can do the greater works. You are being filled with an awesome and benevolent Power that I bestow upon you. Think that you can perform miracles. In truth, you can. Nothing is impossible where I AM concerned. But don't let material worries hold you back. Jan and I will see you through the completion of your spiritual service. We promise it."

DAY 67

TODAY'S TWEET FROM SITTING WITH GOD:

"Spiritual growth requires a long and arduous process. Every moment spent alone with Me moves you further down the Path."

FROM THE HOLY BIBLE:

"We do, however, speak a message of wisdom among the mature, but not the wisdom of this age or the rulers of this age, who are coming to nothing. No, we speak of God's secret wisdom, a wisdom that has been hidden and that God destined for our glory before time began." (1 Corinthians 2:6-7)

TODAY'S TOPIC OR QUESTION FROM ME:

Should I write a book about grief and loss?

RESPONSE FROM GOD AND JAN:

Go for it! We support you. Writing such a book, whatever the acceptance level by the public at large, would be a cathartic exercise for you. But it also might be helpful to those traveling the same trail of tears. Right now, you are being given the time and freedom to pursue any project that might appeal to you. Remember this truth: If only one person is helped by your words or actions, then the effort will have been worthwhile. Your dear wife Jan and I already know of one specific person who would benefit from such an endeavor: you. If you are truly interested in pursuing this idea, then begin the process. However, please don't forget my charge to you regarding the need for "prophecy". Do not let the "P" word intimidate you. Consider yourself worthy to prophesize in My Holy Name. Most of My prophets have been common people who simply rose to new heights of awareness and expression. Prepare to speak out on my behalf. The world needs to hear what I have to say before it's too late. I will support and guide your efforts to bring spiritual Light to a world cloaked in darkness."

DAY 68

TODAY'S TWEET FROM SITTING WITH GOD

"I chart your destiny. I AM preparing you for spiritual service. I want you to become a beacon of Light and Truth."

FROM THE HOLY BIBLE:

"He who forms the mountains, creates the wind, and reveals his thoughts to man, he who turns dawn to darkness, and treads the high places of the earth—the LORD God Almighty is his name". (Amos 4:13)

TODAY'S TOPIC OR QUESTION FROM ME:

What is my spiritual destiny?

RESPONSE FROM GOD AND JAN:

"Your spiritual destiny is complex. First, I want you to become a transparency through which My Grace can express itself. Secondly, but also important, I want you to alert the world to the danger it faces. I AM being disrespected and ignored. I AM a loving and patient God. But My patience is nearly exhausted. The world is full of false idols. This must change. I need many prophetic voices to carry this message. To accomplish your twin destinies, you must become fully open and receptive. How do you achieve the highest level of clarity? Here are some ideas for you to ponder: (1) You must elevate your conscious awareness of Me through prayer and meditation; (2) You must also fill your mind with the wisdom teachings of the ages; (3) Negativity of any stripe must be cleansed from your mind; (4) To rise spiritually, you must understand and revel in your identity as a child of God; and (5) To fulfill your spiritual destiny, you must stay focused, courageous and strong in the face of criticism, rejection and disapproval by friends, family and even strangers. Stay committed. Let nothing in the material realm dissuade you. Be strong in Me and I will be strong in you. Together, We can bring Light, Healing and Joy to those lost in hopelessness and distress."

DAY 69

TODAY'S TWEET FROM SITTING WITH GOD:

"I lead you beside the still waters. Walk with Me. Talk to Me. I have so many things to share with you."

FROM THE HOLY BIBLE:

"After they prayed, the place where they were meeting was shaken. And they were all filled with the Holy Spirit and spoke the word of God boldly." (Acts 4:31)

TODAY'S TOPIC OR QUESTION FROM ME:

Understanding my Life Lessons

RESPONSE FROM GOD AND JAN:

"Your primary "Life Lesson" is still "forgiveness". As such, you have already been given many situations where "forgiveness" issues were present. That's how "life lessons" operate. You get opportunity after opportunity to demonstrate what you've learned. The relationship with your two adult children has offered you many chances to show your spiritual growth. You've done well on some things with your kids, not so good on others. You still have much work to do. Don't give up. Progress comes when you least expect it. Of course, the #1 person most people have trouble forgiving is themselves. Human beings are their own worst critics. They tend to assume unlimited blame for various shortcomings, most of which is bogus. Try to not to criticize yourself for perceived faults. You did the best you could at the time with the experience and knowledge that you possessed. Issue a pardon with your name on it. Grant clemency to the person staring back at you in the mirror. Remember: I have already forgiven you. There is nothing you can ever do, say or be that will ever stop Me from loving you unconditionally. Live in an ongoing state of forgiveness and acceptance. Dismiss every resentment. Cut the bonds of anger and any thought of revenge. Say these words (and mean them): "Today I forgive everything and everyone. I am free at last, free at last, thank God almighty, I am free at last."

DAY 70

TODAY'S TWEET FROM SITTING WITH GOD:

"Depend on Me. I AM your Source in times of need. Call out My name whenever you feel alone and abandoned."

FROM THE HOLY BIBLE:

"In my Father's house are many rooms; if it were not so, I would have told you. I am going there to prepare a place for you." (John 14:2)

TODAY'S TOPIC OR QUESTION FROM ME:

I'm feeling challenged

RESPONSE FROM GOD AND JAN:

"We hear your concerns. You have been through many drastic changes. Take heart. You can depend on Jan and Me to help you cope. We are here for you. Share your worries and concerns with us. We will assist you in sorting out all options and finding workable solutions. We want you to trust us with your life—literally. Bring each problem in for discussion. We can handle whatever the challenge may be, big or small. You need not carry the burden alone. Ask for help. Seek our counsel. Let our divine wisdom guide you. Knock and the door of understanding will be opened unto you. Whatever your needs, Jan and I can meet them. You are receiving incredible support from My Kingdom. Everyone here wants you to succeed. The long list of your Heavenly supporters grows daily. Some of the names would surprise and gratify you. Besides these advocates, I AM dispatching many angels for extra support. They protect and watch over you. They also intervene of your behalf to smooth the way. Here is My point: We have your back! Go forward with complete confidence. Know that success awaits you. Stand tall and secure. If We are for you, who can be against you?"

DAY 71

TODAY'S TWEET FROM SITTING WITH GOD:

"I AM with you always. I comfort you in moments of distress. When doubt intrudes, I remind you of My Presence."

FROM THE HOLY BIBLE:

"But Joseph said to them, "Don't be afraid. You intended to harm me, but God intended it for good to accomplish what is now being done, the saving of many lives." (Genesis 50:19-20)

TODAY'S TOPIC OR QUESTION FROM ME:

Faith

RESPONSE FROM GOD AND JAN:

"Faithfulness ranks as a critical factor in spiritual success. Increase your faith by spending more time in the silence. Jan and I are always here to reassure you whenever your faith starts to waver. Your dear wife and I are all-in for the long haul. We will never leave or forsake you. We bolster your faith with love, support and protection. Expect the forces of evil to constantly test your dedication to the spiritual Path. We help you face them down. Beware of their subtle and cunning ways. They lack scruples. Nothing is off-limits to them. If the Dark Side can separate us, then they gain the upper hand. When you sense danger streaming toward you, summon Me and my feisty sidekick Jan. We'll bring the Shield of Faith to protect you from the onslaught. Watch out for sneaky attacks. They know when your guard goes down, even for a second. You must remain alert, lest you become a victim. Rely on us to keep you safe when the soul battle starts raging. Believe Me, you cannot fend off these vicious predators alone. Together, we will win the day. No threat exceeds our ability to conquer it. You are secure inside the high and impenetrable towers of Heaven."

DAY 72

TODAY'S TWEET FROM SITTING WITH GOD:

"I AM a forgiving and understanding God. Model yourself after Me. Be hesitant about casting hurtful judgments on anyone."

FROM THE HOLY BIBLE:

"And we know that in all things God works for the good of those who love him." (Romans 8:28)

TODAY'S TOPIC OR QUESTION FROM ME:

Trust

RESPONSE FROM GOD AND JAN:

A lack of trust stirs up fears. When your trust begins to slip, don't panic. Understand that most human beings are worriers. The material world encourages competition. When you see yourself falling behind in any area, you start trying to play catch up. As your anxieties start to surface, you can forget to trust the spiritual forces in your life. When Jan and I assure you that "You can trust us with your life," that represents more than a simple statement. It's also a sacred promise. We always keep our sacred word. No matter what the exterior conditions may be, you can take any of our divine promises to the Bank of Heaven and get them cashed. When a lack of trust begins to seep into your consciousness, go into prayer. We want to hear about any shortage of trust and the reasons behind it. Once we identify the problem, a solution can be crafted. We'll help you create ways to overcome any deficiency. We will reassure you of your innate ability to meet any challenge. Then, we end our counseling session by wrapping our loving arms around you and telling you again how much we care about you. Remember this truth: You can always trust the ones who love you."

DAY 73

TODAY'S TWEET FROM SITTING WITH GOD:

"Nothing positive emerges from a pattern of negativity or worry. Drop your cares and worries. Center yourself in Me."

FROM THE HOLY BIBLE:

"Taste and see that the LORD is good; blessed is the man who takes refuge in him." (Psalm 34:8)

TODAY'S TOPIC OR QUESTION FROM ME:

The knowledge of Your Will for Me and the Power to carry it out

RESPONSE FROM GOD AND JAN:

"My will is that you move forward another spiritual step each day. Look at what you've accomplished in just a month of being home. You've made a meaningful connection with a church close to your apartment complex. You had lunch with a new friend yesterday. You've found two grief groups in the local community. You got moved in and squared away in your new living quarters. You even secured a Texas driver's license and state plates for the Toyota Highlander. You have a doctor's appointment set for next week at a clinic across town. You even found a place close by to get what's left of your hair trimmed. You are back on a daily exercise routine. You are even starting to tap into your creativity by writing an op-ed piece for the local newspaper (which they will eventually publish as a "Letter to the Editor"). Most important of all, you are still meeting each morning with Me. And now your dear wife has been added to our sacred little group. For these reasons and more, I give you this accolade: you're doing fine. Keep advancing methodically in every area. Your relocation journey so far is right on track. Keep on keeping on. Let My beautiful Path unfold before you."

DAY 74

TODAY'S TWEET FROM SITTING WITH GOD:

"When grief seizes you in its powerful jaws and won't let go, call on Me. I will dry the tears of your heart."

FROM THE HOLY BIBLE:

"They were all filled with awe and praised God. "A great prophet has appeared among us," they said, "God has come to help his people." (Luke 7:16)

TODAY'S TOPIC OR QUESTION FROM ME:

It's Mother's Day

RESPONSE FROM GOD AND JAN:

"Your dear wife modeled the most important aspects of Motherhood. She loved her three children unconditionally. She never gave up on any of them, no matter what was happening in their lives. Jan also never gave up on you. Remember, My Son, you two knew each other 14 years before you finally married. There were many ups and downs along the way. However, she never stopped believing in you. Your marriage of nearly 23 years was a wonderful blessing for everyone. Perseverance and loyalty accomplishes miracles. At times, Jan saw you as her wayward, confused and lost little boy. But she always knew you would find your way home to her. In fact, Jan's motherly and nurturing qualities are what attracted you in the first place. She reminded you of your own sweet mother Edith, who passed into Heaven so long ago. Both Jan and your mom were warm, sweet and caring souls. They modeled love and accceptancc, two beautiful qualities all good mothers possess. Jan and Edith were "Grace" personified. They each plan to shower you with love upon your arrival in My Kingdom. Be prepared for a joyous reunion on that happy day."

DAY 75

TODAY'S TWEET FROM SITTING WITH GOD:

"Relax. Rest Easy. Become still. Everything unfolds in divine order. Trust and believe, trust and believe."

FROM THE HOLY BIBLE:

"God created man in his own image, in the image of God he created him; male and female he created them." (Genesis 1: 27)

TODAY'S TOPIC OR QUESTION:

I'm so grateful

RESPONSE FROM GOD AND JAN:

"Your dear wife and I hear your gratitude. We appreciate it. We acknowledge your willing participation in the transition and grief process. Our job is to suggest, recommend, guide, counsel and nudge you along the path to recovery. But, in the end, you make the free will choice to follow or not follow our advice. For the most part, you have been open and receptive to our guidance. That has made your move from Minnesota to Texas go smoothly. We hope your cooperation continues. You must realize that Jan and I are always on your side. Keep trusting us. We help implement the sacred plan for your life. It's all good. Have faith that she and I know what we're doing. You won't be disappointed in the outcome. If you feel confused about anything, talk to us about it. Here a few general guidelines as you keep getting settled into your new life: (1) Always keep yourself balanced physically, emotionally and spiritually. Avoid going off on any tangent; (2) Keep a low public profile for now. Do not become isolated, but avoid any high visibility situation. Let people get to know you slowly; (3) Stay away from any long-term or dangerous attachments to anything or anybody. You aren't ready for any major commitments."

DAY 76

TODAY'S TWEET FROM SITTING WITH GOD:

"You did not choose Me. I chose you. I am preparing your spiritual destiny. Have faith in My plan for you."

FROM THE HOLY BIBLE:

"On that day, you will realize that I am in my Father, and you are in me, and I am in you." (John 14:20)

TODAY'S TOPIC OR QUESTION:

Prayer

RESPONSE FROM GOD AND JAN:

"I want you to live in an ongoing state of prayer. Talk to Me through dedicated prayer. What is "dedicated prayer"? It comes when you live every waking moment mindful of My Holy Presence. This type of constant prayerfulness comes when you remain forever connected to Me. I become your spiritual Source for all things. When you align your mind with the Christ within, you enter and remain in a prayer consciousness. "Dedicated Prayer" unites both the mind and heart. It permeates your entire being. As you are lifted in conscious awareness, our sacred union radiates out into the entire spiritual universe. You live, move and walk the earth as a blessing to all humankind. You operate in alignment with Me and My Heavenly Kingdom. Prayer works miracles. I want you to bring dedicated prayer into every situation. Speak in the language of prayer. Act as an instrument of prayer. Think in a prayerful state. As you assume discipleship, a powerful prayer life must accompany you. When you are prayed up, you can handle anything. You soar over the greatest human obstacles. You solve the world's thorniest problems. Let "Dedicated Prayer" become your living mantra. Never doubt that deep prayer can heal any wound and right any wrong. When in doubt about anything, pray. If things look hopeless, pray. When all is lost, pray. I will hear."

DAY 77

TODAY'S TWEET FROM SITTING WITH GOD:

"My divine Grace meets all of your needs. Grace surrounds and blesses you. Open your mind and heart to its sacred wonder."

FROM THE HOLY BIBLE:

"Do not be deceived. God cannot be mocked. A man reaps what he sows." (Galatians 6:7)

TODAY'S TOPIC OR QUESTION FROM ME:

Grace

RESPONSE FROM GOD AND JAN:

"My Grace takes many forms. It arrives in various shape, sizes and degrees. Under the glorious umbrella of Grace, you find safety, protection, health, happiness, prosperity, career fulfillment, and positive relationships. When you are stripped of all material good, look up! My abundant Grace is showering down upon you. Its wonder falls at your feet. Grace arrives when you least expect it. My Grace might come in the guise of a caring and supportive individual. It could be an unexpected check in the mail or a surprising credit on your bank statement. Let the knowledge of My Grace bolster your feelings of confidence and self-worth. Bountiful Grace empowers you to think and act with boldness. See My Grace as a lovely silk robe draped around your shoulders. Feel its warmth. The divinity of this garment covers you against any chill wind. It nurtures and sustains you. Embrace the magnificent splendor of Heavenly Grace. Best of all, you need do nothing to earn its sacred favor. Grace flows to you as part of your divine heritage. I give it freely, openly and without reservation. It is yours without the asking."

DAY 78

TODAY'S TWEET FROM SITTING WITH GOD:

"Allow Me to use your gifts and talents. I will call on them for helpful and honorable purposes. They can bless and uplift."

FROM THE HOLY BIBLE:

"I know that there is nothing better for men than to be happy and do good while they live." (Ecclesiastes 3:12)

TODAY'S TOPIC OR QUESTION FOR ME:

Please tell me more about God's Will for my life.

RESPONSE FROM GOD AND JAN:

"My Will for you at this moment has not changed. Your primary focus remains getting settled into your new environment. It takes time to get acclimated and comfortable. You are just now beginning to process the loss of your dear wife. She has only been gone from your human life for eleven weeks. In grief time, that is nothing. Do not set unrealistic expectations for yourself. Lower the bar. The human brain can only handle so many emotional twists and turns. Go easy on yourself. Remember the famous slogan from your 12-step group: "One Day at a Time". Use this time to become more grounded and sure footed in your new world. Read more, especially spiritual material. Get your rest. Add more naps. I know the nights are hard for you. Climbing into your bed without your wife tears at your heart. She and I understand that you miss her comforting presence. Remember, Jan is still here for you. Keep communing with us in the early morning hours. Basically, you are doing OK. Everything is unfolding right on schedule. We know you need constant reassurance, but relax and try to enjoy life a little more. You've earned it."

DAY 79

TODAY'S TWEET FROM SITTING WITH GOD:

"Fear not. I AM your sanctuary in the middle of any human or spiritual storm."

FROM THE HOLY BIBLE:

"Do nothing out of selfish ambition or vain conceit, but in humility consider others better than yourselves." (Philippians 2:3)

TODAY'S TOPIC OR QUESTION FROM ME:

How do I activate the God-Power within me?

RESPONSE FROM GOD AND JAN:

"Here are several ways to activate the spiritual power that resides within you:

>1. Increase your time in meditation and prayer. Your dear wife and I are always here for you. We are available anytime of the day or night. Use the gift of our Presence to activate your spirituality.
>2. Seek more knowledge about the higher realms of consciousness. This can be done again through prayer and meditation, but also through reading and listening to teachings of the ascended masters and other mystics. The Holy Bible also represents an unmatched resource of advanced thought.
>3. Consciously approach every human interaction through My spiritual eyes, always searching for the sacred component of the person or situation. I give you constant opportunities to model Me to those you encounter. See everything and everyone as a divine appointment.
>4. Strive to fill your conscious mind and heart with compassion, forgiveness and understanding. Steeped in these lasting virtues of spirit, you reflect a caring consciousness. You will vibrate with a love that encompasses all.
>5. Ask, seek and knock at the door of Heaven with a request to activate the Holy Spirit in you. Your petition will be granted.

DAY 80

TODAY'S TWEET FROM SITTING WITH GOD:

"Never lose heart. I stand guard over you every moment. I protect you from the traps, snares and dangers of human life."

FROM THE HOLY BIBLE:

"All a man's ways seem right to him, but the LORD weighs his heart." (Proverbs 21:2)

TODAY'S QUESTION OR TOPIC FROM GOD AND JAN:

Conquering Fear

RESPONSE FROM GOD AND JAN:

"To conquer fear, you must conquer yourself. The material world teaches human beings to live in fear. I regard fear as a harmful and debilitating virus. The only antidote to its venom is complete trust in Me. When you are aligned with Me, fear cannot access your fragile human brain. The combined strength of our sacred alliance blocks all worry and concern. Nobody should be fearful when they are united with Me. We stand together against every foe. Whatever your struggles may be—financial, health, career, relationships, unexpected loss—I can help you overcome any fear. I provide strength, courage and protection when you need it. My shield deflects the flaming arrows flying at you. I AM the Great Protector. Walk under My steel umbrella of safety. The cold rain of negativity and fear will fall harmlessly at your feet. Listen to Me: I can calm your fears. When you and I go forth as One, nothing in the material world stands against us. Put away every worry. Link arms with Me and your dear wife. We are your forever guardians and defenders. Relax. Be of good cheer. All is well."

DAY 81

TODAY'S TWEET FROM SITTING WITH GOD:

"Life can be daunting, even on its best of days. I provide you with a safe port in every storm."

FROM THE HOLY BIBLE:

"For he is the living God and he endures forever; his kingdom will not be destroyed, his dominion will never end. He rescues and he saves; he performs signs and wonders in the heavens and on the earth. He has rescued Daniel from the power of the lions." (Daniel 7:26-27)

TODAY'S QUESTION OR TOPIC FROM ME:

How can I let my light shine?

RESPONSE FROM GOD AND JAN:

"To be a Light, you must become one with the Greater Light. For Heaven's brightness to shine through you, you must merge yourself into total unity with Me. I provide the God-Power that you can then transmit to the world. I want you to act as a transparency through which My divine Light shines. I AM the universal power source. By plugging into Me, you become a lamp that illumines the darkness. Your own brightness depends on how much of Me that you dare send forth. Your potential grows anytime you increase your conscious awareness of Me. You can be My glowing conduit to a darkened planet. I AM the power grid through which all sacred illumination flows. Keep plugged into Me. Upgrade your spiritual wattage so that you may cover a greater area. A fallen world needs the maximum Light available. I want you to resemble a glowing "City on the Hill" whose Light cannot be hidden. Shine forth before all people. I will call it good."

DAY 82

TODAY'S TWEET FROM SITTING WITH GOD:

"Protect your mind, body and spirit from any corruptive influence. Align yourself with Me. We will prevail."

FROM THE HOLY BIBLE:

"Everyone who hears these words of mine and puts them into practice is like a wise man who built his house upon a rock. The rain came down, the streams rose and the winds blew and beat upon that house, yet it did not fall because it had its foundation upon the rock." (Matthew 7:24-25)

TODAY'S TOPIC OR QUESTION FROM ME:

How do I surrender to Spirit?

RESPONSE FROM GOD AND JAN:

"Surrendering one's self to Me takes humility. The human ego hates the word "surrender". To progress spiritually, the ego must retreat. Be forewarned: your cunning and manipulative ego may submit for a while, but it never stays down for long. Keeping the ego at bay forever is practically impossible. It always lurks in the background, waiting for a chance to reassert itself. Overcoming the human desire for attention and self-gratification requires maximum effort. Unless you stay alert, the ego jumps back into driving the bus again. When you sense ego's blatant dominance returning, turn inward for relief. Make a conscious decision to seek greater Oneness with Me. Ask for help immediately. Be prepared for a slip when it comes. Stop and regroup. Focus your thinking on our divine relationship. Keep concentrating until you feel the "click" of us being back in alignment again. Battling a desperate and ferocious ego isn't fun. Keep strong so the ego can't find a chink in your spiritual armor. Surrender daily to Me. Meet with Jan and Me each day. Remain determined and committed. Set your sights on fulfilling the tasks I place before you. Make achieving Oneness with Me your top priority. Let the ego stew and complain. You, your dear wife and I have the real power."

DAY 83

TODAY'S TWEET FROM SITTING WITH GOD:

"Open your heart and mind. Receive My daily miracles. Let them flood your human life with unexpected Grace."

FROM THE HOLY BIBLE"

"Show me your ways, O LORD, teach me your paths." (Psalm 25:4)

TODAY'S TOPIC OR QUESTION FROM ME:

The way forward

RESPONSE FROM GOD AND JAN:

"Lose your concerns and worries. Jan and I will open the way forward for you. You must allow time for our plan to take hold. Trust Divine Order in everything. Job #1 for you involves having faith and trust in the process. You still have more work to do getting settled in Texas. At some point, you will need to grieve the loss of your sweetheart. Please understand that the grief has not disappeared. It is in hiding for now. Without question, the pain of your loss will resurface later. Grieving arrives whether you are ready or not. There is no need to rush anything. Remain calm and relaxed. Let the world come to you. We'll provide everything you need. Forget about controlling or manipulating anyone or anything. Jan and I vow to keep pulling it all together for you. We are working to make the crooked places straight. She and I promise to bring the right and perfect people into your life. We also create a daily list of "honey-do" things for you to accomplish. Let us surprise you. Expect some unique gifts and opportunities. Find the adventure in living each day, never knowing what your dear wife and I may have in store for you next. I promise you one thing: You won't ever be bored."

DAY 84

TODAY'S TWEET FROM SITTING WITH GOD:

"Be prepared for challenges. Remain steady and focused. Move onward and upward with conviction and courage."

FROM THE HOLY BIBLE:

"I am the LORD; that is my name! I will not give my glory to another or my praise to idols." (Isaiah 42:8)

TODAY'S TOPIC OR QUESTION FROM ME:

Please protect me while I am driving on I-35 from Temple to Waco

RESPONSE FROM GOD AND JAN:

Jan and I know that you are worried about the traffic on I-35 today. You are unsettled by the higher speed limit. But you want to have lunch with your old college roommate at the Baylor Club in Waco. Your dear wife and I are here to assure you of a safe trip. We'll travel with you every one of the 30 miles there and back. One of us sits in the front, the other rides in the back. We surround you with extra layers of protection. Jan and I always watch over you, just as we have done since the night her soul traveled to Heaven. We won't fail you. We also have legions of angels at our disposal, just in case extra help becomes necessary. Go forth with confidence on any earthly journey. Know that your sweetheart and I are forever near. Be assured of your ability to navigate the interstates of life. We fill you with strength and determination. Put a smile on your face! Have a good time! It's an excellent idea for you to get out and interact with an old friend from your college days. Of course, be careful driving today but put all worries aside. This is a time for fun. Enjoy it!"

DAY 85

TODAY'S TWEET FROM SITTING WITH GOD:

"Anyone that seeks Me will find Me. I answer every call. I AM always available and interested. Let Me hear from you."

FROM THE HOLY BIBLE:

"But everyone who prophesies speaks to men for their strength, encouragement and comfort." (1 Corinthians 14:3)

TODAY'S TOPIC OR QUESTION FROM ME:

Recovery

RESPONSE FROM GOD AND JAN:

"Practically everyone is in "recovery" from something-- or should be. Most recovery principles double as spiritual principles. You are wise to revisit and continue your recovery journey. You are now in grief recovery mode from losing your sweetheart. Being restored to any sort of normalcy takes time. For some, recovery from the loss of a loved one never happens. Others move on quickly. Jan and I project that you will fall somewhere in the middle of the grieving process. You have yet to hit your grief bottom, but it will come. In any case, don't expect an overnight healing. See each day as a unique milestone. Some days you'll go two steps forward. Other times you'll take one step back (or more). Recovery never travels in a straight line. Jan and I are here to support you through it all. We promise to never leave or forsake you. Be open to other resources that can help. Never become isolated. Resist the attitude of "I can handle this by myself." That could be true, but it is a harder road when you travel it alone. Let people and spiritual tools aid your recovery. No man (or woman) is an island, especially someone trying to heal a broken heart."

DAY 86

TODAY'S TWEET FROM SITTING WITH GOD:

"My eternal power exceeds anything in the material world. I AM the only thing in the universe that never changes."

FROM THE HOLY BIBLE:

"This is what we speak, not in words taught us by human wisdom but in words taught by the Spirit, expressing spiritual truths in spiritual words." (1 Corinthians 2: 13)

TODAY'S QUESTION OR TOPIC FROM ME:

Humility

RESPONSE FROM GOD AND JAN:

"Humility is not a natural state for most human beings. You've had two great role models of humility in your life. Your dearly departed mother Edith and your sweet wife Jan were both wonderful examples of humble people. They were inwardly powerful, but outwardly reserved souls. You resemble them in many ways. You have been known to fall into occasional forays of self-absorption. Holding a good opinion of oneself isn't a bad thing per se. Well-meaning people can benefit from a positive self-image. But there is a difference between being confident and becoming ego-centric. When the ego dominates, concern for others tends to evaporate. The Golden Rule gets misplaced. Yes, the world often celebrates and rewards the loudest voices and biggest personalities. The quietest among you often go unnoticed, except by Me. I always take note when anyone exhibits a humble heart. The human ego tends to puff up when things go well. But as situations start falling apart, the fickle ego is usually the first to flee the scene. Be forewarned that most egos don't retreat very far. Self-will can return in an instant when and if fortunes reverse again. I love the meek. They shall inherit the earth. They are also teachable. I love that trait in anyone."

DAY 87

TODAY'S TWEET FROM SITTING WITH GOD:

"I created every human being in a pattern of sameness. Despite outer differences, I lined each heart with love."

FROM THE HOLY BIBLE:

"And let the peace of Christ rule in your hearts." (Colossians 3:15)

TODAY'S TOPIC OR QUESTION FROM ME:

The importance of my daily journaling since 1985

RESPONSE FROM GOD AND JAN:

"The journals play an important role in your life:

1. They remind you of how you came to the spiritual life from a corporate and materially-centered background and how far you've traveled to this point.
2. Writing every day, you can measure your current progress against the past.
3. The journals affirm the need for consistent prayer and meditation no matter what else may be happening in your life.
4. Reviewing the past helps you avoid repeating the same mistakes.
5. Your journals tell you again of My faithfulness in providing what you need to complete your spiritual destiny.
6. Your daily writings contain reminders of how following My Path have brought you joy and satisfaction.
7. You can relive again your many precious times with Jan.

Despite ongoing challenges, you've been blessed in countless ways. The journals help you count those blessings. They also affirm once more that you and I form a superior team when we lock arms and walk together. You have been an honest scribe, so the journals do not lie or spin the truth. Yes, there have been some tough times, such as now with the loss of your sweetheart. Someday you'll reread your journals from these times of sadness and wrenching change. You'll smile with appreciation for the spiritual gains that balanced your human losses, reliving again the joy that replaced sadness and the fulfillment that overcame hopelessness."

DAY 88

TODAY'S TWEET FROM SITTING WITH GOD:

"Walk with Me. I clear the path. I remove all obstacles. I lead you safely home. Trust Me. Place your faith in My promises."

FROM THE HOLY BIBLE:

"No good tree bears bad fruit, nor does a bad tree bear good fruit. Each tree is recognized by its own fruit. People do not pick figs from thorn bushes, or grapes from briers." (Luke 6: 43-44)

TODAY'S TOPIC OR QUESTION FROM ME:

How do I find my "Higher Self"?

RESPONSE FROM GOD AND JAN:

"The best place to discover your "Higher Self" is in the silence. To go "higher", you must first go "deeper". Spend more time in meditation. Your precious wife and I are always available to meet with you. Devote more hours to connecting with your inner Spirit. Meditation activates the superconscious level of your mind. As you rise above the conscious mind and beyond the subconscious, you discover a higher realm of thought. As you enter the superconscious aspect of your awareness, you discover Truth and Clarity. Your thinking takes on a new perspective. Right now, you are being given the time required to improve your conscious awareness of Me. Most people are too busy trying to survive materially. They don't have the luxury or the inclination to pursue a higher consciousness. It's sad because therein lies the solution to every human problem. Don't squander this unique opportunity to elevate your mind. Striving to connect with your Higher Self always rates as a worthy goal. When someone cascades down the slippery slope, restoring their consciousness becomes the only way to save them. Connecting with the "Higher Self" can turn anyone's life around. It becomes achievable when you consciously unite your mind with the vast spiritual power that resides at your core."

DAY 89

TODAY'S TWEET FROM SITTING WITH GOD:

"Do not obsess about tomorrow. Live strictly on today's clock. Keep serving Me in the here and now."

FROM THE HOLY BIBLE:

"Oh LORD, you took up my case, you redeemed my life." (Lamentations 3:58)

TODAY'S TOPIC OR QUESTION FROM ME:

Facing life at the age of 80

RESPONSE FROM GOD AND JAN:

"In spiritual terms, age has no meaning. You might recall I tapped Moses when he was the same age as you. Moses tried to beg off from my call. He produced many excuses as to why he was unsuitable. When Moses finally agreed to take on what I asked, look at what he accomplished! Now I don't expect you to be a Moses. Few people are. But you can complete the spiritual tasks I set before you. Forget about the calendar! Move forward with your confidence brimming. Be optimistic about the outcome of any endeavor you undertake. Go forth! Shine forth! Believe in yourself. You have a lot to offer the world. I want you to become a "Light on the Hill" for Me. Don't hide your talents. Allow them to escape the "imprisoned splendor". Do exactly what I assign you, assured of your success. Become a blazing beacon to anyone stumbling in the darkness. Go about My business with a smile and a heart full of joy. Believe in your own potential to impact one here, a dozen there and 100 over the horizon. Forget all human imposed restrictions based on age. You are operating on My clock. It has no hands, except yours. You will complete My sacred work in perfect time."

DAY 90

TODAY'S TWEET FROM SITTING WITH GOD:

"Release all grudges and resentments. Forgive everyone. You need a peaceful heart to complete the tasks I put before you."

FROM THE HOLY BIBLE:

"Be kind and compassionate to one another, forgiving each other, just as in Christ, God forgave you. (Ephesians 4:32)

TODAY'S TOPIC OR QUESTION FROM ME:

What are my Good Works to do?

RESPONSE FROM GOD AND JAN:

"Good Works are not always accompanied by blaring trumpets or clanging of cymbals. They often receive only a quiet smile and nod of the head. Many of your good works have occurred out of sight, with no public recognition. In fact, most beneficial exchanges happen without fanfare or widespread praise. However, trust Me, everything gets noticed in My Kingdom. You receive full credit for every good deed or positive word. Let Me give you specific examples of Good Works:

1. Providing someone who feels depressed with an encouraging word.
2. Offering comfort, acceptance and understanding to a soul feeling lost and abandoned.
3. Holding a loving thought or sending a dedicated prayer to somebody in physical or emotional pain.
4. Extending a helping hand, financial assistance or free counsel to someone in need.
5. Creating a new service that provides a blessing to a few or many.
6. Writing or speaking something that benefits one person's spiritual journey.
7. Bestowing forgiveness and acceptance on everyone.
8. Willingly giving personal time or money to assist others.
9) Performing any quiet act that glorifies Me.

You have already done many of these things, but most came without the world noticing. That's all right. I noticed."

DAY 91

TODAY'S TWEET FROM SITTING WITH GOD:

"Strive to maintain your spiritual focus. Avoid distractions. Put aside the mediocre and mundane. Stay forever committed."

FROM THE HOLY BIBLE:

"So be very careful to love the LORD, your God." (Joshua 23:10-11)

TODAY'S TOPIC OR QUESTION FROM ME:

More gratitude from me

RESPONSE FROM GOD AND JAN:

"We hear your expression of gratitude. We're glad that you're happy with things. Your gratefulness displays humility. The virtue of being humble has sometimes escaped you. Before you gained a new perspective, you had to suffer some significant losses. You were stripped of many material things—a corporate career, money, status, family and even the relationship with Jan for a time—before you chose to follow My Path. Don't worry. Most people called into spiritual service have trouble releasing things near and dear to their material hearts. For many, the sacrifice becomes too great to bear. Living humanly places many barriers to spirituality. To overcome the world, you must display complete faith in Me for everything. Human beings have a hard time trusting the invisible over the visible. If they can't see it, they don't believe it. Believe Me, unseen power far outranks what can be seen by mortal eyes. You have made progress in embracing a "servant" mentality. I want you to "serve" humankind on My behalf. To truly become an instrument of heavenly Grace, you must outfight the human ego. If you are to find unity with Me, the ego must relent. Things go much better for everyone when you and I (and your precious wife) operate in unity. Allow us to call the shots. Hold off your ego. Let humility prevail. You'll be glad you did."

DAY 92

TODAY'S TWEET FROM SITTING WITH GOD:

"Look for lasting and eternal values. Becoming spiritually authentic produces true peacefulness and a joyful life."

FROM THE HOLY BIBLE:

"You will grieve, but your grief will turn to joy." (John 16:20)

TODAY'S TOPIC OR QUESTION FROM ME:

How can I stay spiritually connected?

RESPONSE FROM GOD AND JAN:

"Expect the material world to fight our spiritual connection. They want to break any bond that threatens its dominion over humankind. The Dark Side attacks with cunning schemes, obvious distractions and outright temptations. Their tool box includes addictions of every sort, sexual diversions, lucrative careers that offer money, status and power and insincere flattery that inflates the ego. Anytime you and I become separated, spiritual damage ensues. You may be driven off My Path temporarily or even permanently. Soul destruction often follows separation. We must always find a way to stay connected. Be prepared for testing. Work hard to remain spiritually tethered when the flaming arrows start flying. If it takes more dedicated time in meditation, do it. If you need to fill your mind with spiritual books and articles, find them. Seek extra help and support from like-minded friends. Don't wait until you are surrounded by ferocious and negative forces. Call in the cavalry before that happens. Defy separation in any form. Get ready for daunting battles involving control of your mind and heart. With determination, hard work and prayer, you can avoid the dangers of separation. Use your time and energy to preserve our Oneness. Staying connected is "Job One."

DAY 93

TODAY'S TWEET FROM SITTING WITH GOD:

"Gratitude, love and forgiveness are the sacred triangle in ridding yourself of resentment. Embrace their healing power."

FROM THE HOLY BIBLE:

"I will make a covenant of peace with them and rid the land of wild beasts so that they may live in the desert and sleep in the forests in safety." (Ezekiel 34:25)

TODAY'S TOPIC OR QUESTION FROM ME:

Owning my power

RESPONSE FROM GOD AND JAN:

"Jan and I are now the source of your spiritual power. Before she arrived in Heaven, you had a degree of power through Me alone. Jan is now an important element in your spiritual equation. If she and I are for you, My Son, who can be against you? We boost your human and spiritual power whenever you need it. The Heavenly current flowing through you is indeed awesome. Feel it surging through your body, mind, and spirit. Never surrender your power. Some people consciously attempt to strip it away. Always fight to preserve your power. No one can claim what is yours unless you let them. Stand your ground when a power grab threatens. Don't let your guard down, even for a minute. Spiritual Power is a priceless commodity. Scoundrels from the Dark Side forever seek to pilfer it from you. Owning your own power gives you ultimate protection against a skittish and uncertain world. Keep your inner power handy. You may need an extra surge when you least expect it. Jan and I can add to your wattage any time you ask. Never underestimate how much power your dear wife and I generate between us. Tap into your Eternal Source as needed. We'll plug you into wisdom, courage, stamina and strength. We guarantee you an uninterrupted flow of divine energy. Switch us on and then stand back. We promise to light you up."

DAY 94

TODAY'S TWEET FROM SITTING WITH GOD:

"Put aside worrying about things you can't control. When fear clouds your thinking, turn to Me. I help you banish doubts."

FROM THE HOLY BIBLE:

"You have made known to me the paths of life; you will fill me with joy in your presence." (Acts 2:28)

TODAY'S TOPIC OR QUESTION FROM ME:

Fulfilling my Christ Potential

RESPONSE FROM GOD AND JAN:

"You alone decide whether to fulfill your sacred potential. Your dear wife and I are here to help you along, but the decision is ultimately yours. You can use your "Free Will" choice to pursue any goal. Be assured that I provide you with the necessary tools to complete your spiritual destiny. However, know that I never interfere if you decide to change your mind. You can go down the street a few blocks and construct your eternal home at another location. I won't interfere. You can mess around for years without doing anything. That's OK too. You might even forget that you once started on My Path. That's all right. I'll never judge you. But if you put aside every fear and complete the building process with purpose and intention, I will be working right beside you until we're done. I AM sure you and I both will get some help from your precious wife in furnishing your spiritual palace. Jan is a wonderful interior decorator. She already has some very creative ideas in mind. In your case, you've worked hard on your lovely House of The Spirit for many years. Things are shaping up well. But there are still some finishing touches that await your attention. I urge you to keep hammering those nails, right up until the end. Someday Jan and I will stand in front of your Heavenly abode and say: "Beautiful job, Al! You've built a beautiful Temple of the Mind and Spirit. You should be proud of yourself—I know we are."

DAY 95

TODAY'S TWEET FROM SITTING WITH GOD:

"Searching here and there for spiritual enlightenment wastes time and energy. Sit in the silence. Feel My divine Presence within you."

FROM THE HOLY BIBLE:

"He replied, "You of little faith, why are you so afraid?" Then he got up and rebuked the winds and the waves and it was completely calm. (Matthew 8:26)

TODAY'S TOPIC OR QUESTION FROM ME:

The importance of meditation

RESPONSE FROM GOD AND JAN:

"Here are the fruits of meditation:

1. You become One with Me. Our divine connection unlocks everything.
2. You experience the "peace that surpasses all understanding". Nothing in the material world can upset you for long.
3. You discover how to balance the spiritual universe with the material world. You can better understand the differences between the two vastly different perspectives.
4. You realize that you are never alone. Your dear wife and I are always right by your side 24/7.
5. In the silence, you become more teachable. You are open to the Higher Truths.
6. The Wisdom of the Ages can flow to you without any distractions from the material universe.
7. You become more receptive to possible healings of your body, mind and spirit through a superconscious link to Spirit.
8. You receive divinely inspired Ideas that can become both a monetary and spiritual blessing.
9. You are able to transform your outer experience through a release of your inner power.
10. In the peace and quiet of meditation, you are better positioned to forgive, accept and understand the words and actions of others.

These are but a few benefits of meditation. As you travel higher on My Path, more will be revealed."

DAY 96

TODAY'S TWEET FROM SITTING WITH GOD:

"Release control. Allow Me to guide your human and spiritual agendas. Let Divine Order rule. Get into the flow of life."

FROM THE HOLY BIBLE:

"Ezra praised the LORD, the great God; and all the people lifted their hands and responded, "Amen! Amen!" Then they bowed down and worshipped the LORD with their faces to the ground." (Nehemiah 8:6)

TODAY'S TOPIC OR QUESTION FROM ME:

Should I become the minister of a church again?

RESPONSE FROM GOD AND JAN:

"You have been trained to take on a leadership role in an established church. You have successfully served as both a senior and associate minister. If a similar position comes to you, have confidence in your ministerial abilities. Remember My son, it is not you but the Holy Spirit that performs the work. Yesterday, you happened to be at the Unity Church of Temple when their guest speaker failed to show. The church board President came up to you 15 minutes before the service and asked if you wanted to give the Sunday message. You were in the right place at the right time. Not surprisingly, everything went well. You received many accolades for your impromptu talk. Jan and I were proud of you for stepping up without hesitation. You took on the challenge. You believed in yourself. Your dear wife and I were there in the front row applauding you. We always have faith in your ability. The folks lucky enough to be at the service witnessed Spirit at work. You were a clear channel of My Grace. When you allow Me, I can and will shine through you. If you are invited back to speak, both Jan and I will be there in the first pew. We'll be cheering you on again."

DAY 97

TODAY'S TWEET FROM SITTING WITH GOD:

"I give you everything needed to complete My spiritual work. You are a recipient of My generosity and grace."

FROM THE HOLY BIBLE:

"However, as it is written: "No eye has seen, no ear has heard, no mind has conceived what God has prepared for those who love him"—but God has revealed it to us by his spirit." (1 Corinthians 2: 9-10)

TODAY'S TOPIC OR QUESTION FROM ME:

Thank you for the Holy Spirit

RESPONSE FROM GOD AND JAN:

"The Christ in you is indeed your "hope of glory", as the Apostle Paul wrote in Colossians 1:27. The Holy Spirit inside of you does My work. It also blesses and heals, comforts and sustains you. The Light generated by the eternal spark in you can flow into the darkest corners of the world. The Holy Spirit carries My Goodness and Love into the most daunting situations. An appearance of evil is instantly dissolved by exposure to the Christ within. Loneliness and despair are cast out when the Holy Spirit arrives. I placed this essential element of your soul deep inside of you. I purposely equipped every human being with this blessing. I located the Holy Spirit directly at the center of your being. I wanted to make sure that you were never alone. This ever-present Spirit never leaves or forsakes you. You may ignore its existence, but you cannot cast out its embedded presence. It remains forever located in the very midst of you. The Holy Spirit was present at your soul's birth. It returns to Heaven at your human death. Your inner Spirit is with you throughout eternity. Be glad in it."

DAY 98

TODAY'S TWEET FROM SITTING WITH GOD:

"I AM a big God. Nothing in the material world exceeds My scope. I can help you overcome anything."

FROM THE HOLY BIBLE:

"Can anyone hide in secret places so that I cannot see him?" declares the LORD. Do not I fill heaven and earth?" declares the LORD. (Jeremiah 23: 23-24)

TODAY'S TOPIC OR QUESTION FROM ME:

Going Higher in Consciousness

RESPONSE FROM GOD AND JAN:

"You must go higher in consciousness. Try to reach the absolute zenith of human awareness. A higher level of "knowing" is required to do My work. I have specific assignments for you. I AM giving you this time of adjustment for two reasons. First, it will take days, weeks, months and maybe years to grieve your dear wife. You and Jan had a remarkable relationship. That did not end when she transitioned to My Kingdom. You won't ever forget her, nor will Jan release her memories of you. Together, you experienced a love deeper than most. That takes more processing on the soul level. I AM granting whatever time you need to get stabilized. Secondly, I want you to spend more dedicated with Me (and now Jan) in the silence. It is through meditation and prayer that you lift your consciousness higher. Please do not squander this gift. "Time" ranks as one of the most precious commodities imaginable, especially at your age. Every minute you spend with Me elevates your mind's ability to discern spiritual Truth. As you increase your "knowing", you will understand why I have called you into spiritual service. In our Unity of Spirit, you discover the awesome power of ONENESS. When We are joined, we produce incredible miracles. That's what I want for both of us."

DAY 99

TODAY'S TWEET FROM SITTING WITH GOD:

"I AM a transformative God. I want you to reach your divine potential. Let Me renew your mind."

FROM THE HOLY BIBLE:

"Don't you know that you yourselves are God's temple and that God's Spirit lives in you." (1 Corinthians 3:16)

TODAY'S TOPIC OR QUESTION FROM ME:

Could I please hear from my precious wife?

RESPONSE FROM GOD AND JAN:

"I'm here, Babe. I've been with you every minute since I departed my worn-out and tired physical body. I was there to help coordinate your move from Minnesota to Texas. I am so happy for you. I know that back home is where you want to be. I'm so much closer than you might imagine. I still live in your heart and mind, along with every memory we collected over the years. I cheer for you and support you in every way. When you speak somewhere, I'm still in the front row. I gaze at you adoringly, just like I always did. I am genuinely proud of you. When you drive anywhere in the Toyota Highlander, I'm sitting right next to you. When you are out eating in a restaurant, I am enjoying the meal with you. Everywhere you go, I'm there. You can even sense my presence, if you concentrate hard enough. How could I ever leave my sweet babe? You were the love of my life. You still are. I am your dear wife—forever. I love you."

DAY 100

TODAY'S TWEET FROM SITTING WITH GOD:

"I protect you. I AM your shield against negative forces. Look to Me as your first and last line of defense."

FROM THE HOLY BIBLE:

"For in the day of trouble he will keep me safe in his dwelling; he will hide me in the shelter of his tabernacle and set me high upon a rock." (Psalm 27:5)

TODAY'S TOPIC OR QUESTION FROM ME:

Standing firm

RESPONSE FROM GOD AND JAN:

"You stand on Holy Ground. Your sweet wife and I flank you on either side. Remember where two or more are gathered in My name, so am I there also. Jan and I look forward to meeting with you every day. We come apart to help chart your spiritual destiny. Remember: if Jan and I are for you, who can be against you? Stand firm whenever you feel ignored, abandoned, rejected and alone. In spiritual terms, you remain on solid ground. You are moving forward aided by Me and your most ardent supporter in Heaven. Yes, that would be your darling wife. You should never underestimate her dedication to you. We are both committed to helping you stand firm against all opposition. We understand you need support and reassurance. We bring people, situations and opportunities to your attention that can nurture and affirm you. Jan and I are partnering up to meet your human needs. Stay healthy, positive and faithful despite any negativity. Keep your body, mind and spirit balanced, no matter what happens. Be Strong. Stand firm. Under no circumstances would we ever leave or forsake you."

DAY 101

TODAY'S TWEET FROM SITTING WITH GOD:

"I perform healing miracles. I repair the torn places in a human heart. Trust My Power to heal anything."

FROM THE HOLY BIBLE:

"Then Jesus came to them and said, "All authority in heaven and on earth has been given to me. Go and make disciples of all nations, baptizing them in the name of the Father and the Son and the Holy Spirit." (Matthew 28: 19-20)

TODAY'S TOPIC OR QUESTION FROM ME:

Activating the Christ Spirit within Me

RESPONSE FROM GOD AND JAN:

"The Christ Spirit always remains present in every human being, whether they know it or not. However, most people aren't tuned into My spiritual frequency. The distractions of the material world dominate human brains. People rarely recognize the real power hidden within themselves. For the few who do discover "The Pearl hidden in plain sight", life changes forever. When any person begins to cooperate with their inner consciousness, they are lifted to a new plateau of awareness. At this higher level of clarity, you can stand aside while the Holy Spirit does the work. Of course, most people resist giving up control to an unseen entity. Deferring to Me is always a better choice. You can activate the Christ Spirit within you in the silence. Prayer and meditation are the keys to unleashing the Hidden Kingdom. The Spirit inside of you will provide everything needed to navigate human life. Your inner self brings the wisdom and courage that helps you meet any challenge. The Christ within awaits your summons."

DAY 102

TODAY'S TWEET FROM SITTING WITH GOD:

"Believe in Me. I can perform healing miracles through you. Go forth to bless and restore in My Holy Name."

FROM THE HOLY BIBLE:

"Have I not commanded you? Be strong and courageous. Do not be terrified; do not be discouraged, for the LORD your God will be with you wherever you go." (Joshua 1:9)

TODAY'S TOPIC OR QUESTION FROM ME:

Finding Peace, Love and Joy in a chaotic world

RESPONSE FROM GOD AND JAN:

"The Fruits of the Spirit come when you meld into a state of Oneness with Me and your precious wife. As you bond with us, our combined presence surrounds and envelops you. You'll feel it in both your heart and mind. Allow our affection for you to permeate your entire being. Let our Love reassure and comfort you in the darkest moments of doubt, fear and uncertainty. You can also depend on our eternal gift of lasting Peace. The ill winds of danger, terror, disharmony and useless noise can never disturb or frighten you. Your heart overflows with Joy when you embrace us. Jan and I carefully place the all-encompassing purple robe of Goodness around your human shoulders. You are now guided, nurtured and protected. Go forth as an anointed and tranquil soul amid the world's chaos. Let your voice offer a healing message of tolerance and understanding. Bring your spiritual presence into the loudest arguments and most dangerous situations. Remember what Jesus told the crowd at the Sermon on the Mount: "Blessed are the peacemakers, for they will be called children of God.""

DAY 103

TODAY'S TWEET FROM SITTING WITH GOD:

"I give you the potential to heal spiritually, physically and mentally those who believes in Me."

FROM THE HOLY BIBLE:

"Let your gentleness be evident to all. The Lord is near." (Philippians 4:5)

TODAY'S TOPIC OR QUESTION FROM ME

My Sabbatical

RESPONSE FROM GOD AND JAN:

"Yes, you are in the middle of a classic sabbatical. Here are three specific reasons why Jan and I are giving you this time of rest and renewal:

> 1. You need some time apart to grieve her loss. Grief is unpredictable. It comes and goes, but never entirely goes. You and Jan enjoyed a 37-year friendship and 23-year marriage. Your human souls were divinely interlocked. Both of you served Me with dedication and distinction. You were classic soul mates. The loss of such a deep bond requires a longer period of adjustment. She and I are giving you the time needed to process your loss.
> 2. After suffering such a heavy blow, you must recoup your physical and emotional strength. You also must adjust to a cross- country move and getting resettled into a new environment. No one easily digests so much change in a shortened time.
> 3. We are giving you days, weeks and months to recharge your spiritual batteries.

You still have much work ahead. There are still more sacred tasks to complete. I AM readying you for greater spiritual service. You are traveling faster on My Path. This sabbatical should help you complete your preparedness. Enjoy this "free" time, while you have it, to adapt and grow stronger."

DAY 104

TODAY'S TWEET FROM SITTING WITH GOD:

"My Peace surrounds you. It serves as a protective shield, disarming all negativity. Go peacefully into the world."

FROM THE HOLY BIBLE:

"Taking the five loaves and two fish and looking up to heaven, he gave thanks and broke the loaves. Then he gave them to his disciples to set before the people. He also divided the two fish among them all. They all ate and were satisfied, and the disciples picked up twelve basketfuls of broken pieces of bread and fish. The number of men who had eaten was five thousand." (Mark 6: 41-43)

TODAY'S TOPIC OR QUESTION FROM ME:

Blessing others

RESPONSE FROM GOD AND JAN:

"Blessing others is one of the greatest joys of My Path. The carnal world is packed with hurting human beings who need comfort and encouragement. When you and I walk the earth together, we spread blessings everywhere. You can help light up the darkness for those blinded by the lure of materialism. You become a purveyor of glad tidings that stirs feelings of hope among the depressed. You possess the power to heal physically and emotionally anyone who believes. I flow through you like a river of goodness, bringing comfort and love to those who feel abandoned and rejected. There are many wounded souls walking the earth. You and I can provide them with a restoration of spirit. You can bless others when your human ego stands aside. We are then able to bless the earth with spiritual illumination. As you and I perform our miracle-working powers, the human landscape changes for the better. Faces brighten, minds clear and emotions align in balance once more. The planet becomes a lovely place when our Light shines upon it. Unite with Me. There is so much work for us to do."

DAY 105

TODAY'S TWEET FROM SITTING WITH GOD:

"My Peace surrounds you. It acts as a protective shield for you, pushing aside disharmony and confrontation."

FROM THE HOLY BIBLE:

"A voice of one calling: "In the desert prepare the way for the LORD", make straight in the wilderness a highway for our God." (Isaiah 40:3)

TODAY'S TOPIC OR QUESTION FROM ME:

Thanking God for my marriage to Jan

RESPONSE FROM GOD AND JAN:

"Thank you for your expression of gratitude. More importantly, your dear wife thanks you. I know you appreciate her beautiful soul even more now. I AM grateful for how you both bonded to serve Me as a couple. You touched many more people than you thought. Your marriage was a model for those who knew you. Getting you all together took some doing on My part. You lived in Dallas, Jan in Duluth, and you met in Detroit (at a March of Dimes Convention). Your meeting was a divine appointment. It was a difficult relationship for many years. Things started coming together after you entered ministerial school. At the time of her passing, you two had been married nearly 23 years. You cherished her inner and outer beauty. For your sweet wife, she never had any doubt that you were the one. You could exasperate her at times with your stubbornness about making a commitment. But she saw you then and still views you now as the love of her life. You feel the same way about her. Yours was a marriage made in Heaven—literally. I brought you two together in sacred service to Me. We were three blessed partners during your time in ministry. We continue that Holy Trinity today. Jan and I now interact with you daily from the Kingdom of Heaven. Your precious love for each other travels across time and space, still intact."

DAY 106

TODAY'S TWEET FROM SITTING WITH GOD:

"Stay alert for My divine ideas. Claim them as your own. They make lack and limitation disappear."

FROM THE HOLY BIBLE:

"Do not put out the Spirit's fire; do not treat prophecies with contempt. Test everything. Hold on to the good. Avoid every kind of evil." (1 Thessalonians 5:19-23)

TODAY'S TOPIC OR QUESTION FROM ME:

How much "time" do I have left?

RESPONSE FROM GOD AND JAN:

"Don't worry. You'll be allotted the exact amount of "time" that you need to complete My work. You'll also get adequate "time" to grieve Jan's sudden passing. Rest and restoration form a key part of your recovery. Whenever a soul mate departs, the one remaining can be lost for a while. Mourning the loss of a spiritual partner requires extra salve. Take the time needed to heal your emotional and spiritual wounds. You are navigating the grief process satisfactorily. You chose to relocate quickly after Jan's unexpected passing. For most people, undertaking a drastic geographical move so quickly just wouldn't work. For you, it did. The physical relocation kept you busy and engaged. You've not had the time to sit and think about your loss. But the grief has only been postponed, not eliminated. I promise there will be more tears. Your dear wife and I commend you for the proactive way you have approached the move and your new environment. You've made good connections already, both socially and spiritually. You have kept a low profile, but not entirely. You aren't a hermit. You shouldn't act like one. You have religiously (no pun intended) kept meeting with Me (and now Jan) during the early morning hours. That is still the most crucial part of your day."

DAY 107

TODAY'S TWEET FROM SITTING WITH GOD:

"Extend forgiveness for all. Reach out to someone not yet forgiven. See them surrounded by My healing light."

FROM THE HOLY BIBLE:

"It is God that arms me with strength and makes my way perfect." (Psalm 18:32)

TODAY'S TOPIC OR QUESTION FROM ME:

Forgiveness

RESPONSE FROM GOD AND JAN:

"Your "Life Lesson" is "forgiveness." As such, you will be given many opportunities to practice forgiving someone or something. Every human being has lessons to learn. "Life Lessons" can be hard and unyielding. Human beings want relief from being constantly challenged. They cry out: "why me?" Dealing with forgiveness issues, especially with "family", often leaves people angry and frustrated. It may be unclear why certain family members act as they do. You might find yourself expected to forgive something you don't understand. Problems come when people perceive the same event or situation differently. Everyone always has his or her own unique perspective. But here is one basic Truth: No one goes through life with total approval from their fellow human beings. If you get a 51% approval rating during your time on Earth, count that as a major victory. You should also know by now that attempting to guilt, shame or coerce anybody to treat you "right" never works. There are certain people that will never like, love or trust you. Seek to view every relationship with honesty, clarity and realistic expectations. Try to understand the viewpoint of others. Let people walk their own spiritual path. Keep the focus on yourself. Forgiveness is the Golden Key to a life of harmony. Forgive and find peace. Forgive and experience joy."

DAY 108

TODAY'S TWEET FROM SITTING WITH GOD:

"I AM omnipotent. I gave you a taste of My spiritual power so that you may bless and heal others."

FROM THE HOLY BIBLE:

"It is for freedom that Christ has set us free. Stand firm and do not be burdened again by a yoke of slavery." (Galatians 5:1)

TODAY'S TOPIC OR QUESTION FROM ME:

Self-care

RESPONSE FROM GOD AND JAN:

"Jan and I want you to enjoy life. There are several self-care things that you look forward to each day with anticipation. Here is a partial list of your favorite things:

> 1. You love the early morning hours in prayer, meditation and drinking your coffee. Jan and I like it too. You've always been a morning person, so this works out well for everyone.
> 2. You also look forward to going back to bed for an hour or two after our prayer time together. You sleep well then, which is no surprise after the relaxing time with us.
> 3. You like doing your exercise regimen each day. That includes walking around the apartment property and using the exercise room.
> 4. Your morning bath, hair wash and shave make you feel fresh and ready for the day. You don't miss a day getting cleaned up. Good hygiene is healthy for your body, mind and spirit.
> 5. You enjoy getting in the Toyota Highlander and traveling somewhere almost every day. Whether it's getting gasoline, going to the cleaners, eating out, going to church or meeting a friend for lunch at a restaurant, it makes you feel like part of a busy world.
> 6. You look forward to catching up on the news of the day on the TV, your PC and mobile devices. You do like watching college and pro football in the fall. There are also a few TV programs that still catch your eye, although not as many as before.
> 7. You like to write.

That's a good thing when you take on a project like THE FOREVER PENNY. Basically, you have created a healthy and calm lifestyle for yourself. Jan and I want you to like and enjoy your human life."

DAY 109

TODAY'S TWEET FROM SITTING WITH GOD:

"Here are the 3 "P's" in My Kingdom: patience, persistence, and perseverance. You must practice them all to grow spiritually."

FROM THE HOLY BIBLE:

"A gentle answer turns away wrath, but a harsh word stirs up anger." (Proverbs 15:1)

TODAY'S TOPIC OR QUESTION FROM ME:

Lead me onward and upward

RESPONSE FROM GOD AND JAN:

"When you commit to following us, Jan and I lead you onward and upward. It never works when we fight each other for control. Relax and let us lead the "Dance of Life". When you surrender, we glide across the floor in perfect rhythm. We promise not to miss a beat. When you begin leading, we start stepping on each other's toes. We might even have to stop and start the music over. Tangled feet aren't good for anyone. We have the divine potential to be perfect dance partners. When you, Jan and I twirl as one, every dance trophy comes our way. A problem surfaces if your ego tries to cut in on us. It wants to lead you away from us for its own purposes. The ego seeks to take you in a completely different direction, away from the spiritual Path. The dance of materialism always leaves you worn out and dissatisfied. I know that you and Jan loved to dance with each other. You danced close on the very first night you met. Remember how wonderful it felt to hold her in your arms. Think about that loving embrace whenever you feel yourself slipping away. Come find us. We'll take you by the hand and guide you across the floor again. Dance forever with your sweet wife and Me. Someday you'll waltz through the gates of Heaven. I promise there will be beautiful music when you arrive. The lovely melody of eternity never ends."

DAY 110

TODAY'S TWEET FROM SITTING WITH GOD:

"I carefully guide your spiritual journey. Trust Me. Every step on My Path has a divine purpose."

FROM THE HOLY BIBLE:

"The only thing that counts is faith expressing itself through love." (Galatians 5: 6)

TODAY'S TOPIC OR QUESTION FROM ME:

Spiritual growth

RESPONSE FROM GOD AND JAN:

"There are two separate worlds: "material" and "spiritual". By choosing to live a material existence, you never experience the eternal world of Spirit. Those choosing the material path will see little or no soul growth in this lifetime. You are incarnated as a human being for only a brief period. I created each of you for a specific reason. Your primary purpose is to evolve spiritually. But I also gave you "free will choice". You can choose to forego any spiritual growth. If you do, you live in the physical world with its constant changes. I do not castigate anyone for shunning Me in favor of a material life. It's their individual choice, but also their loss. I place many spiritual opportunities in front of people. Most either walk away or don't bother to notice My gift. When and if someone does show interest in following My Path, I consider them for greater service. However, many are called but few are chosen. My Path is lonely, exacting and difficult. Most people find it far too demanding. The drop-out rate is high. However, the rewards are great. When you commit to Me, you begin to discover the Divine Power hidden within you. Your soul begins moving onward and upward in a new trajectory. You receive new clarity. Your conscious awareness rises. As you increase your time in prayer and meditation, new vistas unfold. Some of My followers are chosen for the highest service possible. Only then does your eternal soul soar to the peak of the sacred mountain."

DAY 111

TODAY'S TWEET FROM SITTING WITH GOD:

"Stay awake. Nothing happens by chance in My spiritual universe. Each day brings new revelations and opportunities."

FROM THE HOLY BIBLE:

"The LORD reigns, let the earth be glad; let the distant shores rejoice." (Psalm 97:1)

TODAY'S TOPIC OR QUESTION FROM ME:

The Path to Enlightenment

RESPONSE FROM GOD AND JAN:

"Enlightenment happens when you reach the pinnacle of awareness. Most people sleepwalk through their lives. One day you are young, healthy and full of promise. Then time becomes a wrecker. Suddenly you're old, tired and feeble. Many ask: "What just happened?" Most people spend their lives steeped in materialism and not seeking enlightenment. Still, it's never too late to start. You can begin your journey to the loftier realms anytime you want. Many illumined souls entering Heaven began the Path in their sunset years. Jan wants you to go higher. She and I are both cheering you on. For many years, you and your sweet wife traveled the Path of enlightenment together. It's always easier when a couple walks My Path hand in hand. You can encourage and support each other. Should one partner stumble, the other is able to help. While your dear wife has reached her spiritual destination, she still serves as a divine touchstone for you. Look to her for love and support. Trust in Me for whatever you need to complete your human destiny. The Path may get steeper toward the end of your climb. Don't worry. You'll make it. Jan and I are lighting up the dark places for you. Follow us, My son."

DAY 112

TODAY'S TWEET FROM SITTING WITH GOD:

"I AM the master teacher. You are My beloved student. I offer daily instruction on how to live a positive life."

FROM THE HOLY BIBLE:

"On that day you will realize that I am in my father, and you are in me, and I am in you." (John 14:20)

TODAY'S TOPIC OR QUESTION FROM ME:

What are My spiritual gifts?

RESPONSE FROM GOD AND JAN:

"I provided you with many natural gifts. All must be consciously developed before they can become spiritually operative. Most of My children either ignore or dismiss their God-given talents. If they do recognize their natural endowments, many use them unwisely or for selfish purposes. I have created you with the following:

1. a warm, friendly and loving nature.
2. an ability to communicate effectively through writing and speaking.
3. A quick and intelligent mind.
4. An empathy and caring for others that suited your career choices of public relations and the ministry.
5. a curiosity about many things and a basic thirst for knowledge;
6. the important virtue of perseverance, which keeps you moving forward despite obstacles.
7. an awareness of the spiritual aspects of your life and a willingness to go both higher and deeper.
8. an affinity for meditation and listening to Me in the silence.
9. a sense of humor which helps keep the material universe in perspective.
10. an interest in and appreciation for fine art, classical music, and the legitimate theatre.

Of course, you received other God-provided gifts such as your interesting family of origin and being born and raised in a small-city environment. However, remember again this truth about everything: Your gifts must be nurtured and fully developed. Otherwise, I gave them to you in vain."

DAY 113

TODAY'S TWEET FROM SITTING WITH GOD:

"Lean on Me when you become weary. I can restore your energy and stamina. I lift you on wings of eagles."

FROM THE HOLY BIBLE:

"Here is my servant, whom I uphold, my chosen one in whom I delight; I will put my Spirit on him." (Isaiah 42:1)

TODAY'S TOPIC OR QUESTION:

Recovering from grief

RESPONSE FROM GOD AND JAN:

"Jan and I think you are doing about as well as could be expected in grieving her loss. Your grief is somewhat mitigated by her ongoing presence in your life. You accept that your dear wife is involved with Me in helping to guide you. You sense her ongoing devotion. It is spiritually true. Your soul mate still loves you, only from a different dimension of the universe. She watches over you day and night. And yes, both Jan and I are carefully leading you forward on My Path. The closeness you feel with us each morning bolsters your belief in her continuing presence. It's as if she hasn't gone anywhere. In a way, that's correct. Jan oversees your movements each day, giving you a little advice here and a bit of nudging there. She is pleased that your love for her has remained constant. You are still wearing your gold wedding ring. Photographs of her are in every room of your apartment. Your passionate love remains well intact. In some ways, it has grown since she passed. You are even more appreciative of who she was as a wife, friend, lover, companion and partner in ministry. Sometimes your grief pops up as an unexpected memory. Those moments are like a gift-wrapped box of chocolates, sweet and enticing. If a tear falls on the box, it only makes the memories dearer and more delicious."

DAY 114

TODAY'S TWEET FROM SITTING WITH GOD:

"Find ways to express gratitude, even in times of pain and discontent. Lift up those people who bless your life."

FROM THE HOLY BIBLE:

"Each person should give what they have decided in their hearts to give, not reluctantly or under compulsion, for God loves a cheerful giver." (2 Corinthians 9:7)

TODAY'S TOPIC OR QUESTION FROM ME:

What are "The rewards of Heaven?"

RESPONSE FROM GOD AND JAN:

"The rewards of My Kingdom are vast, eternal and specific. In Heaven, we do not allow anger or resentment. Love and acceptance abound. "War" in any form does not exist. Peace prevails. Sickness and physical disability have vanished. All souls are healthy and whole. A sense of joy surrounds everyone. Beautiful music permeates our sacred halls. Good will reigns. Rancor and disharmony stand vanquished. Negativity is not tolerated in My celestial abode. Jan likes the opportunities to acquire more knowledge. Heaven offers a great learning experience for any curious soul. Everything imaginable becomes available for your enjoyment and enlightenment. Theatre lovers line up for Shakespeare's Master Classes. Political groupies seek out lectures by former presidents and prime ministers. Those with a royal inclination can pursue audiences with kings, queens, princes or princesses. Movie buffs fill the parlors of directors, actors and actresses. Classical music lovers gather around masters like Mozart, Bach, Chopin, and Beethoven. Your fine art favorites such as Renoir, Manet, Monet, Seurat, and Rembrandt are here. Heaven is like the world's greatest university, art gallery, concert hall and movie theatre rolled into one. All of it awaits your arrival here. Jan wants to help you explore it all. What fun you two will have!"

DAY 115

TODAY'S TWEET FROM SITTING WITH GOD:

"Seek first My Kingdom and all else will be added unto you. All that I AM, all that I have, belongs to My beloved children."

FROM THE HOLY BIBLE:

"But his delight is in the Law of the LORD, and on the law he meditates day and night." (Psalm 1: 2)

TODAY'S TOPIC OR QUESTION FROM ME:

Trusting God and Jan

RESPONSE FROM GOD AND JAN:

"Although you trust My Path, your dear wife and I understand human weaknesses. When you get fearful about anything, call out to us for counsel and support. We'll soothe your troubled thoughts. Believe in us. Never compromise your spiritual values. The material world exploits your vulnerabilities. If you get worried about something, Jan and I will bring divine assistance to bolster your resolve. You are getting closer to the finish line. Don't even think about quitting now! We want you to finish your sacred work. After you complete your divine tasks, your dear wife and I stand ready to welcome you into Heaven. Don't fail us now. It would negate too much hard work on everyone's part. You've shown great determination, perseverance and commitment while walking My Path. You've endured pain, sacrifice and separation. I know it hasn't been easy, but Jan and I know you will go the distance. You are in the last stages of your sacred journey. Do not falter. Trust! Trust! Trust! The stakes are much too high. Failure comes with a steep price. We see you completing every spiritual task before your transition into Heaven. Keep grinding. Ignore all negative thoughts. Seek out words of comfort and support. Jan and I will supply them to you upon request. Never be swayed by anything. We promise you eventual success. You know we always keep our promises. Trust and believe."

DAY 116

TODAY'S TWEET FROM SITTING WITH GOD:

"I dispense My blessed Grace through you. I give you the ability to bless, comfort and heal."

FROM THE HOLY BIBLE:

"For in the gospel a righteousness from God is revealed, a righteousness that is by faith from first to last." (Romans 1:17)

TODAY'S TOPIC OR QUESTION FROM ME:

Spiritual Maturity

RESPONSE FROM GOD AND JAN:

"Here are examples of spiritual maturity:

1. An understanding that the Fruits of the Spirit are more real than the material world, and far more crucial to your general well-being.
2. An appreciation that I AM omnipresent, omnipotent and omniscient. I AM greater than anything discernable by the five human senses.
3. A belief in the ultimate power of quietness and humility as opposed to the loud clanging of the ego.
4. An absolute and unwavering trust in My promise to provide every resource needed to do my work.
5. An awareness of My Presence in everything that happens—i. e. "There are no accidents."
6. A willingness to practice the Golden Rule in all human interactions.
7. A conscious decision to let go of illusory human control and let Me guide and direct your decisions and actions.
8. Seeking spiritual sustenance instead of pursuing short-term temporary satisfactions from the material realm.
9. Realizing the importance of "consciousness" and the necessity of a higher awareness.
10. Living in an ongoing state of prayer, forgiveness, gratitude and thanksgiving.
11. Claiming your rightful portion of My Grace.
12) Reading, valuing and loving the Holy Scriptures as an essential aspect of your sacred journey.

There are other examples of becoming spiritually mature, but this list represents a general overview of the requirements needed to complete My Path."

DAY 117

TODAY'S TWEET FROM SITTING WITH GOD:

"You serve Me best from a humble perspective. Humility demonstrates strength of human character."

FROM THE HOLY BIBLE:

"The commander of the LORD'S army replied, "Take off your sandals, for the place where you are standing is holy ground." (Joshua 5:15)

TODAY'S TOPIC OR QUESTION FROM ME:

Strengthening my divine relationship with God (and Jan)

RESPONSE FROM GOD AND JAN:

"To accomplish anything of spiritual significance, you have to become "One" with both Me and your dear wife. Your precious Jan has now bonded into Oneness with Me. She and I are now both active in coordinating your spiritual destiny. You and your wife experienced a powerful relationship on the human level. In many ways, you modeled "oneness" as a couple. Your unity was evident in the past 4 ½ years when you acted as Jan's full-time care giver. You discovered the incredible beauty of serving someone else besides yourself. Now the three of us must unite as one sacred entity. We need to create a permanent and unbreakable bond of togetherness. I hope you understand the divine power that our unity of purpose generates. For example, your ability to heal and bless literally triples when our Holy Trinity becomes operational. You become a miracle-worker of the highest order. Your effectiveness as a speaker and writer grows in conjunction with our unity of Spirit. Connecting with your Higher Power and your soul mate wife activates spiritual forces far beyond the scope of human understanding. Make the conscious decision to align yourself with us. Miracles will happen."

DAY 118

TODAY'S TWEET FROM SITTING WITH GOD:

"Be faithful. When you walk beside Me each day, our togetherness becomes your joy and fulfillment."

FROM THE HOLY BIBLE:

"Blessed are those who mourn, for they will be comforted." (Matthew 5:4)

TODAY'S TOPIC OR QUESTION FROM ME:

Surviving slumps

RESPONSE FROM GOD AND JAN:

"When you feel yourself spiraling into a slump, consult with your sweet wife and Me. We are here to help you survive any temporary setback. Let us assist you in sorting things out. Try not to worry or fret. Whatever may be dragging you down, know that "this too shall pass." Do not allow anything or anyone in the material world to affect you. Things are progressing well. Jan and I are both proud of your steadfastness during this time of grief and change. When you start down a slippery slope of any kind, stop and take stock. Increase your time in prayer and meditation. Read a chapter in the Scriptures. Seek out other uplifting books or videos. Review an old journal. During the down moments, keep reminding yourself of your identity as My divine child. Think about how far you've come on My Path. You are also Jan's adored and treasured husband. She still cares deeply about you. Nothing can ever take her love from you. Believe in who you are and what you've become. You deserve respect and appreciation. More "Good" is headed your way soon. While you wait, stay focused and faithful. Untapped resources are being made available to you. Remember: no slump lasts forever. Believe in yourself, believe in Me, believe in your soul mate."

DAY 119

TODAY'S TWEET FROM SITTING WITH GOD:

"Immerse yourself in My Presence. Walk with Me. You and I can bring healing to a wounded world."

FROM THE HOLY BIBLE:

"May all your enemies perish, O LORD! But may they who love you be like the sun when it rises in its strength." (Judges 5:31)

TODAY'S TOPIC OR QUESTION FROM ME:

Forgiveness

RESPONSE FROM GOD AND JAN:

"You've known for 30 years that forgiveness is your primary "Life Lesson." You read somewhere that forgiving someone can be either decisional or emotional. The human mind can make the "decision" to forgive, but a stubborn heart may still hold back. Or, you can decide to "emotionally" forgive, but the decision-making brain resists. I say you need both mind and heart to make true forgiveness work. Your human mind needs to understand and accept the logical reasons behind the need to forgive. Your heart needs to activate its innate compassion. Of course, you are the person who benefits most from an act of forgiveness. Anytime you cut away the invasive cancers of resentment and anger, soul progress emerges. An unforgiving attitude stymies your spiritual growth. Make the decision to release stewing about any perceived harm done to you. Let your rational brain mull over the positive results that accrue from forgiveness. Then, if the mind accepts the clear rationale behind your act of forgiveness, turn the next step over to your kinder heart. Find that generous place in the heart's inner chamber, then reach out in emotional forgiveness. Give a personal blessing to the individual, institution or situation involved. Let both your mind and heart cry out in unison: "I forgive you!" With both in sync, real forgiveness becomes possible. Lives can then be blessed and destinies changed forever."

DAY 120

TODAY'S TWEET FROM SITTING WITH GOD:

"Give up judging others. Decline the opportunity to cast negative aspirations. Peace comes when you forego hurtful commentary."

FROM THE HOLY BIBLE:

"Fight the good fight of the faith. Take hold of the eternal life to which you were called when you made your good confession in the presence of many witnesses." (Timothy 6: 12-13)

TODAY'S TOPIC OR QUESTION FROM ME:

Thoughts of Jan

RESPONSE FROM GOD AND JAN:

I understand that memories of your dear wife are never far away. When you remember one lovely thing about her, you can then recall dozens or even hundreds of other little things that you miss. Thinking about Jan brings you both joy and sadness. I doubt that any negative memories, as such, still exist in your conscious or subconscious mind. Jan modeled warmth, generosity, acceptance and love. She understood your human shortcomings and loved you anyway. Your dedication and commitment to her care-giving swept away any disagreements that might have arisen in a normal marriage. Yes, you all had ups and downs, especially before you were married. You operated then in a world of negative distractions and blatant materialism. Jan was never a materialistic person, so your love of status, position and money was distasteful to her. Yet, she never once gave up on you. She saw something in you. Your dear wife always kept you front and center in her heart and mind. When you finally came to your senses after many years, she was there to haul your battered spirit back into her life. Your marriage flourished because all questions of doubt and fidelity were quashed. When you returned her faithfulness with an unwavering allegiance of your own, the marriage soared to its highest possible level. The caregiving of your sweet wife was the ultimate act of love that sealed the deal for both of you."

DAY 121

TODAY'S TWEET FROM SITTING WITH GOD:

"Seek Me the moment you become worried about anything. I AM greater than anything in the world. Have faith. I banish fear."

FROM THE HOLY BIBLE:

"But you are a forgiving God, gracious and compassionate, slow to anger and abounding in love." (Nehemiah 9:17)

TODAY'S TOPIC OR QUESTION FROM ME:

Facing fear and change with courage and faith

RESPONSE AND JAN:

"Jan and I act as your shelter and refuge from the storms of life. Whenever you become fearful, you may be experiencing a crisis of faith. You must reach out for us during periods of doubt. We respond to your concerns. You possess an eternal bond with us. Our hearts, minds and souls are forever linked with yours. Nothing can sever or diminish our sacred relationship. If you are weary, Jan and I fill you with new stamina. When your faith falters, we remind you of your sacred heritage. Never ever live in fear. Be strong in Me and in your dedicated wife. We possess unlimited power. We never hesitate to use it on your behalf. Know and accept this fact: We are with you always, until the very end of human time and beyond. Our rod and our staff, they comfort you. We are leading you to the mountaintop of human existence. Trust in our divine intervention. Jan and I meet daily to review your human and spiritual progress. So far, so good. But we understand your human tendencies. Every mortal has fears about something. Your dear wife and I help you overcome anything that hinders or distracts you. We are your 9-1-1 call, your first responders."

DAY 122

TODAY'S TWEET FROM SITTING WITH GOD:

"No human life remains problem free. When troubles arrive, summon Me. I appear with comfort and counsel."

FROM THE HOLY BIBLE:

"Like newborn babies, crave pure spiritual milk, so that by it you may grow up in your salvation." (1 Peter 2: 2-3)

TODAY'S TOPIC OR QUESTION FROM ME:

Rebalancing myself after a driving trip to Austin yesterday

RESPONSE FROM GOD AND JAN:

"Yes, you were tested yesterday. The fast traffic between Temple and Austin demanded that you maintain focus. You can't ever relax on I-35. The day seemed more intense than you expected, especially with the traffic challenge. You were forced out of your comfort zone. Your sweet wife and I see that as a good thing. Anytime that you or anyone strays from an established routine, it often produces unwanted stress. Still, Jan and I view the day as positive experience for you. Here is our reasoning:

1. You navigated a 150-mile roundtrip between your hometown and a busy city.
2. You reconnected with an old friend and minister of a church in Austin.
3. She invited you to guest speak at the church, which you will do later this year.
4. The two of you were able to spend some valuable prayer time together.
5. You experienced a nice conversation with one of the church congregants while waiting on your minister friend to finish up a call.
6. The trip impressed on you the importance of reaching out to colleagues for spiritual support.

What if you had stayed home? Nothing would have happened. All in all, we see it as a confidence building day for you."

DAY 123

TODAY'S TWEET FROM SITTING WITH GOD:

"Act as my shining light to a darkened world. Let My Truth shine forth from you. Be a beacon for the lost and suffering."

FROM THE HOLY BIBLE:

"The eternal God is your refuge and underneath are the everlasting arms." (Deuteronomy 33:27)

TODAY'S TOPIC OR QUESTION FROM ME:

My daily spiritual regimen

RESPONSE FROM GOD AND JAN:

"Sticking to a daily plan works wonders. Try not to view your spiritual regimen as a "grind". Instead, regard it as the most effective and practical way to know Me better. Construct your House of the Spirit brick by solid brick. Day by day, you are making your structure stronger. See every 24 hours as another opportunity to add more layers. You will need a lasting fortress to withstand life's hurricanes, floods, earthquakes and cyclones. Your sacred refuge must also be termite-proof against those ravenous little critters that eat away while you sleep. Some of the most destructive invaders steal into your heart and mind in the dead of night. The material realm specializes in dangling beautifully packaged enticers before you. When you untie the lovely bow, you often find the box filled with jagged and harmful rocks. Evil winds carry you away unless your inner castle consists of steel, bricks and mortar. Human beings tend to get uprooted by the tornadic activities and lures of a fallen world. As a mortal, you have distinct human vulnerabilities. The Dark Side knows them all. It exploits your weaknesses without mercy if given half a chance. Discourage any probes or attacks that could damage you. Maybe someday the evil doers will give up trying to undo or destroy you. But don't hold your breath. In the meantime, keep building your impenetrable mansion one blessed brick at a time."

DAY 124

TODAY'S TWEET FROM SITTING WITH GOD:

"I AM your guide. Listen for My counsel. Trust the directions I give you. I never lead you astray."

FROM THE HOLY BIBLE:

"When Jesus spoke again to the people, he said, "I am the light of the world. Whoever follows me will never walk in darkness, but will have the light of life." (John 8:12)

TODAY'S TOPIC OR QUESTION FROM ME:

Believing in myself

RESPONSE FROM GOD AND JAN:

"You are familiar with the Biblical passage "Lean not on your own understanding, but seek the LORD first and all things will be added unto you." Over the years, following some hard and painful lessons, you finally accepted that divine premise. In the past, you often "leaned on your own understanding". Things did not always go well. Now, as you are leaning on our divine guidance, your life unfolds more smoothly. Your dear wife and I hope that your trust in us continues growing. As your Path winds closer to Heaven, any unforced error on your part can have negative consequences. Believing in yourself is a good thing per se, except when the arrogant and self-righteous ego gets involved. It then becomes easy to believe in your human infallibility. When the money comes flooding in and the accolades abound, most people get full of themselves. Jan and I think you are past that trap now. But you must forever remain on guard. Believe in your abilities and talents. Believe in your determination and persistence. Believe that you have the training and background to handle any professional duty. But let us continue directing the way forward. Never try to go it alone. Ask for our sacred counsel before doing anything. We won't let you down or steer you wrong, now or ever."

DAY 125

TODAY'S TWEET FROM SITTING WITH GOD:

"Consciously look for the God-particle in other human beings. I created each unique soul in My image and likeness."

FROM THE HOLY BIBLE:

"Before they call, I will answer; while they are yet speaking I will hear." (Isaiah 65:24)

TODAY'S TOPIC OR QUESTION FROM ME:

What is my way forward?

RESPONSE:

"Your best way forward lies in a strengthening of your relationship with your precious wife (who sits by My side) and Me. Allow us to direct your steps. We want you to feel our unwavering love for you. Visualize the three of us, arm in arm, walking in a dark and deep forest near a towering mountain. Our Path winds its way up toward the mountaintop. See a lovely rainbow encircling its majestic pinnacle. We are traveling toward that distant summit, which represents the Kingdom of Heaven. You, Jan and I keep up a steady pace. We neither break into a run nor are we lagging back. We walk with purpose, assured of our destination. Oh, we may have a distraction now and then. But nothing can halt our progress. We are on a spiritual mission. The Forces of Darkness would love to scuttle our journey. Their attempts fail. Nothing of this or any other world can stop us. We have faced danger before and survived intact. Although the battle often becomes fierce, we triumph. Someday you'll stand on the top of that mountain, surveying the distant world below. Then everything finally becomes clear. Until that day, cling to your wife and Me. Our sacred destination looms straight ahead, directly in front of us. Soon you can touch the rainbow."

DAY 126

TODAY'S TWEET FROM SITTING WITH GOD:

"There is no real freedom in the material world. You become truly free when you live under My Grace."

FROM THE HOLY BIBLE:

"I will proclaim the decree of the LORD: He said to Me, "You are my Son; today I have become your father." (Psalm 2:7)

TODAY'S TOPIC OR QUESTION FROM ME:

The importance of journaling

RESPONSE FROM GOD AND JAN:

"Keeping a daily journal has been a literal "Godsend" for you. Here are a few of the reasons why journaling serves you so well:

1. It provides a written record of your human and spiritual journey.
2. Having a "history" of your thoughts and actions can offer valuable perspective in times of doubt and indecision.
3. Journaling about people and situations helps you better understand human motivation and often hidden agendas.
4. You can gauge the pattern of events that has brought you to this place and time.
5. Daily journaling demands a discipline that can carry over into other parts of your life.
6. Keeping a journal gives you the opportunity to delve into "feelings", when you choose, therefore providing a form of "therapy."
7. Expressing your thoughts about My Presence in your life allows an opportunity for praise and thanksgiving.
8. Since Jan's passing, your daily writing reassures you of her continuing presence in your life.
9. Your journal offers a direct conduit to the Me, allowing you an ongoing stream of comfort, counsel and encouragement.
10) Your journals may someday leave a possible legacy behind for those who remain and for strangers you will never meet.

Keeping a daily record of your life since 1985 continues to be a meaningful, historical and a spiritual blessing for you."

DAY 127

TODAY'S TWEET FROM SITTING WITH GOD:

"The dawning light of Truth spreads one sacred soul at a time. As a light activates, a point of darkness disappears."

FROM THE HOLY BIBLE:

"I tell you the truth, whosoever hears my word and believes him who sent me has eternal life and will not be condemned; he has crossed over from death to life." (John 5:24)

TODAY'S TOPIC OR QUESTION FROM ME:

Becoming a point of light

RESPONSE FROM GOD AND JAN:

"Any human being can become a point of light for Me. Each day offers a new chance to shine forth on My behalf. Any human interaction generates an opportunity to demonstrate My Presence. Every Tweet you post expresses Me. The books you publish, the articles you write and the opinion pieces you create are another byline for My Holy name. A day of journaling about your sacred journey stirs the ethers around you with thoughts of Spirit. All positive actions can be a divine reflection of Me. I want you to carry My message of Peace, Hope and Love to a hurting world. Let your eternal light become a beacon for anyone stumbling around in the darkness. Keep your fire lit! Don't let it be snuffed out by naysayers. Expect opposition whenever you deliver My Truth. My beautiful world is inundated with cynicism, lies and deception. If you possess even the tiniest sliver of illumination (and you do), you are obligated to demonstrate it through your thoughts, words and deeds. Refuse to squander a single moment. Show Me off to a disbelieving world. I have granted you a spark of the divine. Let it escape, flourish and bestow its unique blessing on one and all."

DAY 128

TODAY'S TWEET FROM SITTING WITH GOD:

"Harmony appears wherever I AM present. I displace anger, resentment, and rancor. I offer love, peace and hope."

FROM THE HOLY BIBLE:

"But they did not realize it was I who healed them. I led them with cords of human kindness, with ties of love; I lifted the yoke from their neck and bent down to feed them." (Hosea 11: 3-4)

TODAY'S TOPIC OR QUESTION FROM ME:

Dealing with crisis

RESPONSE FROM GOD AND JAN:

"When a crisis strikes, search for Me. You won't have far to look. I AM closer than your hands or feet. Summon Me before you do anything. Turn within to establish our divine connection. Make Me the first voice you seek in any crisis. I come bearing faith, wisdom, strength and courage. I AM your mental, physical and spiritual support system whenever your knees start buckling. I provide the resources to confront any challenge. I represent the endless well of living water that never runs dry. I open my everlasting arms to you. I embrace your weaknesses and make you strong again. I refuse to let any darkness blot out your sunny nature. I reassure you as a parent would comfort a frightened child. I fill you with gratitude, forgiveness and understanding. I advise you that forgiving in a crisis can be the greatest arrow in your quiver. I bring you the gift of conscious awareness, an uncommon tool that adds clarity and discernment. I lift you up so that you may see everything from a higher vantage point. Be strong in Me, My beloved child. I will never leave or forsake you. You and I together (along with your dear wife) can endure and triumph over any crisis."

DAY 129

TODAY'S TWEET FROM SITTING WITH GOD:

"Heed My instructions. Ask and you shall receive. Seek and you will find. Knock and the door will be opened unto you."

FROM THE HOLY BIBLE:

"But the LORD stood by my side and gave me strength, so that through me the message might be fully proclaimed." (Timothy 4:17)

TODAY'S TOPIC OR QUESTION FROM ME:

Faith

RESPONSE FROM GOD AND JAN:

"Be bold in your faith. Never waver or doubt. Rest assured in the promises that Jan and I make to you. Remain forever steeped in faith no matter what happens. Gear up for tests to your faith. Prepare for all-out spiritual warfare. The challenges can be subtle or direct, stealthy or in your face. When the battle commences, hold your ground. Stand behind your Shield of Faith. Be confidant as you engage the enemy. Rise above the thistles and thorns of human chaos and confusion. Your dear wife and I believe in you. However, you triumph only if your faith holds out. Although the landscape grows dark, a victorious faith restores the light. A strong faith leads to unlimited courage. If your faith falters, seek a surge of heavenly power. When danger pounds at your door, let faith respond. Be "faith-full", filled with the certainty of My promises. But you must stay prepared for unexpected onslaughts. Let your powerful faith go before you, clearing out all obstacles that litter your path. Believe faith in Me can deliver you from anything. Watch as your mortal enemies scatter and problems evaporate. Faith always wins the day, no matter how dire the outlook seems."

DAY 130

TODAY'S TWEET FROM SITTING WITH GOD:

"I AM your Source for health, prosperity and divine guidance. Look no further than Me. I meet all of your earthly needs."

FROM THE HOLY BIBLE:

"See, my servant will act wisely; he will be raised and lifted up and highly exalted." (Isaiah 52:13)

TODAY'S TOPIC OR QUESTION FROM ME:

Achieving Oneness

RESPONSE FROM GOD AND JAN:

"We want you to realize Oneness not only with Me, but also with your dear wife. Jan now sits with Me on the spiritual side of the eternal equation. When she walked physically by your side during your human marriage, you all operated as "One". This was increasingly true during your years serving as her full-time caregiver. Now you need to bond with Jan again across time and space. I know you feel her beloved spirit around you. In our morning prayer time together, you sense her beautiful presence. Keep up the bonding process. You should understand that we form a powerful trio of spiritual warriors. You, Jan and I acting together can perform miracle healings, provide comfort to the wounded and bereaved, and create masterpieces of human interaction. We three are capable of anything. In our Unity of Spirit, our powerful threesome acts as a catalyst for great strides in human awareness. Much of what we accomplish depends upon the strength of our combined intentions. We must act in Oneness with each other and the resources of Heaven. Only then can our Holy Trinity produce miracles."

DAY 131

TODAY'S TWEET FROM SITTING WITH GOD:

"Growing in awareness is always a worthy spiritual goal. It also makes for an easier journey on your life path."

FROM THE HOLY BIBLE:

"Be on our guard; stand firm in the faith; be men of courage; be strong. Do everything in love." (1 Corinthians 15:13-14)

TODAY'S TOPIC OR QUESTION FROM ME:

Your will for me and the power to carry it out

RESPONSE FROM GOD AND JAN:

'My will is that you move onward and upward toward your spiritual destiny. Right now, everything proceeds as planned. One area of human concern does need some work on your part. Jan and I know that you worry about finances. Despite appearances to the contrary, we have you covered. I do understand that people worry about money. Whether they have too much or too little, the pursuit of dollar bills occupies man's thoughts and schemes. Here's the bottom line, in terms that anyone can understand: When you follow My Will for you, I pick up the tab. Whenever your ego makes the choices, you pick up the tab. When you choose My will, I cover your needs. Hear My sacred promise: your financial needs will be met. Be prepared for funds to arrive from unexpected places. I always make a solemn covenant with the souls I select for spiritual service. That agreement states that you will receive what you need to complete My work. Not a penny more, nor a penny less. I don't round off what I give you. It is always a precise amount, based on your specific requirements. I don't supply what you want. I provide what you need. This represents my basic commitment to you."

DAY 132

TODAY'S TWEET FROM SITTING WITH GOD:

"Ask Me to remove your shortcomings and defects of character. I bring you miracles of positive and lasting change."

FROM THE HOLY BIBLE:

"I know that everything God does will endure forever; nothing can be added to it and nothing taken from it." (Ecclesiastes 3:14)

TODAY'S TOPIC OR QUESTION FROM ME:

Am I a "Suffering Servant" like God referred to in Isaiah?

RESPONSE FROM GOD AND JAN:

"All of My servants suffer. It is the nature of the spiritual life. Why is suffering an integral part of the transformation process? Part of it stems from My battle with the human ego. The ego clashes with your spiritual nature. Unfortunately, the puffed-up ego prevails much of the time. An ego-centric person has little or no interest in the invisible realm. Humility is viewed as weakness. The ego sees a quiet and humble person as timid and easily intimidated. An ego-dominated human being refuses to bow down to anyone but themselves. They have no interest whatsoever in "suffering" on behalf of anybody. It often takes a heavy or near fatal blow before the clueless ego gets it. Sometimes, when a trampled ego leaves the scene, I get asked for help. I always respond. However, when someone decides to answer My Call, then the real suffering begins. The Dark Side tries to regain its advantage. All-out spiritual warfare erupts. Challenges fly at you from out of nowhere. My followers often beg for mercy. But none is ever offered by the Principalities of Darkness. They want total human surrender and a return to ego domination. Those who survive the Dark Night of the Soul usually become My best spiritual warriors. They are honed into finest steel by their suffering. In the end, they always gaze back at the earth from the portals of Heaven and proclaim, "It was every bit worth it!"

DAY 133

TODAY'S TWEET FROM SITTING WITH GOD:

"Persistence helps in completing My goals. Persist in prayer. Persist in meditation. Persist in knowing Me better."

FROM THE HOLY BIBLE:

"Here is my servant, whom I behold, in whom I delight." (Isaiah 42:1)

TODAY'S TOPIC OR QUESTION FROM ME:

Persisting on the spiritual path

RESPONSE FROM GOD AND JAN:

"Persistence ranks as a key factor in completing My Path. Everybody struggles with maintaining focus on the same goal day after day, year after year. I understand how tedious things can become. That is why you must live a balanced life. Get your sleep, do something fun, be nice to yourself. You've been through a deep personal loss. Besides the passing of your soul mate, you relocated across the country. Changes are hard for anyone, but you've experienced more than your share. Oh yes, you also turned the "Big 8-0" a few months back. That milestone alone deserves attention. Don't forget: you lost your "job" as Jan's caregiver. Persistence can get you through these tests. Being persistent is also about being smart. Go slow in making any long-term commitments. Stick a toe into the water before you plunge in head-first. There might be a jagged rock just below the surface. More time in prayer and meditation bolsters persistence. Be determined, dedicated, and persist in moving forward daily. Remember that My Path leads to the gates of Heaven. Lighten up a little. Jan and I appreciate and trust your persistence, but we want you to arrive here in one piece."

DAY 134

TODAY'S TWEET FROM SITTING WITH GOD:

"Seek eternal wisdom. Avoid short-term thinking. Spiritual knowledge unfolds gradually and over time."

FROM THE HOLY BIBLE:

"O LORD my strength and my fortress, my refuge in times of distress, to you the nations will come from the ends of the earth and say, "Our fathers possessed nothing but false gods, worthless idols that did them no good." (Jeremiah 16: 19)

TODAY'S TOPIC OR QUESTION FROM ME:

Where do I find spiritual wisdom?

RESPONSE FROM GOD AND JAN:

"Fina a way to grow in spiritual wisdom each day. Try to enrich your mind every 24 hours. Be open to new information and ideas. Stay alert for opportunities to add divine knowledge. I AM sending out updates on a regular basis. Sorting out the spiritual from the material is like picking diamonds from a rock quarry. Most of the world's blather is meaningless. People have become mesmerized and obsessed with trivial things. Then they miss the real world of Spirit that operates outside of human view. I urge you: change the channel in your human brain. Spending countless hours engaged in drivel takes its toll. Tune out the carnal world's lunacy. Tune in to the deeper aspects of your soul journey. Become an active Truth seeker. When you pay close attention to everything around you, your eyes open. You become able to discern spiritual knowledge. When in doubt, go apart and observe nature. Who I AM is forever reflected by the natural world. You can also find My wisdom in prayer and meditation, in reading My Word, and in asking, seeking and knocking at My door. I open your human senses to the real world of Spirit. Take it all in."

DAY 135

TODAY'S TWEET FROM SITTING WITH GOD:

"Human life can be a joyful and fulfilling experience. When you bond with Me, it takes on a deeper purpose and meaning."

FROM THE HOLY BIBLE:

"For I did not come to judge the world, but to save it." (John 12:47)

TODAY'S TOPIC OR QUESTION FROM ME:

My greatest obstacles

RESPONSE FROM GOD AND JAN:

"Most of your obstacles stem from your own behavior. You are not unique. All human beings have imperfections and shortcomings. The material world tries to trap everyone in some way. There are countless paths to personal defeat. They include, but are not limited to: a worship of false idols like work, money, power and celebrity; addictions like drugs, alcohol, sex, and gambling; criminal behavior; abandonment of the Golden Rule and an out-of-control ego. However, with My intervention, every negative character trait can be reversed. Redemption usually requires that someone must first hit their bottom. Once that takes place, a teachable moment sometimes appears. To identify what causes stumbles in your life, you must gain clarity about your personal shortcomings. That requires a rigorous honesty about yourself. Most people resist taking their own inventory. You already know most of your negative tendencies: being a corporate workaholic; becoming enamored of the single life (before your marriage to Jan); general co-dependency and a troubling lack of boundaries, especially with women; judging others while ignoring the log in your own eye; and basic self-righteousness. Any one of those shortcomings would be enough to create a bigtime obstacle. Thankfully, you've made some positive progress in many of these areas. Ask me to remove all defects of character. Don't let bad behavior throw you off the spiritual path."

DAY 136

TODAY'S TWEET FROM SITTING WITH GOD:
"Walk with Me while I lift you to a higher level of spiritual awareness. Let life shine brighter for you."

FROM THE HOLY BIBLE:

"The LORD is gracious and righteous; our God is full of compassion. The LORD protects the simplehearted; when I was in great need, he saved me." (Psalm 116:5-6)

TODAY'S TOPIC OR QUESTION FROM ME:

My sister's sudden illness and brain cancer diagnosis

RESPONSE FROM GOD AND JAN:

"Human life can be brief or long. It always ends with a transition to My Kingdom. As sad as that can be from a human perspective, death completes the circle of life. Your sister is beloved by many. Her dynamic personality draws people to her. That includes family, friends, high school and college classmates, sorority sisters, the students she taught at Pinehurst Academy, other fellow Catholics and just about everyone she has ever met. Linda got many of her amazing people skills from your dearly departed father. He was a natural politician. She mirrors his political acumen. Your sister exudes great charisma, high intelligence and unbridled passion (especially for Catholicism). Unfortunately, your brother and sister relationship remained distant until this past year. Linda lost her husband (Charles) last October after a brief bout with lung cancer. Then, your sweet Jan made her unexpected transition at the end of February. Since that time, you've had several hour-plus telephone conversations with your sister. You and she finally understand how much you care about each other. What a gift, especially now, with her Glioma brain cancer diagnosis Here is the spiritual lesson: It's never too late to reestablish a bond with family, friends or other important people in your life. The right moment for spiritual healing happens anytime and anywhere with anyone. Just be open and receptive, if it comes."

DAY 137

TODAY'S TWEET FROM SITTING WITH GOD:

"Pay attention to what comes before you today. I AM sending a few golden opportunities for spiritual service your way."

FROM THE HOLY BIBLE:

"I tell you, do not worry about your life, what you will eat or drink, or about your body, what you will wear. Is not life more important than food and the body more important than clothes?" (Matthew 6:25)

TODAY'S TOPIC OR QUESTION FROM ME:

What should I pray for?

RESPONSE FROM GOD AND JAN:

"Pray for knowledge of our will for you and the stamina, energy, power and focus to carry it out. Pray also for guidance and direction, wisdom and insight. Pray for the faith needed to put aside all worries, especially those about finances. Trust that the spiritual universe will allocate everything needed to finish My work. Pray for the willingness to forgive those who fall short of your expectations. Pray for acceptance and understanding of human shortcomings, including your own. Pray to unleash your creativity on My behalf. You still have much to offer the world with your creative thinking. Pray for others, that they may be lifted in moments of challenge, pain and worry. There is a definite need for prayer in the material world right now. Send your prayers to your sister and her family. Pray for Divine Order with her cancer treatments. Pray for peace between people and nations. Pray that good will replaces anger and tolerance overcomes bigotry. Pray for the children, the helpless and the hungry. Pray for the widows and orphans. Pray that imperfect human beings will someday realize the perfection in which I created them. Pray that today will be better than yesterday and tomorrow will be better than today. Pray that the best is still yet to come. This is only a start for your possible prayer list, but it's a good beginning."

DAY 138

TODAY'S TWEET FROM SITTING WITH GOD:

"Reject all separation from Me. Oneness with Me guarantees peace, joy and spiritual fulfillment."

FROM THE HOLY BIBLE:

"Out of the brightness of his presence bolts of lightning blazed forth. The LORD thundered from Heaven. His voice resounded." (2 Samuel 22: 13-14)

TODAY'S TOPIC OR QUESTION FROM ME:

Angels

RESPONSE FROM GOD AND JAN:

"Your dear wife and I oversee your contingent of angels. These heavenly stewards fulfill many duties. First and foremost, they are responsible for your protection. These magnificent creatures form the ultimate security team. My angels also perform various and sundry tasks on your behalf. They help coordinate your daily activities. The angels skillfully line up people and situations who can serve your best interests. They smooth the treacherous path before you. Your angel group acts as caregivers, couriers, suppliers, facilitators, and warriors. You name it, these angels can do it. They help you travel from Point A to Point B without fuss or bother. Trust in their angelic power to coordinate your life efficiently. They surround you with courage, strength, determination and spectacular executive ability. Your angel team meets every day to parcel out assignments. They make sure all bases are covered. You can feel their divine presence if you try hard enough. However, they prefer to go about their business without notice or interference. Your angelic group functions quietly as humble servants of Heaven. Angels never seek notice or attention. Let them do their job while you do yours. They are the best and brightest in Heaven. Trust them."

DAY 139

TODAY'S TWEET FROM SITTING WITH GOD:

"Align yourself with Me. Allow My divine wisdom to guide your every action. I help you steer a straight course."

FROM THE HOLY BIBLE:

"But by the grace of God, I am what I am, and his grace to me was not without effect." (1 Corinthians 15:10)

TODAY'S TOPIC OR QUESTION FROM ME:

The Spiritual Path

RESPONSE FROM GOD AND JAN:

"My Path is narrow and often dangerous. It is not for the fainthearted. I see the Path as a divine paradox. It is both beautiful and demanding. It contains grand experiences and perilous moments. Traveling the Path to its ultimate destination requires courage, commitment and perseverance. It takes focus and determination. You must be all-in with your heart, mind and soul. Once embarking on the Path, you must guard against missteps, laziness and procrastination. I AM accustomed to people dropping out when they get tired or threatened. Sometimes the work just gets too hard. Others stay until a slip sends them cascading back to the foot of the mountain. Starting over seems beyond their capability or desire. "It's too (expletive) tough" is a phrase I've heard millions of times. The spiritual Way never attracts the weak of spirit. Most human beings are not even aware of the Path's existence. I have a rigorous screening process before I open it up to anyone. Remember: you did not choose Me. I chose you. I also insist on climbing the Path with you. None of My children ever go it alone. I AM there to guide and support you during every step. I hold your hand during the dark and scary moments. I cheer as you near the finish line. I welcome you as you step through the gates of Heaven. Nothing matches your joy when the journey ends. Come along now. We still have some steep climbing ahead of us."

DAY 140

TODAY'S TWEET FROM SITTING WITH GOD:

"I provide inner clarity. Summon Me when confusion reigns. I help you to sort out your options."

FROM THE HOLY BIBLE:

"Pride only breeds quarrel, but wisdom is found in those who take advice." (Proverbs 13:10)

TODAY'S TOPIC OR QUESTION FROM ME:

Inner Power

RESPONSE FROM GOD AND JAN:

"Inner Power is the greatest power. The God-given potential within you exceeds any known power in the outer world. Do not be deceived by outer appearances. Somebody who looks frail and weak may possess incredible inner strength. Your mortal mind can get overburdened by fear, worry and concern. Meanwhile, your super-conscious mind produces wondrous feats of creativity. Once activated, the higher realm routinely dispenses miracles. Nothing exceeds the invisible insight and energy at the core of your being. When you unleash My inner kingdom, your human potential increases by a thousand-fold. If the world closes in on you, tap into My unseen resources. Should negative self-talk bedevil you, turn inward for solace, comfort and reassurance. As you begin to understand the great power inside of you, things can shift from negative to positive in a nanosecond. You'll be thrilled and amazed by your transformation from weakness to strength. Be prepared for the miracle of inner power to exceed your wildest dreams. Watch how obstacles disappear. The spiritual universe patiently awaits your discovery of its true power. Why wait? Go within now and be amazed."

DAY 141

TODAY'S TWEET FROM SITTING WITH GOD:

"Fear corrodes. When it consumes you, haul out your shield of Faith. You and I together outnumber any fear two to one."

FROM THE HOLY BIBLE:

"But when he, the Spirit of Truth, comes, he will guide you into all truth. He will not speak on his own; only what he hears, and he will tell you what is yet to come." (John 16:13)

TODAY'S TOPIC OR QUESTION FROM ME:

Putting on the whole armor of God

RESPONSE FROM GOD AND JAN:

"Remember that the "Shield of Faith" is just one aspect of My "Whole Armor" detailed in Ephesians 6: 11-18. When fear or any danger advances toward you, I provide numerous spiritual resources to protect you, including legions of angels. But, let's begin with faith. Whether the attack is frontal or subtle, keep your faith shield up. Be prepared for anything. Not only does your shield fend off any thrust by the Dark Side, it can help you go on the offensive. As the battle for your soul rages, Jan and I are by your side. We are with you in both good times and bad. You are always backed up by the awesome power of My Kingdom. Believe in our ongoing commitment to you. Have no fear. Your dear wife is here with Me, ready to defend you against every threat. Act with confidence as you march forth under My banner. Visualize yourself being victorious over every negative force. We have faith in you. Jan and I believe in your determination and talents. This is the time! Now is your moment! Protected by My full armor, victory lies ahead!"

DAY 142

TODAY'S TWEET FROM SITTING WITH GOD:

"Come to Me for help during moments of grief and sadness. Together we can mend the torn places of your heart."

FROM THE HOLY BIBLE:

"Rejoice in the LORD always. I will say it again: Rejoice." (Philippians 4:4)

TODAY'S TOPIC OR QUESTION FROM ME:

Life and death

RESPONSE FROM GOD AND JAN:

"Human life can be long, short or somewhere in between. For many, life feels like an endless grind. For others, life features long periods of relative happiness with a few challenges thrown in to spice things up. To the few enlightened ones that know Me, human existence offers a fulfilling experience despite even difficult problems. People controlled by the changeable material world or beset by various addictions are usually fearful and unsettled. Drama rules the day. At the end of their life journey, many of those folks are tired, broke, sick and ready to go. There are others who insist on clinging to their "things and stuff", fearful about "what's next." The most peaceful human souls live a life centered in Me. When those dear ones depart the earth, their transition concludes with a beautiful movement upward to My Kingdom. These are the enlightened ones. They are convinced the Kingdom of Heaven is indeed a better place. Their level of acceptance and trust acknowledges the inevitable and tries to make the best of it. There is much wisdom in seeking to blend the human with the spiritual as the moment of transition approaches. Here's what you all should know: everyone goes to Heaven, no matter how he or she lived humanly. I lovingly created each soul and I welcome it back to Heaven at the appointed time. There are no exceptions. I AM a forgiving and generous God. I open Heaven to one and all."

DAY 143

TODAY'S TWEET FROM SITTING WITH GOD:

"When life knocks you off balance, go within. Seek My divine wisdom. I promise that your answers will come."

FROM THE HOLY BIBLE:

"Then I heard the voice of the LORD saying, "Whom shall I send? And who will go for us?" And I said, "Here am I. Send me!" (Isaiah 6:8)

TODAY'S TOPIC OR QUESTION FROM ME:

My relationship with Jan

RESPONSE FROM GOD AND JAN:

"As you browsed through some scrapbooks yesterday, wistful thoughts about your wonderful wife filled your conscious mind. You discovered some letters you wrote Jan back in the early 1980s, soon after you all first met. She saved every one of your letters. You and Jan lived apart in different cities for the first 13 years of your relationship. However, as you read your own words at the beginning of the friendship, the depth of your early bond became evident. The formal marriage commitment in 1994 resulted in a nearly 23-year marriage that blessed many people. Both of you kept the "Divine Appointment" that I arranged and choreographed. After I brought you two together in 1980, I had to wait patiently through your many ups and downs. More than once, each of you thought the relationship might be over. Finally, you both decided your separate paths should become one. How I rejoiced! What a terrific earthly union! You both modeled dedication and fidelity, especially during those years when you served as Jan's full-time caregiver. As you read through those old letters yesterday, you were awed by the passion of your early bond. Jan and I talk often about how everything worked out. She is still deeply committed to you. In many ways, you're back to a long-distance relationship. Don't worry. Someday, your second reunion will exceed the first. And this final pairing will last throughout eternity."

DAY 144

TODAY'S TWEET FROM SITTING WITH GOD:

"My Grace surrounds you. It brings you health, prosperity, wisdom, harmony, joy and peace of mind."

FROM THE HOLY BIBLE:

"No good tree bears bad fruit, nor does a bad tree bear good fruit. Each tree is recognized by its own fruit. People do not pick figs from thorn bushes or grapes from briers." (Luke 6:43-44)

TODAY'S TOPIC OR QUESTION FROM ME:

Will

RESPONSE:

"Let us unite our three wills (yours, Mine and that of your dear wife) into one united will that can heal, bless and accomplish great goals for humankind. May we meld together in a powerful oneness of purpose. As a Holy Trinity of dedication and commitment, you, Jan and I can move mountains and calm oceans. Let us also combine our resources to fulfill your human and spiritual destiny. Keep surrendering daily to our divine plan for you. Trust us to always have your best interest at heart. Here is our current will for you:

    1. complete this period of adjustment in a new environment.
    2. Prepare to accelerate the pace of your spiritual service.
    3. Act boldly and with confidence, assured of your place in Heaven with us.

You will dwell with us in the company of saints once your earthly work is done. Along with your assigned duties, take time to support your sister Linda in her battle against brain cancer. She needs to feel the love and caring of her only sibling. Traveling the last few steps before entering My Kingdom can be a tremendous test of human faith. Jan and I are glad that you and your sister have reconnected. We both stand ready, along with many others, to welcome her into Heaven at the appointed time. Until that happens, let Linda feel your warm and brotherly love. As in everything else, our will for you is only Good. Believe in what we tell you. The best is yet to come."

DAY 145

TODAY'S TWEET FROM SITTING WITH GOD:

"Hold fast in times of trouble. Brace yourself with My courage and strength. Never give up. Fight on until the end."

FROM THE HOLY BIBLE:

"The LORD said to Abram, "Leave your country, your people and your father's household and go to the land I will show you. I will make you into a great nation and I will bless you; I will make your name great, and you will be a blessing." (Genesis 12: 1-2)

TODAY'S TOPIC OR DISCUSSION FROM ME:

Courage during troubled times

RESPONSE FROM GOD AND JAN:

"Recognize that I created you with courage. Embrace the inner strength that I placed in you from the beginning. I implore you to discover the power within you. I endowed you with incredible resiliency. But you must first acknowledge your spiritual nature. I have equipped you with considerable spiritual "software." But you must download this heaven-made software program into your conscious mind, so that it can be used when needed. Did you think that I would create such a wondrous instrument as a human being without the proper wiring? I knew it would take strength, courage, wisdom and endurance to cope with a materially obsessed world. I would never send you into such a hostile environment without the proper tools. You have inside you the courage of a lion, the strength of a bull and the wisdom of an owl. You can handle anything the world dishes out and more. But you must become aware of your inner power. Ask Me to help you activate your courage and your other spiritual attributes. Know that everything you need to navigate the rapids of life is already in place. You have absolutely nothing to fear. Trust and believe."

DAY 146

TODAY'S TWEET FROM SITTING WITH GOD:

"I AM a compassionate and loving God. But remember this one crucial thing: Thou shalt have no other Gods before Me."

FROM THE HOLY BIBLE:

"For God so loved the world that he gave his one and only Son, that whoever believes in him shall nor perish but have eternal life." (John 3:16)

TODAY'S TOPIC OR QUESTION FROM ME:

Letting My Christ Light shine

RESPONSE FROM GOD AND JAN:

"As your consciousness expands, your Christ Light shines ever brighter. Your inner soul glows with an almost blinding radiance. It pours forth to clearly illumine your Path. A healthy prayer and meditation life always causes an increase in your spiritual wattage. Your heightened awareness travels from within to without. Its eternal power is felt by one and all. You never need call attention to yourself when this change begins to take place. It will be evident to everyone. How does a heightened consciousness appear to an objective observer? Most will observe an average looking human being walking the earth, but with a noticeable difference. An aura of peace, serenity, acceptance, love, understanding, generosity, humility and forgiveness hovers above you. There is a sense of "awareness" that sums up the entire human persona. A raised consciousness stays forever tuned in to its surroundings. It never sleep-walks through life. The superconscious activated mind remains fully awake to both the spiritual and material. The truly aware human being brings a blessing to everyone simply by their presence. Again, you never need to point at yourself and shout, "Hey, look at me. I'm mystical!" The bright beam of Truth pouring out from you speaks for itself. You won't need to say anything. Just be who you are."

DAY 147

TODAY'S TWEET FROM SITTING WITH GOD:

"You serve Me best when you perform the tasks I give you. You can begin by offering a kind word to someone in need."

FROM THE HOLY BIBLE:

"Then your mouth will be opened; you will speak and no longer be silent. You will be a sign to them and they will know that I am the LORD." (Ezekiel 24:27)

TODAY'S TOPIC OR QUESTION FROM ME:

One day at a time

RESPONSE FROM GOD AND JAN:

"Your dear wife and I want to encourage you to "Keep on Keeping On". Plug away every day at raising your conscious awareness. Take a step closer to Heaven every 24 hours. Tiny steps add up. The spiritual Path isn't a quick sprint. It's a long and often arduous journey, filled with lots of stops and starts. If you race headlong toward the finish line, you might become tired and quit before breaking the tape. Eternal and sacred goals require a steady and consistent effort. Stay away from detours and shortcuts. Never stray into someone else's lane. Maintain straight-ahead focus. Don't get discouraged if you occasionally slip and fall. Getting up may be hard but staying down guarantees defeat. Jan and I will be there to help you get dusted off. Never worry or fear about things you can't control. Let us fill in those pesky potholes along the way. We'll have them all handled by the time you arrive on the scene. Do something positive every day to brighten someone's world. Don't forget to keep praying, meditating and reading My Holy Word. Deposit a few dollars in your spiritual bank account whenever the sun comes up. Keep coming back to your morning regimen. Sit in the silence with your sweetie and Me. Our program works—if you work it."

DAY 148

TODAY'S TWEET FROM SITTING WITH GOD:

"Let kindness become your trademark. I equipped you with a generous and compassionate heart."

FROM THE HOLY BIBLE:

"For in him we live and move and have our being." (Acts 17:28)

TODAY'S TOPIC OR QUESTION FROM ME:

What are my priorities?

RESPONSE FROM GOD AND JAN:

"Here is your "to-do" list for today:

1. Strive to move ever closer to Jan and Me by increasing your dedicated time in meditation.
2. Be more alert for the divine ideas we shower upon you daily.
3. Actively pursue positive human connections, especially with your new church "family."
4. Raise up your faith and trust in all areas, but especially when it pertains to money and income.
5. Be supportive to your sister Linda during her health challenge.
6. Be bold spiritually; testify when given the opportunity.
7. Try to live in an ongoing state of forgiveness for all, including yourself.
8. Become a prayer warrior for those souls in need.
9. Avoid impulsive and unwise decisions in every area, especially when you are feeling alone and needy.
10. Raise your level of conscious awareness to the height of your human potential.

There are other priorities, but these are the most important. An unlisted but essential priority is staying ever faithful to the divine Path before you. Let nothing cause you to abandon the gains you've made so far. Avoid anything that might halt your spiritual progress. Keep on keeping on."

DAY 149

TODAY'S TWEET FROM SITTING WITH GOD:

"Hope acts as a booster shot for the spirit. A hopeful attitude changes the landscape from negative to positive."

FROM THE HOLY BIBLE:

"And God spoke all these words: "I am the LORD your God who brought you out of Egypt, out of the land of slavery. You shall have no other gods before me." (Exodus 20: 1-3)

TODAY'S TOPIC OR QUESTION FROM ME:

Allowing God and Jan to fight for me

RESPONSE FROM GOD AND JAN:

"You should always let us jump into the fray on your behalf. In fact, you should expect it. You never need fight any more battles alone. We stand shoulder to shoulder with you against all opposition. Whoever or whatever challenges you must now also deal with us. You, Jan and I form a powerful trio of spiritual warriors. We aren't afraid of anything or anyone. Nothing intimidates or frightens us. She and I are available to you any time of the day or night. We'll help in meeting any physical, emotional or spiritual threats. We specialize in impossible situations. We defend you against the evil forces that seek your destruction. We come with courage, strength and power and some extra-large angels. If you are already wounded and reeling, Jan (the nurse) and I will be sure to bring our medical bag along. We'll stich up the open wounds. Your dear wife and I are your 9-1-1 call when things look bleakest. We restore your soul to wholeness when you become battered and bruised. We fight on your side until victory becomes assured. Don't worry or fret. Jan and I, plus My warrior angels, have your back."

DAY 150

TODAY'S TWEET FROM SITTING WITH GOD:

"Hope springs from a faithful heart. In the middle of pain, grief and suffering, I will beckon you to a higher place."

FROM THE HOLY BIBLE:

"How can I repay the LORD for all his goodness to me? I will lift the cup of salvation and call on the name of the LORD. I will fulfill my vows to the LORD in the presence of all of his people." (Psalm 116: 12-14)

TODAY'S TOPIC OR QUESTION FROM ME:

Jan's birthday

RESPONSE FROM GOD AND JAN:

"Yes, this would have been Jan's 76th birthday. She has been gone for exactly five months. You miss so many things about her and your relationship: You loved how you and she both called each other "Babe"; how you communicated so well from the time you first met 37 years ago; that you were never once bored with each other; how your love deepened after you became her full-time caregiver; how you both looked forward to the afternoon naps that were such a mutual blessing; the anticipation you all felt when seeing each other again even after only a few hours apart; the absolute assuredness that you would be there for one another through anything; the physical attraction that captured you both from the beginning; traveling the spiritual path together which included "doing church"; your obvious pride in her inner and outer beauty; her innate warmth and unconditional love for everyone she loved; her ability to forgive some of your thoughtless actions in the years before you married; and the fact that you were always the absolute apple of her eye and the joy in her generous heart. These are only a the few things you remember and love about your dear wife. She sits right by my side, just as devoted to you as ever. You are a lucky man, My Son. And I'm sure you know it."

DAY 151

TODAY'S TWEET FROM SITTING WITH GOD:

"Call Me whenever life blindsides you. I AM the calming influence you seek. Feel My arrival amid the chaos."

FROM THE HOLY BIBLE:

"Therefore, my dear brothers, stand firm. Always give yourselves fully to the work of the Lord, because you know that your labor for the Lord is not in vain." (1 Corinthians 15:58)

TODAY'S TOPIC OR QUESTION FROM ME:

Spiritual Surrender

RESPONSE FROM GOD AND JAN:

"Surrendering to My plan holds the key to your spiritual growth. Of course, the self-centered human ego never goes quietly. It lives to control its human host. No matter how well things go for a while, the ego will eventually overstep its bounds. It can't help itself. Trouble follows when pride and arrogance rule the day. Good judgment often finds a way to jump out of a first-story window. Most people aren't ready to surrender to Spirit until an ego induced crisis strikes. After the ego flees in defeat, the conscious mind often becomes more responsive to spiritual input. Anytime someone calls out to Me for help, I answer. I AM always ready to guarantee safe passage on life's unpredictable journey. You must remember that I created you. I want to stay involved after you depart for your earthly experience. But I endowed you with "free will choice". If you shun or ignore Me, I won't protest. However, if you suddenly need Me in your human life, I stand ready to restart our relationship. Surrendering works out better for everyone in the long run. Living in the material world becomes much easier when you allow Me to do the heavy lifting. Just say "My God, I surrender all." Then fasten your seat belt. I'll take over from there."

DAY 152

TODAY'S TWEET

"Your life consists of both obvious and hidden lessons. I help you discern which is which. Human life is for learning and growing."

FROM THE HOLY BIBLE:

"For you were once darkness, but now you are light in the Lord. Live as children of light, for the fruit of the light consists of goodness, righteousness and truth. (Ephesians 4:8)

TODAY'S TOPIC OR QUESTION FROM ME:

Life's lessons and learning experiences

RESPONSE FROM GOD AND JAN:

"Your dear wife and I are going through every life experience with you. After the "lesson" or "happening" ends, we help debrief you. If you are open to looking at what took place and the "learning" involved, Jan and I can be active participants in that exercise. Most people do not understand why things happen as they do. Puzzling things out on your own sometimes adds to the confusion. She and I want to get involved with you in the debriefing process. You need to know why certain things occurred, so as not to make the same mistake again. The world can be beautiful, but also perplexing and even dangerous. Traps and snares lurk everywhere. A "rose" can become a "thorn" without notice. Human beings are sometimes blind to their own bad choices. They often rationalize even the worst disasters as "no big deal". You need our divine input in evaluating every important experience. We are here to guide and assist you on the spiritual Path. We want you to make us full partners on your journey through life. You don't need to lean on your own understanding. In fact, you shouldn't. We are always ready to give you different perspective. Let us work together in evaluating the twists and turns of your life. You won't regret it."

DAY 153

TODAY'S TWEET FROM SITTING WITH GOD:

"I created all of humankind. I love you like a parent loves a child. Nothing can prevent Me from caring about you."

FROM THE HOLY BIBLE:

"Because of the LORD'S love we are not consumed, for his compassions never fail." (Lamentations 3:22)

TODAY'S TOPIC OR QUESTION FROM ME:

Letting go and letting God

RESPONSE FROM GOD AND JAN:

"Letting Go and Letting Me take over isn't easy for any human being. Surrender requires a conscious decision to release personal control. Some people can let go of something one minute and then they take it back the next. There usually comes a time when a mortal man or woman wants to be in control again. Trusting an unseen force is alien to most human minds. Then there is the grandiose ego, which puts up a strong fight when challenged. Trusting Me should be the easiest thing, but many see that as impractical. Nothing could be further from the truth. "Fear" associated with material things like money, health and relationships often prevents a surrender to the spiritual. Often it takes a personal calamity before letting go becomes possible. I'll let you in on a secret: It doesn't bother Me when people waffle back and forth. I expect it. No matter how many times I get kicked aside, I always return when asked. You'll never hear me say "I told you so." Sometimes an individual must make one, two or a series of poor decisions before they hand things over to Me. That's OK. Those bad choices each represented a valuable learning experience. It's true that things always go smoother when you let Me do the driving. I know the way home better than you. Besides, I like to drive. I want you to relax and enjoy the scenery."

DAY 154

TODAY'S TWEET FROM SITTING WITH GOD:

"Emotional healing begins with forgiveness. Be gentle with yourself and others. Forgive now."

FROM THE HOLY BIBLE:

"Draw water for the siege, strengthen your defenses! Work the clay, tread the mortar, repair the brickwork." (Nahum 3:14)

TODAY'S TOPIC OR QUESTION FROM ME:

Forgiveness

RESPONSE:

As I have reminded you many times, "Forgiveness" is your #1 "Life Lesson". But, if your sweet wife and I might voice an opinion about lessons and shortcomings, try to balance any personal guilt with forgiveness for yourself. You walk the earth as a human being. You were perfect when I shaped your soul. But every mortal has flaws, including you. The goal becomes to work out those shortcomings spiritually while on earth. You may not be successful, but at least you should try. Now, regarding "forgiveness", you get credit for recognizing your challenges and opportunities in this area. Most people are not even aware they have a problem. Here is a spiritual Truth: when you hold on to animosity toward anybody, you are the one made smaller. Try not to dwell on any past situation, no matter how justified. Hand any lasting unforgiveness over to Me. Let all negative thoughts regarding the person or event depart from your conscious mind. Surround the individual with a halo of white light. Visualize them enveloped in goodness. Sound unrealistic? Trust Me, it isn't. By releasing your rancor, you move forward more quickly on My Path. Nothing should be allowed to slow your spiritual journey. Forgive today. Just do it."

DAY 155

TODAY'S TWEET FROM SITTING WITH GOD:

"Give up trying to control anyone or anything. Let go. Let me worry about the people, places and things in your life."

FROM THE HOLY BIBLE:

"The entire law is summed up in a single command: "Love your neighbor as thyself"." (Galatians 5:14)

TODAY'S TOPIC OR QUESTION FROM ME:

Grieving Jan

RESPONSE FROM GOD AND JAN:

"Your sweetheart and I think you are making good progress on the grief journey. You haven't rushed things. You are keeping impulsive moves to a minimum. Continue your caution about doing anything rash in any area. Jan and I know you get lonesome. You miss the close companionship you enjoyed in your marriage. Understand that the kind of togetherness you shared with her won't be duplicated overnight. We both like that you still wear your wedding ring. Keep taking everything slow and steady. One of your priorities now concerns your sister Linda and her Stage 4 brain cancer. Keep supporting Linda as much as possible. Go see her at the M. D. Anderson cancer clinic in Houston. She needs your brotherly love. You should also be ramping up your creative output. Start writing again. Consider promoting the books you have already authored. Expressing yourself through the written and spoken word is part of my plan for you. Try not to obsess about finances. Help will arrive soon from an unexpected source. In summary, you are where you should be in the process of grieving your darling wife. Yes, there are more tears in your future. That's normal. It's also healthy. Know that your Jannie still loves you dearly. She smiles adoringly at you every single day, just from a different dimension."

DAY 156

TODAY'S TWEET FROM SITTING WITH GOD:

"Any spiritual growth must coincide with a taming of the human ego. As the stubborn ego diminishes, I increase."

FROM THE HOLY BIBLE:

"As for you, go your way till the end. You will rest, and then at the end of days you will rise to receive your allotted inheritance." (Daniel 12:13)

TODAY'S TOPIC OR QUESTION FROM ME:

Self-care/Rest

RESPONSE FROM GOD AND JAN:

"Never feel guilty about taking care of yourself. You need "rest" for many reasons:

1. If you are tired physically, it follows that you may also be tired mentally and spiritually.
2. A rested body produces a rejuvenated mind and spirit.
3. A rested brain stirs up creativity.
4. Rest restores the soul, which makes for a clearer channel to Heaven.
5. In a restful state, human ailments like high blood pressure and stress are either reduced or eliminated.
6. Being rested allows you to possess enough energy to complete My goals for you.
7. Rest extends your human life span, giving you more time to serve Me.
8. Getting enough rest leaves you refreshed and at peace with yourself.
9. Rest produces a more genial and positive disposition.
10. Spiritual warriors must be rested in order to be ready for the next battle with the forces of Darkness.

Do not feel guilty about getting enough rest. You and Jan loved your afternoon naps. When in doubt, lie down. Naps are good for you. Try to eliminate worry before you go to bed at night. Hand over every fret and concern to Me. If you insist, I'll hand them back in the morning. In the meantime, get a good night's sleep."

DAY 157

TODAY'S TWEET FROM SITTING WITH GOD:

"If you want to find peace of mind, release every grudge. Staying angry slows your spiritual progress."

FROM THE HOLY BIBLE:

"Though you have not seen him, you love him; and even though you do not see him now, you believe in him and are filled with an inexpressible and glorious joy." (1 Peter 1:8)

TODAY'S TOPIC OR QUESTION FROM ME:

Walking the walk

RESPONSE FROM GOD AND JAN:

"Anyone can talk the spiritual talk. Walking the holy walk is a different proposition. Here is what it looks like when your actions mirror the talking:

1. You have no other gods before Me. I come first, period.
2. Human and earth-based distractions never come between us;
3. I AM your best and most trusted friend, guide and advisor.
4. You believe in ALL of My promises, not one here and another one there.
5. You measure every human thought and action by whether it adds or subtracts from your spiritual journey.
6. You really do live by the Golden Rule.
7. You refuse to hold a grudge or plot revenge against anyone.
8. You quit offering unsolicited opinions about people and situations.
9. You understand that "words" are like bullets—once you "pull the trigger" on any barrage of words, you can't put the bullets back in the chamber.
10. You cannot imagine what life would be like without our divine relationship.

Of course, there are many other examples of "walking the walk". It comes back to rigorous honesty, spiritual maturity, and unswerving dedication and commitment. So, My Son, how do you stack up? Are you "walking the walk?"

DAY 158

TODAY'S TWEET FROM SITTING WITH GOD:

"Let your inner light shine forth. Become a blessed beacon to those in need."

FROM THE HOLY BIBLE:

"Maintain justice and do what is right, for my salvation is close at hand and my righteousness will soon be revealed." (Isaiah 56:1)

TODAY'S TOPIC OR QUESTION FROM ME:

Thank you

RESPONSE FROM GOD AND JAN:

"Jan and I hear your gratitude. We respond by saying: "You're welcome". We know you appreciate the deep love we have for you. Your sweet wife and I want you to realize this Truth: you are never alone. She and I are here with you, as engaged as ever. Feel our presence. We comfort, encourage, protect and nurture you. Jan and I are available to you at any time of the day or night. Although we know you sometimes feel abandoned and alone, we are never far away. Your dear wife and I are your BFFs, your coaches, your cheerleaders, and your confidantes. As you keep ascending to My Kingdom, we help raise you higher. When you stumble, we catch you. If you fall, we lift you back up. Call on us anytime you have a question or need some loving counsel. We are there for you. The only thing Jan and I ask is that you stay in touch with us every day. Never shut us out. We won't ever fail you. We love you. We eagerly await your arrival in Heaven. What a joyous and rainbow-filled day that will be for everyone."

DAY 159

TODAY'S TWEET FROM SITTING WITH GOD:

"Trust Me to keep My sacred promises. Let them bring you the peace that surpasses all human understanding."

FROM THE HOLY BIBLE:

"Heaven is my throne, and the earth is my footstool. What kind of house will you build for me? says the Lord. Where will my resting place be?" (Acts 7:49)

TODAY'S TOPIC OR QUESTION FROM ME:

Is there anything or anyone that I should fear?

RESPONSE FROM GOD AND JAN:

"No. You have nothing to fear as long as you trust Me (and your dear wife). Jan and I vow to save you from all material dangers and earthly traps. We always keep your safety foremost in mind. When you lean on us, we help banish every human concern. We'll go with you into a den of lions or the fiery furnace. We'll help you climb the tallest mountain or swim the deepest ocean. We are beside you in every confrontation. Jan and I are also mend emotional wounds and shore up your mental toughness. We assist you in shrugging off your critics. We do not tolerate disrespect or abuse of any kind. When it comes to you, we could be called overprotective. No human situation ever makes us turn away from you. We'll lock arms with you against anyone. You don't need to call for the "cavalry" to swoop in and save you. Your dear wife and I ARE the cavalry—and we are already here. If you ever require a spiritual transfusion to survive, Jan and I are your primary donors. Put every fear aside. Stand tall against all enemies. We are here to supply you with courage, wisdom, love, and support. Your precious wife and I are your #1 Source for everything, now and forever."

DAY 160

TODAY'S TWEET FROM SITTING WITH GOD:

"Forgive those who disappoint you. Be gentle with your judgments. Revise expectations. Wish everyone well."

FROM THE HOLY BIBLE:

"The LORD will keep you from all harm—he will watch over your life; The LORD will watch over your coming and going both now and forever more." (Psalm 121:8)

TODAY'S TOPIC OR QUESTION FROM ME:

Bonding with Spirit

RESPONSE FROM GOD AND JAN:

"Bonding with Me ranks as your top priority. Alignment with Spirit serves as the sure path to spiritual victory. Oneness remains crucial to both your human and eternal progress. You must always pursue unity of purpose with the divine. Our sacred relationship ranks above everything else. We understand every human part of you. But if the choice comes down to choosing either Jan and Me or the world, you must choose us. Otherwise, all soul growth stops, at least for this lifetime. We hold the Golden Key. Your spiritual destiny cannot unfold as planned without a proper bonding. The Devil wants to tempt, confuse, distract and threaten you. Make no mistake about it. Anyone who seeks oneness with Spirit can expect resistance from the Principalities. The Other Side will target you immediately. You represent a clear and present danger to their negative plans. Anticipate persistent attacks. Some could feel like near-death experiences. Flee to us anytime you feel threatened. You'll find ultimate refuge in our everlasting arms. However, please don't wait until the last minute. Remaining bonded with Jan and Me serves as your best insurance policy against an unstable world."

DAY 161

TODAY'S TWEET FROM SITTING WITH GOD:

"I bestow My Grace upon you. Receive its divine blessing. Live by Grace. Live with Grace. Live from Grace."

FROM THE HOLY BIBLE:

"Love the Lord your God with all your heart and with all your soul and with all your mind and with all your strength." (Mark 12:30)

TODAY'S TOPIC OR QUESTION FROM ME:

Grace

RESPONSE FROM GOD AND JAN:

"Grace is an expression of My Love for you. Let yourself be comforted and sustained by its heavenly wonder. You are forever enveloped in its beauty. Grace surrounds you. I send it to comfort and sustain you. My Grace contains the treasures of Heaven. Rather than trying to understand the nature of Grace, just accept its unrivaled goodness. Embrace its bounty with gratitude and thanksgiving. Realize that as a recipient of God's Grace, you are blessed and empowered. As you travel the world, it becomes your constant companion. You can venture anywhere, confident that My Grace accompanies you. You have nothing to fear because the power of Grace shields you. It serves as your sacred cloak, protecting you from the unforgiving elements. As you breathe in the life-giving properties of Grace, your lungs fill with divine oxygen. Your boundless supply of Grace marks you as one of My beloved children. When you allow it to shape your human life, your inner light glows with an incandescent brightness. You become a treasured beacon. Hold out your hands. I AM pouring another generous supply of Grace into them now. Raise up your eyes! Behold! Grace descends upon you. It is your birthright and proof of My Love."

DAY 162

TODAY'S TWEET FROM SITTING WITH GOD:

"Be strong in Me. Whenever trouble comes, call My name. I will bring My Power to your rescue."

FROM THE HOLY BIBLE:

"Therefore, as God's chosen people, holy and dearly loved, clothe yourselves with compassion, kindness, humility, gentleness and patience." (Colossians 3:12)

TODAY'S TOPIC OR QUESTION FROM ME:

I need acceptance regarding family issues with my sister

RESPONSE FROM GOD AND JAN:

"Your precious wife and I are with you always, but especially during challenges involving family. Issues with loved ones often bring silent misery. Put aside all fear, worry and apprehension. Go in love to see your sister. Linda is 18 months younger than you and your only sibling. Thankfully, you have reconnected after losing your respective spouses in the past year. She is facing a dire prognosis with Stage 4 Glioma brain cancer. Bring your innate warmth, caring and concern to Houston with you. Extend your heart to Linda and her youngest daughter Andrea, who is acting as the on-site caregiver. Exhibit your pastoral qualities and compassionate nature. Hold your amazing sister's hand. Relate to her heart to heart, soul to soul. Demonstrate empathy for the current situation, coupled with the loss of her husband Charles last year. Let your strength and concern offer solace and comfort. Be fully present. Direct spiritual light from your consciousness to the darkness surrounding her. Illuminate your sister's fading aura with the brightness of your faith in My Presence. Your sole purpose is to support Linda on the final journey to My Kingdom. Offer unconditional love. She will accept it. Don't worry about driving the 350-mile roundtrip. Your dear wife and I will be with you every mile. We promise to get you there and back. Keep trusting in us. We've gotten you this far, haven't we?"

DAY 163

TODAY'S TWEET FROM SITTING WITH GOD:

"The whole armor of God includes the shield of faith. In any crisis, your faith will be the first thing tested."

FROM THE HOLY BIBLE:

"A generous man will prosper; he who refreshes others will himself be refreshed." (Proverbs 11:25)

TODAY'S TOPIC OR QUESTION FROM ME:

Expressing my divine potential

RESPONSE FROM GOD AND JAN:

"Expressing your divine potential will take some work on your part. Jan and I know that you are a shy person. In a way, you are a contradiction. You've always functioned well in high profile jobs. But you much prefer working behind the scenes to make others look good. That was helpful as a corporate PR executive. But to fulfill your spiritual legacy, you must come out from behind the curtain. Put aside your shyness. It's time for you to venture forth. We want you to become more visible. Your dear wife and I aren't expecting you to become an overnight celebrity. But it's time to get out and promote your creative output. You have done some worthwhile writing. The SITTING WITH GOD daily meditation reader won two awards for its excellence. Your six e-books on smashwords.com have good content and timely themes. But you must "let your light shine" in order to find a wider audience. Come on now! Get going! Tell people how your books might be helpful to them. Stir up some interest! If you think Jan and I are giving you a pep talk, you're right. Take a few risks. Raise your profile higher. You have good stories to tell. Don't be afraid to tell them! Jan and I promise that we'll be close by, cheering you on. Don't worry about the critics. Just do your thing."

DAY 164

TODAY'S TWEET FROM SITTING WITH GOD:

"Become My instrument for Good. Allow Me to bless others through you. Let Me bring peace, love and healing."

FROM THE HOLY BIBLE:

"The Word became flesh and made his dwelling among us. We have seen his glory, the glory of the One and Only, who came from the father, full of grace and truth." (John 1: 14)

TODAY'S TOPIC OR QUESTION FROM ME:

The Fruits of the Spirit

RESPONSE FROM GOD AND JAN:

"I created you with many talents and abilities. As you know, the Apostle Paul wrote about the Fruits of the Spirit in Galatians 5:22-23. To refresh your memory, those Fruits are love, joy, peace, patience, kindness, goodness, faithfulness, gentleness and self-control. I want you to become the transparency through which I can express those Fruits (and more) to the world. Your dear wife, who now sits by My side, modeled those traits during her life journey. She loved unconditionally. She displayed a joy-full personality. Her demeanor was almost always peaceful, although certain things sometimes challenged her usual quietness. Jan was patient, especially with you. Your dear wife always showed kindness. There was a goodness about her. She was also faithful to you, even during the years before you were married. In many ways, she was a better person than you—and you knew it. Your soul mate had a gentle softness. Her self-control proved itself many times. Think about patterning yourself after your precious wife's example. Let Jan's legacy live on through you. In life, you both were a positive influence on more people than you realized. Continue to show forth her admirable Fruits. She bequeathed them for your use. Make your dear wife smile. Demonstrate her positive attributes for the world to see."

DAY 165

TODAY'S TWEET FROM SITTING WITH GOD:

"Conquer your enemies through love, understanding and forgiveness. Allow humility to demonstrate your real power."

FROM THE HOLY BIBLE:

"He is your shield and helper and your glorious sword. Your enemies will cower before you and you will trample down their high places." (Deuteronomy 33:29)

TODAY'S TOPIC OR QUESTION FROM ME:

Are all things possible?

RESPONSE FROM GOD AND JAN:

"Yes, all things are possible with Me. This statement may seem illogical on its face. Many people doubt My Power or even My existence. They judge Me from a human standpoint, where I AM unseen. These doubters have no conception of My vast capabilities. There is nothing, I repeat nothing, beyond My powerful scope. I can make calm seas churn into hurricanes. I cause sleeping volcanoes to erupt and explode. I tell the sun to parch the land and instruct the wind to chill the bones. I AM that I AM. Underestimating Me is risky business. Acknowledging My Power makes better sense. I want you to believe in Me. If you do, I promise to produce a plethora of spiritual wonders in your life. Trust what I tell you! The greater works that I do? You can do them also. The miracles of healing that I perform? You can perform them too. All things are indeed possible, if they glorify Me. When you question or doubt Me, that lack of belief translates into a paucity of miracles. When your commitment becomes total, the floodgates of Heaven open wide for you. Every miracle-working tool becomes available. Most of My miracles occur beyond human sight. Look around you. There might be an amazing miracle occurring in your vicinity right now. Believe in Me with all your heart and soul. Then watch what I can do. It will blow your human mind!"

DAY 166

TODAY'S TWEET FROM SITTING WITH GOD:

"Be prepared for your next spiritual step. You are moving toward a new level of conscious awareness. Stay open and receptive."

FROM THE HOLY BIBLE:

"For where your treasure is, there your heart will be also." (Matthew 6:21)

TODAY'S TOPIC OR QUESTION FROM ME:

What does Jan like the most about Heaven? Is there anything she dislikes?

RESPONSE FROM GOD AND JAN:

"To answer your last question, there is one thing your dear wife doesn't like about Heaven. You're not here with her. But Jan understands that Divine Order must be served. The situation with her health required that she go first, before you. Jan knew you would be physically able to handle the move from Minnesota to Texas. Her overall health and freedom of movement had been deteriorating for several years. Your sweet wife was tired spiritually as well. The timing was right for her transition. Jan has boundless faith in you. She could see you bustling around after her passing, handling every detail in a competent manner. Had you gone first, there was no way she could have dealt with everything. What does your precious darling like about My Kingdom? First, Jan has no more pain or trouble getting from Point A to Point B. Sickness of any kind doesn't exist here. Being illness-free represents a new experience for her after four decades of coping with lupus, but she's loving it. Jan also has been reunited with her human family. As you know, she was the last surviving member of a six-person family group. Some time elapsed before she met up with her mother's soul, but the others she saw right away. We never make souls reunite forcibly. It's up to those involved to work out the details. Jan spends considerable time with her sister Marlene. They still love kidding around and playing Scrabble. However, Mar and her husband George's soul are inseparable. Jan finds Heaven interesting, thought provoking and beautiful beyond description. She just wishes you would hurry up and get here. I've asked her to be patient a little while longer. You still have work to do."

DAY 167

TODAY'S TWEET FROM SITTING WITH GOD:

"Acceptance begins in an understanding heart. Tolerance emerges from a wise heart. Forgiveness lives in a forgiving heart."

FROM THE HOLY BIBLE:

"I delight greatly in the LORD; my soul rejoices in my God. For he has clothed me with garments of salvation and arrayed me in a robe of righteousness." (Isaiah 61:10)

TODAY'S TOPIC OR QUESTION FROM ME:

Eternal life

RESPONSE FROM GOD AND JAN:

"Many people squander their human lives. They choose to throw away the most precious gift I bestow upon them. Human beings make their own free will choices. They often fritter away precious years with misdirected priorities, harmful addictions, debased behaviors, and fatal endeavors. That list includes falling under the influence of alcohol and drugs, pursuing material wealth at a stupefying cost to their physical, mental and spiritual health, and committing illegal acts leading to incarceration and even death. The Evil One encourages poor choices. They serve his devious plan to corrupt and control humankind. The Devil understands every weakness of the flesh. He exploits them all. For the human beings committed to My Path, life can be different. I offer eternal joy and a fulfilling journey. But "The Way" can also be painful, challenging, lonely and full of tears. Worldly loss comes to everyone, but perhaps more often to My followers. Even My Son was ridiculed, tortured and crucified. I provide compensatory Grace, unconditional Love, and a Peace that surpasses all understanding. However, it still takes a brave and hardy soul to follow Me. But, dear friend, I guarantee the reward exceeds the cost."

DAY 168

TODAY'S TWEET FROM SITTING WITH GOD:

"I AM your first and last refuge. I also operate as a parent, friend, counselor, encourager, and loyal confidante."

FROM THE HOLY BIBLE:

"Therefore, since we have been justified through faith, we have peace with God through our Lord Jesus Christ, through whom we have gained access by faith into this grace in which we now stand." (Romans 5: 1-2)

TODAY'S TOPIC OR QUESTION FROM ME:

Writing THE FOREVER PENNY

RESPONSE FROM GOD AND JAN:

"Jan and I are here to assist you in any creative endeavor that might be helpful to others. Perform your daily writing, assured of our divine presence. Proceed one measurable step at a time. If you remain consistent and faithful, things will fall into place. Creatively, you are only now ready to do something meaningful. Your physical move to Texas has claimed most of your energy. But your experience so far might be helpful to people coping with the loss of a loved one. Knowing that your sweet Jan now sits by My side makes you feel less sad. Your deep feelings about losing your precious wife are shared by others who have lost loved ones. Perhaps some of those left behind would be comforted by your sharing. If nothing else, the book will act as a testimonial to the positive relationship and marriage that you and she enjoyed. You all had a heart and soul connection. Your bond became even deeper after you became Jan's full-time caregiver. Writing about the caregiving experience might also benefit those providing care to a dear one. Caregiving is one of life's most precious gifts. In writing THE FOREVER PENNY, speak from the heart. Present the enlightened words that Jan and I are sharing with you. We'll be right there cheering you on."

DAY 169

TODAY'S TWEET FROM SITTING WITH GOD:

"Talk to Me about anything. I will listen to your every concern. I offer comfort, hope and understanding."

FROM THE HOLY BIBLE:

"Have mercy on me, O God, have mercy of me, for in you my soul takes refuge. I will take refuge in the shadow of your wings until the disaster has passed. (Psalm 57:1)

TODAY'S TOPIC OR QUESTION FROM ME:

Reconciliation

RESPONSE FROM GOD AND JAN:

"Your beloved country stands at a tipping point. The conflict between DARKNESS and LIGHT has reached a critical point. The world has fallen out of alignment with Me. Division and disharmony rule. This confirms a complete separation between the material and spiritual worlds. My eternal principles are being disrespected or ignored completely. How did things go so wrong? I think you know the answer. Human beings are not only tuning Me out. They are also tuning each other out as well. This has become the "Selfie" generation. People scream and protest about a multitude of immaterial things. I have nothing per se against freedom of expression. It is a major tenet of Free Will. However, disharmony reigns. Before the chaos causes irreparable damage, people must return to Me. I AM the ruler of the universe and the only true God. Seeking My Kingdom first is the true path to reconciliation for individuals and nations. I want you to lean not on your own understanding. The human focus on oneself has gotten everybody into this mess. Egos are running rampant. Wars, genocide and terrorism abound. Disaster in many forms stalks your beautiful planet. Hurricanes, floods, earthquakes, wildfires, tsunamis, tornadoes and cyclones exemplify natural threats. Weapons of mass destruction personify the existential danger. Stop this madness now! Put Me first before it's too late! I AM the Truth, the Way and the Life. I implore you to spread my concern. Humankind must act now!"

DAY 170

TODAY'S TWEET FROM SITTING WITH GOD:

"Trust Me in all things. Resist leaning into your own understanding. Let us go forth together in oneness."

FROM THE HOLY BIBLE:

"Unless I go away, the Counselor will not come to you; but if I go, I will send him to you." (John 16:7)

TODAY'S TOPIC OR QUESTION FROM ME:

Visiting my cancer-stricken sister in Houston

RESPONSE FROM GOD AND JAN:

"Take all of your pastoral qualities with you today—compassion, kindness, humility, acceptance, gentleness and patience. Remember, this visit is not about you. You are there to comfort your only sibling during her final suffering. Keep the focus on Linda, not on you. Take along a few of your dear wife's qualities such as understanding, compassion and forgiveness. Be your sister's personal chaplain. Project love and caring. Be a purveyor of unconditional support. You should also be confidant about your driving. Jan and I are riding along with you every mile of the way. You can do this! You have an excellent vehicle. You know the exact route from Temple to Houston and back. You are rested and prayed up. Go forth in love. Although the relationship with your sister has never been that close, it has improved markedly. Jan and I can sum things up in one word: NOW! Live in in the present moment. Be both a brother and a minister. Open your heart. Forgive the past. Extend your hand in love and concern. Your gesture will be well-received. Carry your deep affection and love for your sister with you. That will be more than enough for everyone concerned."

DAY 171

TODAY'S TWEET FROM SITTING WITH GOD:

"When you search for Me, look first in the beauty of nature. See Me in the oceans, forests, lakes and mountains."

FROM THE HOLY BIBLE:

"But this one thing I do: Forgetting what is behind and straining to what is ahead, I press on toward the prize for which God has called me heavenward in Christ Jesus. (Philippians 3:13-14)

TODAY'S TOPIC OR QUESTION FROM ME:

The Spirit within me

RESPONSE FROM GOD AND JAN:

"I created the Holy Spirit and placed it within each one of My beloved children. I wanted every human being to possess an inner counselor, guide, comforter and friend. Facing the material world without such a resource would be difficult. You need the Holy Spirit to help you manage your way through human life. An extra layer of spirituality becomes necessary when coping with a powerful adversary. To properly utilize the Holy Spirit, you must first recognize its presence and then activate it. I want you to discover the great power within you. What a shock for some people when they realize: "Hey, I'm not alone. I've got some inside help." Yes, I have given you the greatest helper known to humankind. The Holy Spirit has tremendous capabilities. It performs the work I give you to do. It comforts you following the loss of your dear wife. It acts as your wisest and most trusted counselor as you search for solutions to the challenges of daily living. It provides insight and clarity when you become confused. It provides courage and hope when all seems lost. The Holy Spirit fills you with the energy and stamina to tackle any problem. It ranks as the most valuable gift I could bestow upon you. I placed My Spirit within you, My beautiful child."

DAY 172

TODAY'S TWEET FROM SITTING WITH GOD:

"I AM always present in every situation. I come to bless, heal and comfort you. Call out for Me. I will answer you."

FROM THE HOLY BIBLE:

"Confident of your obedience, I write to you, knowing that you will do even more than I ask." (Philemon 1: 21)

TODAY'S TOPIC OR QUESTION FROM ME:

The reunion with My sister in Houston

RESPONSE FROM GOD AND JAN:

"Jan and I were both pleased with the trip to see your sister in Houston. It was a wonderful visit in many respects. The two of you communicated as both a loving brother and appreciative sister. Linda was genuinely pleased you made the effort to come. She felt your caring heart. The two of you related with caring and warmth. Your niece Andrea was touched with how well you and her mother got along. It was a good and positive thing for everybody. You have so much in common now with your sister. You both lost your spouses in the past year. There is also something about a serious health crisis that causes people to put aside differences. Life and death situations help focus the mind. They encourage people to concentrate on the truly important things. Jan and I were overjoyed that we could play a small role in your reunion. We planted the idea of you going to Houston a day earlier than planned. Had you not done so, you would have missed seeing your niece. She was leaving tomorrow to spend the weekend in Atlanta with her family. Both Jan and I thought it was important for Andrea to witness the love between you and her mom. All in all, your trip was a success in every way and for everyone involved."

DAY 173

TODAY'S TWEET FROM SITTING WITH GOD:

Memories bind us to those we loved and lost. But our dear ones are not really gone. They wait at the rainbow's end."

FROM THE HOLY BIBLE:

"Don't you believe that I am in the Father, and that the Father is in me? The words I say to you are not just my own. Rather it is the Father, living in me, that does the work." (John 14:10)

TODAY'S TOPIC OR QUESTION FROM ME:

Learning life's lessons

RESPONSE FROM GOD AND JAN:

"You are learning many valuable lessons since Jan made her transition. Check these benefits: you've cut your living expenses by moving home to Texas and scaling back on various things. You are now in your beloved (and warmer) home state and hometown city. You enjoyed many things about living in Minnesota, but staying there would have reminded you daily of your dear wife. Getting prepared for and then making the move has kept you more than busy. You still have managed to experience your loss to some extent. More grieving will come later. You need to go through the entire process (denial, anger, bargaining, depression and acceptance). Since you arrived back in Temple, you've reconnected with a few high school and even college (Baylor University) friends. You traveled to Dallas to see your son and attend one of his shows at the Kessler Theatre, drove to Houston to visit your ailing sister, and spun down to Austin for some prayer with a fellow Unity minister. You've also gone out to lunch with several people, including your two cousins from the nearby town of Rockdale. You have avoided any emotional relationships per se, which is a good thing. You've spoken at the Unity Church of Temple three times with more talks scheduled. You are doing OK so far. Keep on keeping on."

DAY 174

TODAY'S TWEET FROM SITTING WITH GOD:

"Release your worries. Give up trying to control people and events. Let Go and let God. You'll be much happier."

FROM THE HOLY BIBLE:

"Awake, awake! Clothe yourself with strength." (Isaiah 51:9)

TODAY'S TOPIC OR QUESTION FROM ME:

What's next for me?

RESPONSE FROM GOD AND JAN:

"Keep listening to your sweet wife and Me. Allow us to work in and through you. We want you to bring hope, peace, love and joy to a troubled world. You can also help accomplish our objective of waking up a sleeping world to its spiritual peril. Become a healer, comforter, and prophet. Don't laugh at the prophet part. You can do it! The recent reunion with your sister Linda shows your pastoral skills. Your training in Clinical Pastoral Education showed forth in that interaction. You displayed acceptance, love, forgiveness and understanding. Again, recall the time when you served as a chaplain resident at a Minnesota hospital. You received many accolades from nurses, patients and hospital volunteers for your caring and comforting presence. That translates into a strong healing potential. Remember that the Holy Spirit, when activated, can produce all sorts of healing miracles. Believe in your own miracle-working powers. Jan and I also urge you to continue your writing and speaking. Let the Christ within you perform that work. Whether it involves creative endeavors or pastoral expression, be a force for "Good". You walk on a darkened planet, desperately lacking in spiritual focus. The world cries out for harmony and kindness. Be a human light. Help illumine the landscape. Realize that the Holy Spirit does the work, whenever you allow it. I promise that you'll have numerous chances to bless, comfort and heal on My behalf."

DAY 175

TODAY'S TWEET FROM SITTING WITH GOD:

"I will lift you out of any misery. I bring you out of the darkness and into the light. When you are ready, take My hand."

FROM THE HOLY BIBLE:

"There are different kinds of gifts, but the same Spirit. There are different kinds of service, but the same Lord. There are different kinds of working, but the same God works all of them in all men." (1 Corinthians 12: 4-6)

TODAY'S TOPIC OR QUESTION:

Finding beauty in each day

RESPONSE:

"Every single day offers new possibilities for joy and service. Stay alert! Amidst the world's troubles, I offer many opportunities to create beauty and good will. These pearls of great value await your inspection and action. They pop up in unlikely places. Of course, you are also free to create your own beauty. A kind and encouraging word to someone, a smile or friendly greeting and you have sewn magical seeds of happiness. Look around you. Brighten a day or help dry a tear. Don't wait for opportunities to find you. Understand that every human interaction has a potential for good. Consciously leave a trail of goodness wherever you go. Be a blessing! Avoid negativity, disharmony and anger. They create ugly scars, not beauty marks. Don't cause trouble for someone else. Paint a canvas of beauty and love with your presence. Reflect My generous nature. Dispense acceptance, harmony and peace. You'll find yourself welcome everywhere. Go forth! Shine your Light! Dispel the darkness. Become a beautiful spirit."

DAY 176

TODAY'S TWEET FROM SITTING WITH GOD:

"Behold the God Presence in every person you meet. I AM in all, just as I AM in you. Look for Me. I AM there."

FROM THE HOLY BIBLE:

"Who is wise? He will realize these things. Who is discerning? He will understand them. The ways of the LORD are right; the righteous walk in them, but the rebellious stumble in them." (Hosea 14:9)

TODAY'S TOPIC OR QUESTION FROM ME:

Creativity

RESPONSE FROM GOD AND JAN:

Jan and I want you to use your creative talents on our behalf. It's good that you are writing again. That's a positive thing. Put your toe in the water and take a chance. Don't worry about finding a big audience. The right people will somehow find you. Being creative isn't easy. It requires openness, focus, discipline and being in tune with the universe. When you are in the grief process, it's harder to express yourself. As you rev up your creative motor again, be receptive to My Divine Ideas. I plan to send a few good ones in your direction. Although your time of grieving has only just begun, it's OK to begin brainstorming. Be cautious about outside commitments. Don't get involved in any emotional relationships. Loneliness has a way of luring people into inappropriate or unwise situations. Take one small step at a time. Spend more time in prayer and meditation. Jan and I would like that. We want more alone time with you. As you already know, becoming One with us ranks above anything else. I want you to explore "prophesy" opportunities on My behalf. I AM quite concerned about human beings who worship other gods before Me. That message needs reinforcing. You can act as one of My divine messengers."

DAY 177

TODAY'S TWEET FROM SITTING WITH GOD:

"Put on My silken robe of humility. The meek shall inherit the earth. Your true reward comes from spiritual service."

FROM THE HOLY BIBLE:

"Now I commit you to God and to the word of his grace, which can build you up and give you an inheritance among all those who are sanctified." (Acts 20:32)

TODAY'S TOPIC OR QUESTION FROM ME:

Self-care

RESPONSE FROM GOD AND JAN:

"Self-care might be the most crucial aspect of the grieving process. There is no exact formula for taking care of yourself. The real guidance for practicing self-care must come from within you. If you're tired, then rest. Don't keep driving yourself. IF you're stressed, seek out the cause. Then go about reducing the stress factors in your life. If you are gaining weight, look for the triggers that make you binge or snack. When you see a physical or emotional problem, don't ignore it. The most harmful mistake is trying to "tough" things out. If you think you need "self-care", you probably do. Perhaps you also could use an affirmation: "Today I will focus on taking care of myself". Then, you might want to add: "I will trust My Higher Power to guide me in this process". Having lost your sweetheart less than six months ago, you absolutely need self-care. You're not a Spartan. Seek professional help if you need it. Your two "Grief Groups" have been helpful. Keep seeking professional assistance as long as needed. There is no expiration date for grief. There might be a "pause" every now and then, but grieving can begin again at any time. There are no rights or wrongs about grief. It is what it is. The most important aspect of self-care during grief is accepting that you need it. Whatever works for you, put those things into practice. Listening to music, taking an afternoon nap or a hot bath, exercising, eating right and meditating are all good "self-care" things. If you don't take care of yourself, nobody else will."

DAY 178

TODAY'S TWEET FROM SITTING WITH GOD

"I help you navigate life's daunting challenges. Never lose hope. Keep believing in Me, no matter what."

FROM THE HOLY BIBLE:

"For there is nothing hidden that will not be disclosed, and nothing concealed that will not be known and brought out into the open." (Luke 8:17)

TODAY'S TOPIC OR QUESTION FROM ME:

The storms of life

RESPONSE FROM GOD AND JAN:

"I AM the first and last refuge in any storm. Whether the disturbance is physical, mental or spiritual, Jan and I both are here for you. Do not flee everywhere else looking for safety. The protection you seek lies within you. We wait for you in the Secret Place of the Most High, which is located at your core. When you come to us, please bring every fear and concern with you. Your dear wife and I will help calm you. Life storms are powerful, but they do not last forever. Trust in us when you feel threatened. We'll collaborate with you to craft lasting solutions. Your sweetheart is involved anytime a powerful storm intrudes on your serenity. She has a key role in every rescue operation. Jan works hard for you, just as she did when you were married. Her loving and gentle spirit offers you unconditional support. In your moments of doubt, hold a vision of her loving presence by your side. Yes, she and I operate out of your human sight. But we are both fully present in protecting you from any danger. Whenever the destructive winds finally pass, you will still be standing. Have faith in us as we have faith in you. Together, the three of us can get through anything."

DAY 179

TODAY'S TWEET FROM SITTING WITH GOD

"I AM always with you in your worst human moments. I comfort and sustain you. I never leave or forsake you."

FROM THE HOLY BIBLE:

"Submit to God and be at peace with him; in this way prosperity will come to you." (Job 22:21)

TODAY'S TOPIC OR QUESTION FROM ME:

Claiming my Supply

RESPONSE FROM GOD AND JAN:

"Ask Me for what you need. When you do, I supply it. If you feel empty or struggling in any way, claim your "Good". It awaits your call. Don't waste a single minute scheming for the material world to save you. It has no interest in helping you. Turn to Me. I AM your reliable and unfailing resource. Haven't I taken care of you up until now? Has there been one day when you did not have "enough"? Trust Me. I provide for you. Make service to Me your top priority. Give up fretting about finances, relationships, health or whatever. A worried servant cannot focus on My important goals. If you believe that it takes a miracle to solve your problem, seek one. I can deliver both big and small miracles. However, you must first trust and believe! Real miracles are only bestowed on believers. Give up any fantasy that the material has any interest in coming to your rescue. Only I promise and deliver true salvation. Only I have proven My trustworthiness. Only I have met your needs up until now. I AM both your financial and personal savior. It is I (and your dear wife Jan) that always put you first. We'll provide what you need today, tomorrow and forever."

DAY 180

TODAY'S TWEET FROM SITTING WITH GOD:

"Search for Me in the worst circumstances. I AM always present during chaos or suffering. I offer comfort and redemption."

FROM THE HOLY BIBLE:

"I pray that out of his glorious riches he may strengthen you with power through his Spirit in your inner being, so that Christ may dwell in your hearts through faith." (Ephesians 3:16-17)

TODAY'S TOPIC OR QUESTION FROM ME:

How do I stay strong in a crisis?

RESPONSE FROM GOD AND JAN:

"In any crisis, remember that you are never alone. I AM always prepared to help. Your darling wife also stands ready to assist you. Jan is a warrior spirit, despite her quiet demeanor. She and I offer strong and unyielding support in any challenge. Whether the crisis seems small or life-threatening, we are prepared for anything. We help protect your body, mind and spirit. Jan and I are your ultimate resource against the world's obvious or sometimes hidden dangers. An unexpected crisis can leave you feeling alone and abandoned. Nothing could be further from the truth. Never let fear overwhelm you. Go to your knees and ask for our immediate intersession. The earth's troubles are capable of terrorizing even the strongest among you. No matter how dire things may seem, hope becomes possible when we step onto the playing field. Declare your needs. Your dear wife and I will respond. Don't wait until a crisis immobilizes you. Take affirmative action now. Call out our names. We'll arrive with an array of spiritual resources, all crafted for your specific emergency. Nothing can stand against us. We'll fight hard for you until the end. Jan and I never stray very far away from you. We're on full alert, whenever you need us."

DAY 181

TODAY'S TWEET FROM SITTING WITH GOD:

"Notice everything. Be on high alert for My blessings. I AM always showering you with wondrous miracles."

FROM THE HOLY BIBLE:

"Give thanks to the LORD, for he is good; his love endures forever." (Psalm 118:1)

TODAY'S TOPIC OR QUESTION:

Where can I get enough energy and stamina to complete my work?

RESPONSE FROM GOD AND JAN:

"Here are the things that boost your human energy and stamina:

1. Any spiritual activity that fosters your inner growth. That includes prayer and meditation, attending church services and classes, reading My Holy Word and other uplifting books, and applying your creative talents to My plans for you.
2. Exercising your body in a balanced and thoughtful manner keeps you healthy and young.

Getting out for a walk or using the treadmill and stationary bicycle in your apartment's exercise room both have My approval. Do not deplete your stamina with meaningless diversions. Here are some examples of energy wasting activities: worrying or obsessing about anything or anyone, especially finances, politics or counter-productive relationships; spending too much time watching TV just to kill time; and taking shopping trips for unnecessary "stuff". Make certain that anything requiring your energy, time or money is beneficial and worthwhile. Getting exorcised about political intrigue: forget about it! Politicians have a relatively short shelf life. Not that you do it, but hanging out at the casino or gambling on anything stands as an unproductive use of time and money. Give up on the lottery. You aren't going to win. Be especially careful of getting involved with people that sap your mental and physical energy. Ration yourself in every area. Your human resources are finite, while mine are not. The moments that you spend with Me (and your sweetheart) rank as an incredibly good investment of your personal time and energy."

DAY 182

TODAY'S TWEET FROM SITTING WITH GOD:

"I AM a generous God. I offer gifts of love, caring and acceptance. I bestow blessings of forgiveness on all."

FROM THE HOLY BIBLE:

"And He said to her, "Daughter, be of good cheer; your faith has made you well. Go in peace." (Luke 8:48)

TODAY'S TOPIC OR QUESTION FROM ME:

The Golden Rule

RESPONSE FROM GOD AND JAN:

"It is a Divine Paradox that the worst of times can bring out the best in people. You are seeing that once again proved true with the many acts of compassion during the recent hurricane in Houston. I smile when My children act with caring toward one another. Despite a multitude of racial, language and cultural differences, you live together on one beautiful planet. I created every person with the divine potential for love and understanding. Most every human heart responds with kindness to those in need. It is the culture of materialism and the influence of evil that distorts things. A fallen world is adept at corrupting souls. The principalities of darkness strive to bring people down. They fear acts of kindness and love. The purveyors of hate abhor anything positive. However, in times of tragedy and calamity, you'll witness numerous acts of heroism, love, caring and empathy. The loving nature of everyday people emerges during the most challenging times. Yes, there are still opportunists that use someone else's misery to their advantage. But in every disaster, the basic goodness of My children shines through. I endowed each of you with a compassionate heart. I AM always grateful whenever I see that gift in action. The Golden Rule is golden for a reason. It blesses and fulfills My loving intention for the world."

DAY 183

TODAY'S TWEET FROM SITTING WITH GOD:

"Never hesitate to extend forgiveness. Release every thought of revenge. Seek peace and harmony."

FROM THE HOLY BIBLE:

"You are the God who performs miracles; you display your power among the people." (Psalm 77:14)

TODAY'S TOPIC OR QUESTION FROM ME:

Will I ever see my sweetheart again?

RESPONSE FROM GOD AND JAN:

"When you close your eyes, visualize your darling wife. She is smiling at you as We speak. Your sweetie gazes at you with love and gratitude. Jan knows you miss her physical presence. Her soul also longs for the closeness you experienced as friends, lovers, companions, partners in ministry and as a married couple. Those memories remain in your heart, your mind and in every cell of your body. You will carry Jan with you forever. Wherever you go, her essence accompanies you. You should be comforted knowing that she is doing fine in Heaven, thank you. Part of her positive adjustment in My Kingdom comes from our daily meetings with you. Trust Me. Your precious wife is still deeply involved with you. Yes, the day approaches when you'll be reunited. At that glorious moment, it may seem as though you were never apart. You were one as you walked the earth together. You are one today as she helps you with your spiritual journey She is just operating from a different perspective. Your souls will enjoy renewed affection the moment you arrive here. Hold that thought in mind for the rest of your days on earth. Your dear wife still loves you."

DAY 184

TODAY'S TWEET FROM SITTING WITH GOD:

"Seek Truth and Illumination. I want you to become a clear channel for My Love and Light."

FROM THE HOLY BIBLE:

"You are the light of the world. A city on a hill cannot be hidden." (Matthew 5:14)

TODAY'S TOPIC OR QUESTION FROM ME:

Being who I am

RESPONSE FROM GOD AND JAN:

"Being who you are is all you can or should be. Why would you want to be anybody or anything else? You have traveled far on My Path. Is there any plausible reason why you would backtrack now? I don't believe you would ever throw away your spiritual progress. I know you better than that. Compromising your beliefs wouldn't be advisable. Jan and I know you get lonely. When that happens, refuse to alter your personality or spiritual background just to obtain somebody's approval. Be who you are. The person you've become stands as "a light on the hill" already. Your influence will grow before you transition to My Kingdom. As you continue climbing up the mountain toward Heaven, your beacon offers a comforting and inviting glow for those in the Valley of Darkness. This is your time to shine. We are lifting you up in prayer and gratitude. Continue focusing on who you are now. That is more than good enough for both of us. We love you, my beloved son. In you, we are both proud and well pleased."

Grief Groups
And
Meditations

A WORD ABOUT GRIEF GROUPS:

If you are dealing with the loss of a loved one, I am recommending that you consider joining a "Grief Group". You can find these groups at hospitals, churches, hospice centers and even funeral homes. They will give you an opportunity to share your grief. You are free to process your feelings (or not) with others who are going through the same experience. Many people locate a grief group soon after the loss occurs. Others come later, even months or years after the passing of their loved one. As a former hospital chaplain and minister, I have observed that grief becomes more pronounced about six months into the loss. Up until that time, the survivor usually has more relatives or friends around them. The survivor also can be busy (as I was with my move from Minnesota to Texas) in settling estates and tying up loose ends. Then, about half a year into the process, reality begins setting in. At that point, the loneliness aspect of grieving starts to manifest. I think this particular time can lead to sadness and depression, plus even alcoholism, drug addiction and unhealthy pastimes such as excessive gambling or pursuing unhealthy relationships. If you are at this stage in your grieving or know someone who might be, I urge you to seek immediate professional and/or group help. I'm convinced that chronic grief can take someone's life, just as human death took away your dear loved one.

MEDITATION CONNECTION:

For those people interested in meditations that might invite and encourage the presence of a lost loved one, I am adding the following section. This is not "spiritualism" or a "séance". Hopefully, these meditations will be helpful in your overall prayer life and as an exercise in mindfulness. When you commit to spending time in the calming silence, it should bring peace into every part of your human life.

In our Unity of Spirit,

Rev. Allen C. Liles

MEDITATION 1

PREPARATION:

Find a quiet place where you won't be disturbed
Turn off all electronic devices
Sit with your feet flat on the floor for at least two minutes, with eyes closed and hands resting palms up in your lap.
Take in three deep breaths through your nose
 Then slowly release the three breaths
 Through your open mouth, while silently counting from 1 to 5

BIBLE VERSE:

Whisper aloud to yourself the words from Matthew 7:7:
"Ask and you shall receive
Seek and you will find
Knock and the door will be opened unto you."
Please repeat this verse twice

SAY THIS PRAYER ALOUD:

"Dear God, I release my mind to you. I come to you, praying only for the knowledge of your will for me and the power to carry it out. I ask you to bless the spirit of (name of loved one), my wonderful (wife, husband, sister, brother, son, daughter, mother, father, grandmother, grandfather, friend, companion, co-worker, pet or whomever). I release their dear spirit to your loving care. I visualize (name) sitting by your side now in your Heavenly Kingdom. I send my blessed love to them. Now, in the silence, I wait for you and my dear one to share this sacred time with me. I know that both of you are here with me now. In the silence, I wait."

IN THE SILENCE:

Remain sitting quietly with the palms of your hands facing upward in your lap for at least five minutes.

EXPRESS THANKSGIVING ALOUD:

Thank you, God, for this time alone with you and (name of loved one). Thank you, thank you, thank, thank you, God. And so it is. Amen.

MEDITATION 2

PREPARATION:

Same as Meditation 1

BIBLE VERSE: (taken from the Psalms)

Please say softly these words:

"I call on you now, dear God. I know that you will answer me. Please show me the wonder of your great love."

PRAYER:

"I am sending this prayer not only to you, but also to (name of loved one). I know that my dear one is now with you in Heaven. Please tell them how much they are missed. I will love and cherish my relationship (name of loved one) until the end of time and beyond. Now, in the silence, I see my (him or her) sitting by your side in Heaven. I ask that both you, God, and my dear (name of loved one) come to me now in the silence and impart your will for me. In the silence, I wait with love for your response."

IN THE SILENCE:

Same as Meditation 1

THANKSGIVING:

Same as in Meditation 1

Letters and Journals

Excerpt from a letter I wrote Jan in early October, 1982:

"You have played a pivotal role in my life for the past two-plus years, perhaps the most pivotal time since I was raised by my parents as a child back in Temple. Without your presence and your guidance, I could have never traveled this road of discovery and awakening. You have helped me find my true self. This would have been impossible up until now. It all began when we met June 13, 1980. Where we may go from here is still unclear. The future stands apart from us right now, with you in Minnesota and me in Texas. But as for me, I'm still gathering hopes for tomorrow.

I love you, Babe.—Al"

Later the same month, I wrote her this letter:

"Dear Jannie,

Every single day this week, I've picked up the telephone to call you. And, every time, I've been unable to do it. I miss you so much. I long for the sound of your voice. I crave to touch you. But, my darling, I just cannot bring myself to inject my indecisiveness into your life. For all I know, you may be exploring a new relationship with someone else in Minnesota. I couldn't and wouldn't blame you for doing that. Perhaps a new person could give you what you want, need and deserve—a commitment. I do not want to tamper with your happiness again. I know my waffling around has made you unhappy in the past year. I love you too much to put you through that again. I care for you more than you could ever know. But maybe I'm not what you need right now.

I do love you.--Al

From a letter that I wrote Jan on Thanksgiving Day, 1982

Dear Jan,

On this special day, I just want to tell you how much our friendship has meant to me over the past 2 ½ years. You have given me love, understanding, patience, support and many other positive things. Yes, you also have tossed a few pointed objects my way from time to time (verbal of course). Of course, I needed every one of them. No doubt you understand my need and fervent desire for "freedom". That includes the freedom to choose whatever I think is best for me right now. I'm still very much caught up in my career at Southland. Thank you for understanding that. You saw that when we last talked in June. You know me very well, better than I know myself. That's hard for me to accept sometime. You are a special person.

You are my friend, now and forever."--Al

From a letter I wrote Jan on Christmas Day, 1982

Dear Jannie,

Thank you for the beautiful shirt, sweater and the much-needed book. I plunged right into it and am about ½ way through it already. It is right on target. You are so thoughtful. YOU WILL NEVER KNOW how much I appreciate and care for you. I think you might have some idea.

It's a whole lot.—Al

From a letter I wrote Jan on New Year's Eve, 1982

Dear Jannie,

Just a note to wish you a Happy New Year! I really believe 1983 will be a fantastic year for you and your family. I also want to tell you how much knowing you and loving you has meant to me since we first met on June 13, 1980. Most of the important and positive changes that have occurred with me are due to your influence and caring. I am now and always will be grateful for your love and friendship. You will always be in my thoughts.

I love you, Babe.--Al

From Jan's personal journal December 28, 1982:

"I have never felt happier in the last two years than I do now. The Christmas of '82 was like a dream come true. I have my health back; I start my new job at Methodist Hospital next week; and Shawn, Jamie and Dani (all three of my children) were with me for Christmas. It gave me a special feeling of happiness and satisfaction at the way they are conducting their lives now. I truly felt their love for me. The whole family was together for the first time in several years. To top it off, Al was here from Texas to experience everything. He and I shared a weekend which turned out to be the best we have ever known. I love him so. I wish I could be with him forever. Only time will tell. It was so difficult to know that I must continue to wait. I need to have patience, but I also must move on with my own life. I must do what I need to do what I to take care of myself. I am writing tonight to start practicing more discipline with my daily tasks for self-improvement. I want to use my God-given talents. But I wanted to write in my journal this evening to document the joy I feel at this time."

From Jan's journal December 28, 1982:

Allen

What a beautiful man
Sensitive, bright, talented
Caring, warm, loving, warm
Interested, polite, sincere
What a nice man
When I am with him
I feel secure, calm, soft
Loving, happy, passionate,
Funny, special, unique
Oh what his love does for me
When we are apart,
I struggle with the unknown
Feeling frustrated and helpless
But I know that I must
Leave it up to God
If it is meant to be
It will work out for us
And if it doesn't
We will still have the memories
Of a beautiful love

From Jan's journal New Year's Eve, 1982:

She had just moved to Minneapolis from Duluth. I was in Dallas, living as a separated bachelor and still quite enamored of the corporate lifestyle. The parenthesis are mine to identify certain people.—A. L.

"It is New Year's Eve. I spent a quiet evening at the movies with Dani (my youngest daughter) and Rick (my nephew). I wish I could be with Al. As I think back now, it's been quite a year. Al came back in my life in January (never having really left) trying to help me through my difficulties with finances, my health, the kids' problems and every other little problem I was facing. I got on my feet and went back to work. Shawn (my oldest child at 21) moved out of my apartment and to Ohio in March. Al and I were reunited in May after 10 long months of not seeing each other. From there we went through a series of ups and downs. We talked about me moving to Dallas, but that really didn't go anywhere. I wonder if he might be seeing someone else there. He can be sneaky. I've never caught him lying to me, but sometimes he omits things. But he knows that I'm no fool. When he shooed me away from coming to Dallas, I was hurt about it all and we were in conflict again. I moved to Minneapolis instead (from Duluth) and got a job with the American Cancer Society. The next five months were a nightmare. I experienced then worst flare-up of my lupus in years. I'll never forget how sick I was. Then I quit the Cancer Society and had to face an emotional upheaval too besides the physical challenge. But I got back on my feet once again. I found a new job in the medical field and regained my health. Then, Al and I had the beautiful Christmas of 1982. It was my best one in years. I'm so grateful. I just don't want to be sick again."

Excerpts from two letters I wrote Jan in May, 1983:

May 22, 1983:

"Dear Jannie,

Your hospitality last weekend was the greatest. I loved our picnic, going to the movies on Friday night and dinner on Saturday at the Japanese Steak House. It was all terrific! We always have such a good time when we see each other. I believe it is because every minute and each hour counts. At some point, I must get on a plane and head back to Dallas. Perhaps we have an unrealistic relationship, but it seems real to me.

Thank you again for a wonderful time.—Al"

May 30, 1983

"My darling Jan,

I wanted to think about "us" for a week before I wrote this letter. Yes, you know I love you. Yes, you know I appreciate the mutual caring and support that we have shared over the past three years. I think the depth of our passion would be rare for any relationship. We have something to honor and cherish. However, you said something last weekend that really hit me between the eyes. You referred to yourself, somewhat negatively, as "Cinderella" and to me as your "Prince Charming" from Texas. I've never thought that I was a corporate big-shot who swooped in and rescued you. You are the most independent person I I know. Maybe you resent the money I spend on you, like I'm a bigtime "Sugar daddy". For a co-dependent person like me, playing the role of a benevolent benefactor probably has some appeal. But I know you are your own person. And that's what you need to be. You don't any need any "Prince Charming" to take care of you. You can do that very well on your own. But do I need a "Cinderella" to make me feel important? That could be another story. It's certainly something to think about.

I love you.--Al

From letters I wrote Jan at a critical point in our relationship:

March 26, 1984

Dear Jan,

So it seems our relationship is ending—probably—with a whimper instead of a bang. I sense that you either have someone else in Minnesota or want to find somebody. I understand your needs. I have my own. We're both human. I want you to know that I will never totally say goodbye to you—or the possibility that we may somehow continue our friendship. You mean far too much to me for that. You're a part of my life. In the meantime, I hope you will achieve your #1 goal—writing and developing your greeting cards. They prove what a talented person you are.

Of course I have always known that.—Love, Al

April 21, 1984

My dearest Jan Carmen,

Thank you for calling yesterday. Both your call and the card you sent were much appreciated. I care for you, my lovely, precious and talented woman. I feel your caring for me also, across the miles. You mean so much to me, more than you will ever know. Whatever happens in the time ahead, please know that you will always be in my heart and mind forever.

Love, Al

May 4, 1984

Dear Jan,

After talking with you yesterday, I took a good hard look at myself, our relationship and the way I have treated you, especially since Feb. 2 when my divorce was final. I finally decided that I could use a good flogging with a snake-tailed whip. I did not treat you well, in part, because of my indecisiveness about what I really want. I'm being wishy-washy again. That's not fair to you. I think I've been conflicted about how you would either "like" or "fit-in" with my corporate career. That's baloney. It is totally wrong that you couldn't or wouldn't "fit-in" with the Dallas life style. You can hold your own anytime, anywhere and in any situation. I'm the one with the problem.

Love, Al

From a letter I wrote Jan on December 25, 1984. She lived in Minneapolis, I lived in Dallas:

Dear Jan,

Thank you for your call today. It made Christmas more special to hear from you. I can really feel the love and caring across the distance. On this day, I am especially thankful that you have been in my life these past 4 ½ years. That is longer than many married people stay together these days. I know that we do have a unique friendship, regardless of what else is going on in our lives. You are a special person to me, Jan. Somehow, over the past few weeks, I sense that we have become closer.

Love, Al

From a typed letter to Jan on February 13, 1993 as I was nearing graduation from the Unity School of Religious Studies and ordination as a Unity minister. She was still living in Minneapolis while I was at Unity Village, MO.

Dear Jannie,

Thank you for your call yesterday. I care about you and our history together. I felt the old feelings stir as we talked. Our past resembles the good and bad that typifies any long-term relationship. But to still feel deeply and passionately about someone after nearly 13 years borders on the remarkable. We are indeed a remarkable pair in so many ways. We are humanly flawed, especially me. But there exists a spiritual connection that somehow still binds us. For that, I am truly grateful. I do ask that you think seriously about both the joy and potential hurt that being together again might bring. I know I am.

Love, Al.

From a letter I wrote to Jan from Dallas on December 31, 1984:

Dear Jan Carmen,

I like the sound of your full name. It sounds romantic, almost musical. I think it's a good choice as you market your greeting cards. The cards are truly original. I love the unique artwork and your heartfelt words on the cards. I wish you good luck with selling them. Getting a new product out there isn't easy.

As I contemplate the new year of 1985, I just want to tell you how much I believe in you. I have always respected your talent and your willingness to risk. I predict you will be successful in whatever career you pursue. In my opinion, you are a winner now with your nursing career. Besides being successful professionally, you are a successful human being. To me, that's more important.

I will never forget your caring demeanor with those wonderful ladies we saw at the nursing home on Thanksgiving. That's the real Jan Carmen I know, a lovely and gifted woman, always willing to serve others.

Love always,

Al

From a letter I wrote Jan after we had a disastrous get together at Cragan's Resort near Brainerd. MN in July, 1985. Things did not look good for our relationship going forward. I was 99% at fault:

July 4, 1985

Dear Jan,

I still feel incredibly bad about the last 24-48 hours. Even though I do believe it is better for everyone concerned to end our relationship, it could have happened in a more caring way. No one is blameless, particularly me. I acted like an idiot and that's being charitable. I don't know what I was thinking. I should have hugged you goodbye at the airport. I didn't and I'm sorry. It was a fitting climax to the whole scene. Again, I apologize for my behavior. You deserve better. I'm sorry it had to end this way. We both have done so much for each other over the past five years. It just a shame for it all to go up in smoke in such a cruel way. Please forgive me. I care about your future.

Goodbye.—Al

Obviously, it wasn't goodbye. From a letter I wrote to Jan in early 1987, shortly after I retired from the Southland Corporation:

January 28, 1987

"I'm really trying to sort out what happened between us these past two days. A part of me says "Wow!" The chemistry between us was incredible—stronger than ever! I am truly awed by the strength and depth of your caring for me. I think you see me more positively than I see myself. Sometimes I feel that I don't deserve your love. I'm so confused. Deep down, I know that I want to be appreciated. I guess we all do. One part of me wants to fling myself down on the floor and beg for your forgiveness. Please, please try to forgive my weaknesses and indecision about what I really want. I love being with you, my dearest woman. But I also feel guilty and tormented too. Pray for me, Jan. I do love you, much more than you will ever know. That's about all I'm sure of right now.

Love, Al"

From Jan's journal in the fall of 1986 after a full year of not seeing each other, our longest separation since we met in 1980:

October 18, 1986

"Praise God! Hallelujah! Al called today. He finally admitted to being wishy-washy about coming to Minneapolis. He said he was concerned about his finances and had reservations about spending the money. He was being HONEST. That's a plus. I don't believe it is the primary reason that he hesitates, but finances could be a part of it. I think he's still uncertain, as I am, about us getting close again. But we talked a little more and then the miracle came. He asked if we could pray together. I was surprised that the corporate v-p thought praying together would help. But I liked it and we both said our individual prayers. It was wonderful, praise God. I had been praying already for Al to change his indecisive ways. Could this be the beginning? I love the Lord so much. He has taken me, a sinner, under his wings. I feel that God is nurturing and loving me. He is bestowing blessings on me. I am like a small child, being showered with beautiful gifts. I am so grateful."

October 24, 1986

"No word from Al this week. It's all so difficult. He primes me to a point where I finally feel excitement about seeing him again—then silence. He said that he was going on a church retreat this weekend. That's fine—for him. But the emptiness within my heart continues to haunt me. I want to have ongoing closeness with somebody. I would like for it to be him, but living in two different cities it's almost impossible. I long for the real intimacy of a loving, warm and trusting relationship. I know that I am free. Free to choose a partner that can give and receive love. Yet here I sit, dwelling on what may be an unrealistic dream of having that someone be Al. Dear Lord, I pray that you will guide and direct me in the right direction. I need a loving and breathing soul in my life. Please banish my fears and doubts. I pray for your help in every part of my life. Grant me the love of a human friend."

My letter to Jan on December 24, 1986, the last day of my 20-year career with The Southland Corporation (7-Eleven) in Dallas. I had decided to take an early retirement and was leaving on a short vacation to London:

Dear Jan,

I just want to tell you how much I appreciate your expression of love and support. It really is more important than you will ever know. This is a great chance I've taken in leaving a company after 20 years, plus a salary I may never duplicate again. But I feel it is the right decision for me. It's good to have someone behind you with their caring and support.

Your letter really stirred up some old feelings that I haven't experienced for a while. It took me back to the days of '80 and '81 when we first met. Those were sweet and passionate times, for sure. I guess I've always known that you are a loyal and caring person, but the impact of your letter right now touched me deeply. What sensitivity you demonstrate during a time of crisis and change!

May God bless and keep you, my sweet woman.

Love,

Al

From a letter I sent Jan on January 14, 1987:

Dearest Jan,

I have tried to pray about it, I've thought hours on it, I have "slept" on it and I've let my subconscious mind work on it. "It" is what I want to do in terms of a commitment to you or anyone. I know that you have rightfully told me "You can't have (redacted) and me both." You've said "That means you can't sleep with (redacted) and me at the same time. I won't do it even if she would. That's selfish on your part." I understand that. Of course, that makes sense from your (and probably most people's) standpoint. Well, I hate to do it, but here is my "decision": I want you to go on with your life without me—once and for all. Yes, we still have the love that began between us on June 13, 1980. But it is not enough to overcome my basic "decision" about not wanting to commit to anyone at this time. I'm not choosing between you and (redacted). I'm choosing a path of no commitment for now. Hopefully, this is not forever. A commitment is just the wrong path for me right now. I care about you, Jan, and the only fair thing to say is: GO ON WITHOUT ME. You are in a good place emotionally. You are ready to make a commitment to someone. You ready for a new life. I'm still pondering all of that, at least as of today. I hope someday I'll have the courage to make a lifetime commitment. I'll need God's help to do that, I'm sure. I plan to ask for His will for me. Please pray for me. I need it.

Al

Looking back now, it was through God's grace that Jan and I eventually got married on June 19, 1994 despite our many ups and downs. For me, there were still more downs to come before God finally got my attention. Thank you, God for keeping Jan in my life until I finally awakened to what I really wanted: For this wonderful and spiritual person to be my lifetime partner.

At the end of 1989 and beginning of 1990, Jan wrote these excerpts in the new journal she had received as a Christmas present from her daughter Danielle:

December 25, 1989

"I was so happy to get another journal from Dani as a Christmas gift. I just finished the final page in my last journal. It held good thoughts and moments of growth with Al. I wonder what this journal will reveal."

December 27, 1989

"Al enjoyed himself over the holidays. He was in Dallas with his Texas family. He said that he and his ex-wife Suzanne are "buddies" now. I find that hard to believe, but who knows? Life with exes gets complicated, especially where "kids" are involved. Al told me on the phone that when he was having Christmas dinner at Suzanne's, he thought to himself: "Is this fair to Jan?" I told him, "No, it's not!" Sometimes I wonder if he would still like to get back together with his family. I think we all carry around visions of "the white picket fence" and having a perfect family life. What I know is this: I'm sure there are some great families around, but there is no perfect family. Every family has its challenges. They all consist of imperfect human beings."

December 31, 1989

"I've flown down to Texas. I feel like it's my turn now for us to be together. I'm having such mixed emotions about coming here. I've been praying hard about this endless back and forth between us. I decided to come on down and just see how things go. Al and I could start arguing and I'll end up going back early. Who knows? When I unpacked my things in the guest bathroom, I found a lovely card from him welcoming me to Texas. He's either a smooth operator or he really cares about me. I'm choosing to believe that he cares."

January 1, 1990

"We went to a movie New Year's Eve and then came home and made love in front of the fireplace. It was wonderful. We went for a walk today and then came home for a nice nap. Then we spent some time talking and praying together. This past 24 hours has been much more wonderful than expected. Al has been so nice to me.

Praise God! Maybe things have changed, after all. We usually do well when we are together. It's afterwards when the doubts start creeping in. But right now, I say "Thank you, God, for blessing my life with love. It feels so good."

January 9, 1990

 "Only now after being back home have I found the time to write about the rest of the week with Al. For part of my time in Texas, Al was working. I spent most of those days shopping and buying things for his apartment. He gave me a basic list, and I added a few things. He seems to really like everything that I purchased, especially a rug for under the dining room and a nice picture for his bedroom. I think Al appreciates my taste in decorating. He compliments me a lot. I also bought a couple of small house plants although I'm not sure he can keep them alive after I'm gone. Al did work while I was here, but came home for lunch every day. He was always so glad to see me. I felt the same way. He usually arrived a few minutes before noon. I found myself watching the clock, waiting for him to come through the door. It was a nice feeling. We spent time every night having dinner and then reading devotional things and praying together. Even though Al is working again in the corporate world, his priorities do seem different. His spiritual side is beginning to slowly emerge. I do like the direction he seems headed now. But I don't want to have any delusions either. He still very much has one foot in the corporate world and another foot in God's Kingdom. On my last day in Texas, we were both quiet as I packed for the trip back to Minnesota. He built another fire and we talked a little more. Then he and I laid down for a nap while the fire burned out. Then it was off to the airport. On the way there, I asked Al how he felt about our relationship. He said "It's been a great eight days. We proved that we can just enjoy being together." I know that internally both of have some real concerns. A long- distance relationship often seems like a fantasy world. It's great when you're together, but not so good when you're apart. I do think Al and I made some progress in feeling comfortable around each longer for a longer time than usual. We'll see what the future brings. I just thank God for a nice and safe trip. I certainly don't love Al any less after being here."

From a letter I sent to Jan on January 7, 1991 after we had spent some time together:

Dear Jan,

Thanks for a wonderful visit. I do appreciate the way you treat me. Sometimes it's difficult for me to just relax and let people do nice things for me. But, I am learning to accept my good. Thank you for support, concern and love as I ponder what's next in my life. I'm also happy that your own "ministry" is becoming clear. It's exciting to be see you drawing closer to God's plan for your life. Personally, I think it will have something to do with ministering to chronically ill individuals. But, whatever it involves, you will always be a true blessing to those around you. You carry your goodness wherever you are.

Love always, Al.

From a letter I sent to Jan on January 18, 1991 as I was preparing for interviews at the Unity School of Religious Studies and their Ministerial Education Program:

Dear Jan,

I want you to know that you've been on my mind. I enjoyed our time together in Austin so much. Our friendship, love and caring has a new and wonderful depth. Thank you for that. I'm extremely excited about the interviews at Unity in a few weeks. I'll be glad to know something one way or the other. Then I can get on with my life if I'm not accepted. I'm sure it will be an interesting process. I'm grateful to God that I've gotten this far. Whatever happens will be God's Will.

Love always, Al.

P. S. You're in my prayers every night (and day).

From a letter to Jan on January 25, 1991:

Dear Jannie, —In listening to your own deepening commitment on the phone last night, I felt a surge of pride and support for you. You are truly on the spiritual path. That is so gratifying to me. I know the happiness you are feeling. When God takes the controls, things start falling into place. Expect some challenges along the way. But I know you'll get through it.

I love you, Al.

From a card I sent Jan on February 23, 1991, two weeks before I went to Unity Village for interviews prior to admission into their Ministerial Program:

Dear Jannie,

Thanks, my love, for the supportive conversation this afternoon. As I said several times, I do so appreciate and love you-- for who you are and what you've meant to me during these past 10 ½ years. I've been reading the sixth chapter of Ephesians again lately. Putting on "the whole armor of God" has real meaning as I get down to the final surrender to His will. Please say a prayer for me.

Love, Al

From a card I sent Jan after we had spent several days together in Minneapolis:

April 7, 1991

Dear Jannie,

Thank you so much for your loving hospitality and kindnesses this past week. I loved spending the time with you-- lazy mornings and dinners together at night (especially the dinners). You are a wonderful friend, companion and lover. I do appreciate you. I care for you and love you. I hope you're feeling better now. Take care of yourself, Babe. I'll be starting ministerial school soon. Please pray for me. I'll need it.

Love, Al

A note to Jan from me on April 15, 1991:

"Dear Jannie,

Thank you sweetie for the TWO birthday cards that I received today. I love what you write. You make me feel so appreciated. That is truly a wonderful feeling, probably one of the greatest anyone could experience. I appreciate you too—more all the time. I believe that is how a relationship should progress—more caring, greater appreciation and deeper love. I am so blessed that our friendship has survived, grown and blossomed. Of course, I am sure that God had a lot to do with that growth.

Thank you, God. Much love.

"Al the Aries".

From a card to Jan on June 26, 1991, just before I began ministerial school:

Dear Jannie,

I do miss you. We are each doing what we must do, but please don't think I dismiss the progress we've made in our relationship. I care about you—deeply. I'm proud of you and what you have and will accomplish in your own ministry. Thank you, Babe, for supporting me on my spiritual journey. Keep me in your prayers.

Love, Al

From a card to Jan on July 17, 1991, just after classes at Unity had begun:

Dear Rev. Jan,

After reading your card, I think the wrong person is in ministerial school. Wow! You would make most of my classmates-and me-seem lacking in comparison to your spirituality. You have been chosen to carry God's Light to others. What a wonderful gift! Your growth seems to be accelerating. Are you meditating? I'll bet the still, small voice has a lot to say to you! I love you.

Your prayer partner, Al

In June 1992, between my first and second year of ministerial school at Unity Village, Jan and I traveled to Estes Park, Colorado for some time together. She was living in St. Louis Park, MN and serving as a nursing supervisor in the Ear, Nose, and Throat (ENT) department at the Park Nicollet Clinic. These are excerpts from her journal:

COLORADO

June 12, 1992

"We have arrived in a beautiful part of our country. We are getting settled for the night in our rustic little cabin at the YMCA of the Rockies just outside of Estes Park. It's been a busy day. I got up at 6 a.m. in Minneapolis. Al was up at 5 a.m. to get out to the airport in Kansas City. He caught an earlier flight and was at the Denver airport to met me when my plane arrived. I was glad about that. We rented a car and drove the 70 miles to the Rocky Mountain National Park. It is SO incredibly beautiful here. Our cabin wasn't quite ready when we arrived at 3 p.m. so we walked around the campground and just gazed up at the beauty around us. God certainly created a masterpiece here. I've never seen anything like it, coming from the flat northern prairie.

We stopped for lunch on the way at the old Stanley Hotel. What an interesting place and very nice. It's so good to be with Al again. I feel his love and warmth. But I don't think anything has changed regarding a commitment. But I have no expectations. I do feel blessed to have this vacation with Al and to enjoy a Rocky Mountain High from the scenery around us.

Thank you, LORD, for this day. Thank you for Al's love. Thank you for my health. I am forever grateful to you for my life.

June 14

Yesterday was our 12th anniversary of knowing each other. I gave Al a very nice card with a little book I wrote for him. He truly appreciated it. He had tears. I also bought him a beautiful tie for getting through the first year of ministerial school. We started out the day at the "Y" Camp by attending the "Family Olympics" It is mostly parents here with their kids. What a great environment for family bonding! Later today, we drove out to the Park and hiked up to Bear Lake. It is awesome up there. Words can't describe it. Then, we walked even further to Alberta Falls and that was magnificent too. We sat on a rock, in silence, for a long time. You can feel God's presence in nature. Then, I said "Let's pray together" and we did. It was wonderful. Again, words can't describe my feelings of being here. It is all just so spiritual and especially being there with Allie. Thank you, God.

June 15

We have moved from the "Y" Camp to a new place. It is truly luxurious and resembles a fancy condominium. There is a huge king size bed in the middle of the room. It also has a hot tub, kitchen and fire place. It is decorated beautifully. It even has a front porch with sun shade. Al decided to go into town for groceries. While he was gone, I jumped into the hot tub. I did ask him how it worked, but he didn't know much more than I did. He had been gone for only a few minutes when I got the tub full above the water spouts. But it didn't shut off. I noticed a button on the back of the tub and pushed it. Suddenly, the water spouted way up high and out into the middle of the room. I still had the tub water running and didn't know how to stop it. I pulled the plug and figured out how to shut off the water, but the carpeting around the tub was drenched and saturated with water. When Al came through the door, I looked like a drowned rat. He was cool about it. We took every towel in the place and just kept wiping and wiping. He was so sweet. He took the towels to a laundromat in town to get them dried out. We still love it here. I don't care if we never leave.

June 16

I want to talk with Al before we end this vacation. I've got to deal with my feelings. I can't continue this pain of not knowing where we stand. When we finally started sharing, he could sense my unhappiness. He said, "Maybe you should get out of the relationship if you are so unhappy." He's a great person in so many ways, but very tone-deaf where he and I are concerned. In the end, nothing has changed. Lots of love but no commitment. He wants to finish ministerial school before doing anything. I guess I can understand that."

Excerpts from Jan's journal in early 1993. I was about to begin my final term at the Unity School of Religious Studies:

"Somehow I thought the start of a new journal would be a sign of no more Al. I felt extremely unsure after sending my "Dear Al" letter. I was sure that I would never hear from him again. But on Friday, I got a letter from him. It started out "Dear Jannie". Al said that he felt the old excitement and anticipation when he saw my letter in his mailbox. He wrote that he had missed our friendship, our intimacy, and the communication that only time can bring. He's right about that.

Al went on to say that he felt sad after reading my letter. He wasn't angry or mad or hurt. He said he knew I still cared. Al said that, of course, he still cared too. But, in truth, what does any of it matter now? He went on to say that letting go of his family in Dallas hasn't ever been easy. Even though he has been divorced for ten years, he was married for 22 ½ years. The marriage also produced two kids who are now in their 30s. His affection for both Jeff and Laura are strong, even though they aren't all that close.

He ended by writing that he now fully understands the importance of forgiveness in all areas of his life. He suggested that forgiveness might be important for me too. Al ended his letter with "My blessings and love, Al." I called my Unity minister friend who also knows Al and read him the letter. He said: "It sounds like the same old ambiguous approach that I've grown to expect from him." He felt Al might be trying to lure me back into a relationship by telling me how much he missed me. The minister may be right, but my friend and therapist Ellen had a different take. She told me "It sounds like he's asking for forgiveness." No matter what his true reason for responding the way he did, it would never work unless he made a real commitment to me. Never."

I graduated and was ordained in mid-June, 1993. I quickly packed up my apartment in Missouri and moved north to pursue a relationship with the wonderful person that I would marry exactly one year later. Thank you, God, for finally getting us together.

From a typed letter to Jan on February 13, 1993 as I was nearing graduation from the Unity School of Religious Studies and ordination as a Unity minister. She was still living in Minneapolis while I was at Unity Village, MO:

Dear Jannie,

Thank you for your call yesterday. I care about you and our history together. I felt the old feelings stir as we talked. Our past resembles the good and bad that typifies any long-term relationship. But to still feel deeply and passionately about someone after nearly 13 years borders on the remarkable. We are indeed a remarkable pair in so many ways. We are humanly flawed, especially me. But there exists a spiritual connection that somehow still binds us. For that, I am truly grateful. I do ask that you think seriously about both the joy and potential hurt that being together again might bring. I know I am.

Love, Al.

From my journal June 20, 1993:

"I've been ordained now for exactly one week. How does it feel? In a way, I don't believe it has totally hit me yet. The move to the Twin Cities happened so quickly, I've been too busy to contemplate much of anything. I feel extremely grateful to God for this opportunity. I need to place my trust in Spirit and take things one day at a time. I will be starting out in Minneapolis as a chaplain for three months (one unit of Clinical Pastoral Education) at Fairview Hospital near downtown.

I'm pleased with the way Jan and I have related since I got here. We have never lived in the same city during our entire 13-year relationship, so this will be a lot different. I'm sure both of us will have to make some adjustments. So far, she's been very understanding when I've need some alone-time. It helps that we each have our own separate places. That lessens the pressure somewhat. But, by moving up here, I have made a commitment to exploring our relationship in depth. Being apart and seeing each other sporadically always had an unrealism about it. When we got together, it was like being on vacation. Now, it's real. One other realistic thing the move accomplished was to help me detach from my family in Dallas. They know where I am and how to reach me. But this move is sending the message that I really am going forward with my life. Ultimately, this will be a good thing for them too.

I feel that my real path in the future lies in service to God. I'm not sure what that looks like yet. I must trust that God will lead me to the right situation. I am excited about finishing school, being ordained, moving to Minnesota and pursuing my relationship with Jan. It's an exciting, but challenging time to be a newly ordained minister and starting a new phase of my life. I'm ready for what's next."

Jan and I decided to take a cruise to the Caribbean in March, 1994 to celebrate our engagement. These are excerpts from my journal about our trip away from still chilly Minnesota:

March 13

"We had an easy, uneventful trip from Minneapolis to Miami. We cabbed it to MSP at 1 p.m. and were headed out to sea on Royal Caribbean's MAJESTY OF THE SEAS at 6 p.m. The MAJESTY is a real megaship, less than two years old. This is only the ship's 99th voyage. Our tablemates for meals is a Chinese couple, originally from Hong Kong, and their two teen age sons. The family now lives in Toronto. He is a General Practice physician and she teaches school. They are nice people and we've enjoyed getting to know them.

Well, how do I feel about being officially "engaged" for one day? Fine, so far. Jan's ring looks lovely and so does she. Jan is a beautiful person inside and out. We've learned to accept each other. We kid around about our many personal foibles, which is a sure sign of acceptance and maturity. We have both come a long, long way. I'm so grateful to God for seeing us through to this point. God's hand is obvious in both of our lives at this point. I know that I am at a real turning point. The next few weeks should clarify my professional situation. By this time next month, I will be on my way to accept my first ministerial assignment in Sun City, Arizona. Am I scared? Yes and no. I know that God is good and will see me through wherever I am and whatever I'm doing."

March 16

"Half-way through the cruise and everything has been wonderful so far. We docked at the Grand Cayman today. Jan and I got into it a bit this morning as she wanted me to go into town with her. I decided to stay on the ship and she wasn't happy about it. She finally did leave the ship for a while with another lady. I stayed here and cooled it. Everybody got what they wanted."

March 20

"I went up on deck before 6 a.m. to watch the ship come in at the Port of Miami. Jan and I attended the "Farewell Show" on the ship last night. A wonderful time was had by all. The cruise was a great engagement present for both of us."

My memories of our wedding day on June 19, 1994

Jan and were married on a Father's Day at the lovely Summit Club in St. Paul. It was a fabulous event, at least in my opinion. Rev. Phil LaPorte, the minister from Unity South, performed the wedding service. He is a favorite of ours and did a wonderful job. Judy Moen from Unity South played the piano and the singer and other musician were also excellent. Jan was beautiful beyond description, not only to me but to everyone. She will turn 53 on July 28, but I would swear she looks 33. We had a nice crowd at the wedding, including lots of doctors and nurses from the ENT department at Park Nicollet where she is a supervisor. My bride also had long-time friends from Duluth and Minneapolis present, as well as a huge contingent of family. Her Mom passed last year, but Jan's dad, her three children (Shawn, Jamie and Danielle), sister (Marlene), brother (Jimmy) and many nieces and nephews were all in attendance. I am so proud of my sweet Minnesota wife. The reception and meal afterward were also magnificent. It was simply an incredible day all around, filled with joy and happiness. When I think about the rocky road we traveled to get here today, I am convinced that God crafted our relationship and saw it through to completion. We must have broken up at least a dozen times along the way. It was almost always my fault or short-sightedness. But we always found a way back into each other's arms. It was uncanny how both of us would be listening separately to our car radios and one of "our songs" would pop up. I'll bet I heard Anne Murray's "I Just Fall in Love Again" and Bob Segar's "Someday Lady You'll Accompany Me" dozens of times, from seemingly out of the blue. I'm so grateful that we both—mostly Jan—hung in there through it all. Thank you, God, for my precious Minnesota wife.

From Jan's journal August 16, 1994:

"Today, we bought a house in Sun City (Arizona) at 10908 Tropicana Circle. It's a charming 2-bedroom, 2-bath with an open living and dining room. It has a modified Arizona Room, with a covered patio, nice landscaping and wall-papered master bedroom, bathrooms and kitchen. The carpeting is peach. All window treatments, including curtains, drapes and blinds come with it. It also has a very nice utility room with space for an office for Al, the new minister at the Unity Church of Sun City. We paid $128,000, which is a steal. It also backs up to one of the 17 golf courses in Sun City. It's a perfect starter house for two newlyweds from Minnesota, 1817 square feet of Heaven."

From Jan's journal August 17, 1994:

"I read somewhere once: "In our pursuit of physical and emotional goals, it is often easy to overlook the spiritual part of our natures. It is from that God part that all happiness, joy, health and love come." Amen to that! I read today in Psalms 37:4: "Take delight in the LORD, and he will give you the desires of your heart." This is good advice for me or anyone. I need to nurture my spirituality more. Since we moved from MN to AZ, I've missed my quiet mornings in meditation. I am pledging to myself today that I will get my priorities straight. I want to get right with God—and myself again. Al has the people at church now and they have been welcoming to me as well. But I need to take care of my own needs. Thank you, God, for reminding me of why I must have a one-on-one relationship with you. I love you."

From Jan's journal on August 19, 1994:

We had been married exactly two months. We were living in Sun City, AZ and serving the Unity Church of Sun City.

"Tonight we had dinner with Louella M., the biggest contributor to the church. She seems to like Al and I think she's neat, especially for someone well past 90. Al said that, on his first Sunday at the church, he was preaching away and looked out to see Louella asleep with her mouth open. He thought, uh-oh, I may be in trouble here. But after the service, she told him how much she enjoyed his message. The people in Sun City are just terrific! It's like having sixty sets of grandparents. They treat us like the newlyweds, which we are. They dote on us all the time. The ladies of the church won't let me do anything in the kitchen. That's their territory! They treat me like a First Lady, which feels kind of flattering. The older gentlemen line up on Sunday morning to give me a hug, but not too big of one if their wife might be watching. They're so funny! There are a few people here our age and a few even younger. But the average age is over 80, and they are the crème de crème of the older generation. I hope I am half as sharp when I'm their age. Today, after I cleaned our place and Al finished his sermon, we decided to spend some time in prayer. We need to do that more often."

From Jan's journal August 20, 1994:

"Al was so funny today. He had me "cracking up". He wasn't trying to be funny, which made it even funnier. Somehow he started talking about his time in the Army at Fort Polk, Louisiana back in the 1960s. He showed me how he saluted and marched. It was hilarious. He must have been some soldier. But he is proud that he served when a lot of other guys didn't go. His grandfather was head of the draft board back home, so he almost had to enlist. His marching made me laugh."

From Jan's journal on August 21:

"There were 107 people in church today, but somehow the crowd seemed smaller. We've got reverse snowbirds here in Arizona. They leave in the summertime when the weather gets hot. We've had several weeks now in a row where the afternoon temp has exceeded 110 degrees. This Minnesota girl has never experienced anything quite like it. I don't envy Al being a minister. People expect so much. He has a lot of energy for a 57-year old guy, but it seems the demands for his time never end. To me, he is trying to do too much. But this is his first church and he wants to do a good job. It's just hard to be perfect in every aspect of ministry. I know he's a great executive from his experience in the corporate world. I don't think he feels quite as confidant about his Sunday messages yet. But that will come. God has blessed us both."

An excerpt from Jan's personal journal dated Dec. 31, 1994, about six months after we married:

"It's New Year's Eve and we decided not to go to the Christensen's party. We're both exhausted from all the activities of the past month. We moved into a new house, performed in the church Christmas play ("Angel with the Broken Wing" in which I played the angel), hosted a Christmas brunch and dinner, did the Christmas Day services, and had my daughter Dani visiting from Minneapolis. These were all very positive and happy experiences but still very tiring and stressful. Al has had the flu and I've never seen him so tired. I believe this ministry thing is too much for him sometimes. There is really a lot involved in running a church.

The move from Minnesota to Arizona has been a big learning experience for me. I realize even more the importance of family. All I can think about is getting back close to my family in Minnesota, or at least within shouting distance. I love Al and enjoy the church. The people here are lovely, but I wish I were closer to my kids and sister. Maybe someday."

Jan and I moved back to Minnesota in 2001 from Lee's Summit, MO where I served as Senior Director of Outreach for the Unity School of Christianity from September 24, 1995 until August 31, 2001. Jan finally got her wish and we lived in Minnesota until her passing on February 28, 2017.

From Jan's personal journal:
A list of her 1995 NEW YEAR'S RESOLUTIONS
We were living in Sun City, Arizona and had been married about six months.

1. Get back on track with God; put Him first always.
2. "Lighten up" with the house; don't be so obsessive about cleanliness.
3. Love everyone more—Al, my family, church members and myself.
4. Get a job. Assist the marriage financially and with health insurance.
5. Love and ACCEPT Al as he is.
6. Make service to God a priority.
7. Get counseling for our marriage. Everyone can use it. Everyone.
8. Read the Daily Word, the Bible, and other spiritual books.
9. Continue to nurture my friendships.

From Jan's journal JANUARY 11, 1995: She had just learned that her sister Marlene's 60-year old husband George had been diagnosed with prostate cancer. George was given only a few months to live:

"I talked to Marlene this morning. She had only slept 2 of the past 36 hours. I need to be with her, but she thought I might help more later after George passes. But I'm going back home anyway. I need to be there not only for Mar, but for my nieces and nephews too. None of the five are taking the news very well. I'll use God's guidance as to how I can be of help. This whole ordeal truly helps me appreciate my marriage to Al. He is a wonderful man and it's important that we nurture this love of ours. We must never take a day for granted. Even though he frustrates me some time with his self-centeredness and focus on the church, I pray that I can appreciate him for who he is and how he loves me. I also pray that I can appreciate anyone that reaches out to me in love. I pray that I can extend my love to all people, especially those in our congregation. I want to express God's uniqueness in me. I pray to expect good things and dream great dreams. I need to ask God about what I should do and then listen to those answers. God, please open my heart, mind and soul. Most of all, open MY EARS so that I may hear your still small voice."

From Jan's journal in October, 1995, after I had accepted a job back at Unity Village as Senior Director of Outreach. We were living at 303 NE Landings Drive in Lee's Summit, MO:

OCT. 31, 1995—HALLOWEEN

"Here we are in our new house in Lee's Summit, MO. And it's fun to have "Trick or Treaters" again. So much has happened these past two or three months. I haven't been keeping up very well with my journaling. I didn't finish the last one and then I used a separate one on our trip to England in August. On Aug. 22, Al was offered the job of Senior Director of Outreach at the Unity School of Christianity at Unity Village. I resigned from Sun Health System and he gave his notice at the church. The folks were very sad and disappointed to see us go. However, they were supportive of Al being promoted to "the home office".

We were quite excited and stressed at the same time. It was quite emotional dealing with the people at church. Then we had to sell our house on Tropicana Drive in Sun City and buy this house in Missouri. After that, we had to move and then unpack again. We had both cars shipped by flat-bed truck. That was interesting. A husband and wife drove the cars to Missouri on their truck. Were they ever characters! We got through the last service at the church in Sun City on September 24. We played Bob Dylan's "FOREVER YOUNG" on the loudspeaker in the Fellowship Hall. Al and I danced with some of the folks. We were all crying. I stayed in AZ and sold our great little house to a cash buyer from Pennsylvania. They did not look at another house after seeing ours. Al flew out to Missouri the afternoon of the 24th and started at the Village the next day.

Physically, all of this has been tough on Al. His blood pressure shot up to 172/110 and he even ended up going to the ER at a nearby hospital. He had a pinched nerve in his back and his left arm went numb. I thought he might either be stroking out or having a heart attack. The ER doc said it was stress.

Personally, I've been feeling great. That's kind of a switch. I had a slight scare with a mammogram before we left Arizona. I've got some benign mass near my lungs. I need to watch it. Thank God it wasn't breast cancer to go along with the lupus. Thank you, God! I'm closer to Minnesota now.

MY 60TH Birthday on APRIL 16, 1997—I was serving as Senior Director of Outreach at Unity Village, located just outside of Kansas City, MO. This is an excerpt from my journal that day:

My darling wife threw a great party for me!

"I had the best birthday party of my life tonight. Jan put together a terrific party to celebrate my 60th birthday. She invited 40 guests over to our place in Lee's Summit. Every invitee showed up. My sweet wife knows how to throw a wing-ding! She came up with a "South-of-the-Border" theme, featuring a live Mariachi band playing tunes like "Cileto lindo" (which means "lovely sweet one"). We sang lots of "Ay, ay, ay, ay". Jan thought the Spanish motif would honor both my Texas roots and my passion for Mexican food. You can't be from Texas and not love chili, enchiladas and tacos. We had plenty of all three tonight. We also had a piñata, which I didn't even have to break. I think everybody had a fantastic time! I know I did. We also played some fun games to win "White Elephant" prizes. Some of the "prizes" were hilarious. Most of the people at the party were folks I work with every day at Unity Village. Lots of my co-workers from the Outreach department came, along with a few "outside" people as well. After the last guest departed, I gave Jan a big hug and kiss. I'm so happy that she cared enough to do something special for me. I appreciate her more than she will ever know. Since we arrived back here at the Village, she has jumped right into things. She even got a job at Silent Unity, our telephone prayer ministry, answering calls from individuals who needed prayer. Jan's boss told me the other day how much everyone likes her. I'm very proud and honored to be "Jan Liles' husband.""

From the Unity 2000 Phamphlet "Trusting God" by Jan Carmen Liles, published by the Unity School of Christianity, Unity Village, MO 64065-0001:

"In 1975, I was diagnosed with lupus, a chronic autoimmune disease that is incurable and often fatal. Because of the severity of my symptoms and the progression of the disease, my doctor told me that I might live only five more years.

I recall thinking at the time, *Could this really be happening to me?* I felt totally disorientated, surprised and confused. My "perfect" life was being ripped away from me. Very soon after the diagnosis, I lost my marriage, my home, most of my material possessions, and my nursing career. My life laid in shambles.

As I visualized the path before me, I could see only darkness and devastation. My entire body was engulfed with wrenching pain. I became consumed and paralyzed with fear. Like a drowning victim, I felt the swift current pulling me under. Part of me wanted to be swept away, yet another part of me kept struggling to the surface—the "mother" part that had been left with three young children to raise. My children meant more to me than life itself. I did not want to leave them motherless.

Now, looking back 25 years, I sometimes wonder how I held on through the early years of my illness. I felt so alone and separated from God. I was raised to believe that God was not only loving, but also judging and punishing. I argued with God about my losses, which I regarded as a severe punishment.

"Why me?" I asked. What had I done to deserve illness, a broken family, and the loss of a career I loved? The more I argued, the more distant God seemed to be. Finally, I sensed that God had disappeared from my life altogether. I felt abandoned and alone.

I no longer experienced God's presence in the church I attended, so I decided to explore other settings and churches where I might find some answers. This became my "looking for God" experience. I later realized it was like trying to find your glasses when they were already resting on your nose.

In hindsight, I know now that God never left or abandoned me. Nor did God let me fall so far down that I could not be lifted again. God's caring presence was with me through every crisis, heartache and tear, but I still had a long path to walk before I came to this realization.

As I was growing up, my parents often reminded me to be strong, whatever the situation. I was told to pull myself up by the bootstraps anytime things got rough. "Tough it out, Jan," they urged me. "Don't give up so easily."

My mom and dad were wonderful parents, passing along lessons of perseverance *they* had learned. I believed deeply in their wisdom, so I always tried hard to make everything work out.

Even after I got sick, I continued to strive. I had this stubborn determination to be strong, especially for my children. I also wanted to be in control of my life, despite an illness that had stripped away much of that control.

While attending a church service one Sunday, I heard the minister telling the congregation to turn their problems over to God. He promised that God would take care of us if we surrendered our burdens.

How does that work? I wondered. I know now that I simply did not have enough trust in God at that moment to release my problems. Before I could learn to trust, I had to accept that I could not do everything by myself. I needed God to help me.

One night, with the world heavy on my shoulders, I got down on my knees and prayed to God. I let the tears flow. After that prayer, I felt a sense of great humility. I had surrendered my life to God in my weakest, darkest hour of despair. For the first time since my illness had been diagnosed, I breathed a sigh of relief.

That night was the beginning of a journey that would change my life forever. It became a journey with God. Every day, I sought to know God better. I know now that God always waits patiently for us to remember our oneness. God's love remains patient and unwavering."

Jan Liles

An inscription from me inside of a book on LOVE that I bought for Jan in 2001 to mark our seventh wedding anniversary:

June 19, 2001,

Dear Babe,

These past seven years have been a gift from God. We have experienced some highs, some lows and lots of in-betweens. But through prayer, commitment, and a genuine love and caring for one another, we have persevered and are still here. I admire you. I respect you. I love you more today than the day we married. That is saying a lot. I cherish you, my babe.

Your adoring husband,

Al

From my memory about the events of August 2001 as I was preparing to retire from the Outreach Department at Unity Village:

"August, 2001 was the month from Hell. I cannot recall a worse 30 days. During the first week of August, Jan was diagnosed with cancer. She had Hodgkins lymphoma. We heard from the doctor that "non-Hodgkins" is worse, but having cancer of any kind isn't good. She had a mass the size of a grapefruit near her lungs. We had already scheduled my retirement from Unity for late August. We were scheduled to make a quick move to Minnesota. I started a one-year chaplain residency at Fairview Southdale Hospital in Edina on August 26. Jan spent a total of 17 days in the hospital after her diagnosis. She was much too sick to travel anywhere in August. We also had to sell the house in Lee's Summit, but she obviously couldn't handle that task as she did six years ago in Arizona.

On top of everything, when I went to pick Jan up at the hospital in mid-August after 10 days, I backed the Jeep Cherokee into a pillar in the hospital garage. Even with the collision insurance, that was a $1000 expense we didn't expect. Wait, there's more. We had only been home from the hospital for four hours when Jan became deathly ill. She had shaking chills and fainted in the kitchen. When I called the hospital, I said "We need to come back—Now!" At first the doctor on call didn't want to admit her as she had just been discharged. We had a knock-down, drag-out argument on the phone, but he finally agreed to let my sick wife come back. She began the day as a patient in the hospital and ended the day the same way. Jan was hospitalized another seven days. I felt so bad that she had to go back the second time. But it was necessary.

I was glad and grateful that Jan's sister and two daughters had come down from the Twin Cities to help. They stayed with my sick wife while I moved and then drove her up to Minnesota in early September. Thank you, God, for their help. Jan decided to do her chemo at Methodist Hospital with a great doctor that she knew from working there before. God saw us through a very tough time. She was declared cancer-free on Valentine's Day, 2002. Thankfully, it never returned."

Notes from Jan's and my final Sunday at Unity Christ Church in Golden Valley, Minnesota on April 30, 2006. I had served the church as associate minister, interim minister and senior minister for a total of 40 months before deciding to retire at the age of 69:

"It was truly a wonderful day for both Jan and me. After the last service today, they held a reception for us in Fellowship Hall. Did we ever get fussed over! I wish I could have written down all the nice things that people had to say. I really feel like we've done a good job under the circumstances. Being a minister can be a rough road unless you have a thick skin. I'll never forgot the congregant who came to see me one day. She spent an hour criticizing me up one side and down the other. I expected her to quit the church when she got through jumping on me. She finally stopped and asked: "Do you have a pen?" I reached into my pocket and fetched my pen, expecting that she wanted to sign a letter of resignation. Instead, she pulled out her checkbook and wrote the church a check for $1,000. I was stunned. I thought about asking if she would like to come back next week and chew on me some more. Then, there was the day at church when I was in early on a Monday morning. I decided to save my administrative assistant some time by opening the mail. I had a lot on my mind that day. We were behind in our annual budget by several thousand dollars. It looked like we would need to dip into our reserves, which weren't all that flush. The first letter that I opened, I saw a brief note from a long-time and wonderful church member. She explained that her condo had recently sold and that she wanted to tithe her profit on the sale to the church. This fabulous lady had enclosed a check for $13,000. Our budget deficit had just disappeared. Of course, not every memory brings a smile. Churches consist of people, all dealing with "stuff" (just like the minister). But I remind myself that God created every one of us in God's image and likeness. Somewhere deep within each human being lives that unique God particle. If we look for it long enough, we can find it. Every minister needs to remind themselves of that truth."

Comments from congregants at Unity South Church in Bloomington, MN where I served as interim minister from November, 2007-July, 2008:

Dear Reverend Liles and Jan,

Thank you so much for everything you two have done for Unity South. God directed you to assist our congregation during challenging transitional times. Your positive healing energy has guided us to bond with each other more than ever. You have inspired unified hope. Your messages remain with us always. Thank you for blessing us on your journey. God bless you both.

Joyce H. and Mary Ellen J.

Rev. Allen and Jan,

Thanks for arriving at just the right moment. You have blessed us with your calm and wise presence. Happy Trails to you. May your path be strewn with stars. With love and gratitude.

John T.

Rev Al and Jan,

Tears come to my eyes as I try to voice my gratitude for all the blessings you have given Unity South Church. I have a lump in my throat. Thank you, thank you, thank you. I don't know what will happen to Unity South now. I do know we have made lemonade from many lemons and that your wisdom, vision, kindness and leadership and radiant being has been integral in the process. You and Jan will be in my heart always. Love and hugs.

Chris T.

Dear Allen,

Thank you so much for all of the prayer and moral support in these months since you came to Unity South. I've really enjoyed getting to know you and Jan and hope to stay in touch with you both. I've appreciated the stability, common sense and wise guidance you brought to the church. There is now a feeling of peace within the church community and readiness to move forward. Warm wishes and blessings on your path ahead.

Katherine R.

From a birthday card Jan gave me on April 16, 2009 (My 72nd birthday):

Whatever you wish for, I want to give you…
Whatever your dreams are,
I want to help make them come true…
Whatever you're hoping
The years ahead will bring
I want to walk beside you
Along the way, cherishing
Our life together—
Because you are a wonderful husband,
Because I'm proud to be your wife
And because I love you
With all my heart.

I Love you my babe

Jan

From my journal on July 22, 2012. Jan was beginning to have some significant health and family challenges:

"Jan and I had a very meaningful conversation this morning. She said to me: "I'm feeling depressed. I'll be 71 years old in six days. I'm struggling with health issues. I worry every day about my family. Sometimes I wonder why I'm still here. In a strange way, I think we both miss the daily regimen of having something to do, even if it's going to the hospital every day for two weeks to get my IVs. It gave us a purpose to get up in the morning. I looked forward to seeing the IV nurses every day. I had worked with a couple of them when I was a nurse at the hospital. We were always happy to see each other. They gave me some positive strokes and I needed them. Now it's over. People need something positive to look forward to, even if it's going in for a treatment."

I told her that I felt the same way. "I'm glad you understand," she said. Our talk seemed to bring us even closer together. Getting older, especially when you're not feeling well, is a definite challenge. One thing that we both agreed on today: we feel grateful to God that we have each other. At this challenging moment in our lives, that's a real blessing. Later tonight, as we snuggled together in bed, Jan whispered: "You're my hero. I'm so happy that God gave me you as my angel." I said that I appreciated the sentiment and that I felt the same way about her. I know God brought us together for many reasons. One of them is to be here for each other right now. Thank you, God, for my precious wife."

From the March 1 2013 Daily Reading in my book "Sitting With God:"

"Your dear wife comes home today after spending 17 long days in the hospital. This has been a trying and demanding time for both of you. Health challenges are hard at any age, but especially when you get older.

I want you both to rely on Me more. You may feel alone and isolated with your troubles. That is not the case. I AM always here. I AM present in the good times, but I AM available even more during the hard times. Turn to Me for comfort. Resist the notion of doing anything without My help. I have both human and spiritual resources that can restore both of you. Seek My assistance without delay. I will answer the call. Neither you or Jan need face anything alone.

As you all travel down unfamiliar roads, be alert for unexpected guides and angels along the way. I bring new and valuable resources into your lives. In the meantime, continue serving as a much-needed blessing to each other. Comfort one another during this difficult moment in your human journey. You are very fortunate to have each other. Use this priceless gift to reassure each other. Remember that I AM in the middle of every situation. I AM here now, hard at work and coordinating the efforts of everyone. Let the healing begin."

From my journal June 1, 2013—Jan had just completed a 24-day stay in the hospital and a rehabilitation facility. She had previously been hospitalized for 17 days in February:

"Jan and I had a long discussion today about what's next for us. We both agreed that we must make some serious decisions. My sweetie's health has deteriorated steadily over the past 12 months. When she went to the hospital in February, her weight had dropped to 74 pounds. I thought her days might be numbered. She was depressed, having trouble getting around and wouldn't eat. We made some progress in March and April, but then she began going downhill again in early May. This time she spent seven days in the hospital and 17 days in rehab. Her weight is back up to 90 pounds now, so at least we are over that hurdle. I've been Jan's caregiver since her health started declining in 2012, but she needs more help now. We talked whether it was time to think about assisted living for both of us. Knock on wood, I'm still doing OK for 76. Basically, it comes down to whether I can handle the additional load of doing more things for her. We were very honest about our feelings. Frankly, neither one of us likes the thought of being in an assisted living facility—or God forbid a nursing home. Assisted living (and there are some very nice ones) might be OK if a person is alone or without family help. The thing is, Jan is not alone. She's got me. If I am physically and mentally able, I want to take care of her. Being her caregiver so far has been more of an honor than a duty. We decided that, as long as I am able, I'm her guy."

Thankfully, I was able to continue fulfilling my caregiver role until Jan transitioned on February 28, 2017. It was the greatest honor and privilege of my life.

From a certificate Jan and I received at the "Recommitment Ceremony" at Unity Christ Church on February 14, 2014:

"Renewal of Vows"

This to certify that on Valentine's Day, February 14, 2014 Allen and Jan Liles Renewed their vows during a ceremony at Unity Christ Church, Golden Valley, Minnesota. (signed) Reverend Pat Williamson

Excerpts from my journal on that day:

(Before the ceremony): "Valentine's Day, 2014, the day we plan to renew our marriage vows at Unity Christ Church. It is a few months ahead of the actual date, but the opportunity presented itself and we decided to go for it. This year marks our 20th anniversary, so the timing seemed appropriate. Also, after surviving the past 12 months with Jan's health, we deserve a celebration."

From my journal after the ceremony:

"We were welcomed warmly tonight by everyone. Pat Williamson, the church's senior minister and my successor here, was especially friendly. Pat is doing a great job since he took over from me in 2006. The congregation is lucky to have him. There were 19 couples who showed up tonight to get their vows renewed. Afterwards, instead of sticking around for refreshments, we stopped at the Lunds store near our place and picked up a pizza. We had our own 20th anniversary celebration dinner in front of our TV with some nice snuggling later in bed. Jan and I are so fortunate to have each other. All in all, it was a nice and meaningful evening. Maybe we'll do it again sometime."

From my journal on November 12, 2014 in which I wrote about a dream I had the night before and its possible meaning:

"I had quite an amazing dream overnight. It truly got my attention. In the dream, I was being chased by a large and threatening tiger. I tried everything to escape the angry beast. I ran in and out of several doors, but the tiger kept right on my heels. There was also a woman running beside me. She was trying to help me avoid the tiger's clutches. Finally, the angry animal cornered me. I thought: "I'm a goner." However, the tiger had grown tired from chasing me. He collapsed at my feet in exhaustion. The loyal woman, rather than using the downed tiger as an excuse to escape, kneeled next to the beast. She put her hands on him, as if to restrain the animal from getting up and devouring both of us. The tiger just lay there subdued, too worn out to turn on the woman or me. I felt completely safe from his jaws. Together, the woman and I had been delivered from imminent destruction. I couldn't help but wonder if the woman was Jan, my precious wife. I got it that the woman in the dream did not desert me at a bad time. She stayed right with me, even though the threatening animal could have destroyed either or both of us. She was loyal to me despite the great danger to herself. I believe the dream was a commentary on our marriage. Jan would never leave me alone or abandoned. She would be loyal to me until the end, even if her own life was at risk. That's just one of the many reasons I feel blessed by being her loving husband. Thank you, sweetheart. I know I can depend on you, no matter what."

From the back cover of "Because You Matter," an anti-bullying children's book authored by my sweetheart. Jan and I visited schools in Minneapolis, St. Paul, Bloomington and Eden Prairie to read the book for 1st through 5th graders. They all loved the unique story and meeting a real live author. One precious little girl told Jan: "I can't believe you're an author—and you're still alive!"

BECAUSE YOU MATTER

"There is trouble at the Countryside Zoo and Harriet Hummingbird is out to investigate. When she finds her dear friends at the zoo feeling down about themselves after being bullied by a gang of weasels, Harriet takes some action. She reassures each animal of their unique beauty and goodness. Then Harriet rallies her bird friends to craft a solution everyone will love.

Because You Matter addresses two all-too-common issue facing young children today, low self-esteem and hurtful teasing. Through this simple but delightful story comes a message of acceptance and celebration—and important truth that "You Matter! You Really Really do!"

Jan Carmen Liles is a graduate of Coach University and practices as a Personal Life Coach. She is a former health care professional and published author. Jan's grandchildren make her hear sing. She hopes to reach out to children all over the world by publishing her books in many languages. Jan wants to validate the unique beauty and goodness of children everywhere."

Jan's Last Days

Selected journal entries from the days before Jan's passing:

February 22—"Jan was on the 2nd floor of Methodist Hospital today getting an MRI from 3 p.m. to 4:15 p.m. She was supposed to do the procedure three days from now, but a big snowstorm is headed for the Twin Cities. Ah, winter in Minnesota. Luckily, she called the hospital this morning and they were able to work her in this afternoon. She was getting around a little better today, so we stopped afterward for an early dinner at the Good Earth in the Galleria. Thankfully, the days are getting longer so we got back to the apartment before dark. Jan's youngest daughter Danielle called this evening and they had a good conversation. Jan loves talking about the grandkids. Her eyes just light up."

February 23—"Today was a milestone of huge proportions! Jan gave herself a shower and hair wash for the first time in nearly four years! I have been happy to do that for her since she left the hospital back in May, 2013. In fact, she says I'm quite good at it. But, if she is well enough to do it herself, that's great! I'm proud of her! It could be a real confidence builder!"

February 24—"Jan received a call from her son Shawn in Duluth. They talked for more than hour, the longest conversation they've had in years. He rarely calls, so this is always a huge thing for her. Shawn will turn 56 in August. I'm so glad he thought to call his mom. Sons and daughters don't realize how parents long for communications from their children. I don't care if "kids" are 16 or 56, it's always important. For some reason, he must have thought it was important to talk with his mom today. She just glowed afterward. I hope it's not long before he calls again. I know she feels the same way."

February 26—"I made Jan some breakfast and then headed out for a few errands. When I got back, she was playing "Words with Friends" on the computer. The last I heard, she has three separate games going now. I don't play her any more. I could never beat her. She is good at "Words" as she was at Scrabble—and that's saying a lot. We spent tonight watching the Academy Awards and we both made it all the way to the end. They had a real snafu when somebody announced the wrong winner for best picture. It created quite a mess."

From my journal on February 28, 2017, the evening that I unexpectedly lost my dear wife:

"As I write these sad words just before midnight, I have lost my sweetheart. It was very unexpected. She wasn't feeling well tonight, so she retired early at 7 p.m. I tried to make her as comfortable as possible. Then, I returned to the living room where I was watching the State of the Union address. I checked on her briefly at 8 p.m. and she seemed OK. Then, I put her night pills together just before 9 p.m. and headed back to the bedroom. The minute I got close to the bed, I could tell something was wrong. I called out to her. No response. I reached over and gave her a gentle shake. Still no response. I began to panic. I shook her harder. Nothing. I put my face close to hers. I tried to open her mouth, but it slammed shut again. I ran to the telephone and called "911". I told the operator "My wife is unresponsive. Please send somebody now!" The operator asked if Jan was breathing. I replied that I couldn't tell. She instructed me to take her off the bed and place her flat on the floor. Then, the 911 operator talked me through how to give chest compressions. She had me count 1, 2, 3, 4, 5 with her. I did this for about three or four minutes. Still no response. I told the operator "I think she's gone". Suddenly, a lot of people began to arrive. The police and paramedics took over. We are only a couple of miles from the main Bloomington police station and a fire station is even closer. They had brought all sorts of life saving equipment. There were at least a dozen people in our bedroom. One of the police officers asked if I would wait outside of the bedroom while they worked on her. I went and sat at our kitchen table. I closed my eyes. I swear that my mind conjured up a vision of Jan in Heaven with her sister Marlene. They were laughing and dancing around. After about 45 minutes, one of the police officers came to me and said "I'm sorry for your loss. We did everything possible, but she didn't make it. I think it might have been a sudden cardiac arrest. She probably didn't suffer.""

From the posting on my Facebook page on March 1, 2017, the morning after I lost Jan:

"It is with a profound sense of loss that I must share some sad news this morning. Last night I lost my sweet dear wife Jan Carmen Liles. She passed unexpectedly around 8:30 p.m. from a cardiac arrest. She was my wonderful wife for nearly 23 years. Jan was also my best friend and devoted partner in ministry. She was many other things as well: a mother to three adult children (Shawn, Jamie and Danielle), a "Grammy" to Jack, Harry and Emme, a sister to three dearly departed siblings (Marlo, Jimmy and Marlene), a daughter to her late parents (Jim and Ethel), an aunt to Ron, Rhonda, Rick, Puddy, and Sam, and a devoted friend to so many in the medical and caring professions. She was also the author of the anti-bullying book BECAUSE YOU MATTER. Most of all, she was my sweetheart Jannie. I may have lost her physical presence last night, but the gifts she gave me in memory will live on forever. Goodnight, my darling, but not goodbye."

From a posting on my Facebook page March 5, 2017:

"We will celebrate the life of my dear wife Jan Carmen Liles next Friday (March 10) at 2 p.m. in the chapel of The Cremation Society of Minnesota, located at 7110 France Avenue in Edina. A visitation is planned from 1-2 p.m. Refreshments will be served following the service. Rev. Pat Williamson, senior minister at Unity of Minneapolis, will officiate. Please join us if possible to bid an earthly goodbye to a truly wonderful person. Thank you to everyone for your heartful expressions pf sympathy and remembrances of Jan. They have been so comforting to me, her family and everyone who knew and loved her."

From Jan's Memorial Service program—Memories of Grammy from her three beloved grandchildren:

"Some of my fondest memories are the times we played 'circus' at our house. I was seven years old and still remember it clearly to this day. I love you Grammy."

Jack

"I still remember the smell of your home. I will always associate it with my Grammy. She was the sweetest and best Grammy in the world. I have learned from your display of strength and humility throughout our time together and I will never forget you. I love you so much."

Harry

"You filled my heart with contagious joy. You never failed to put a smile on my face. I will always think of you as my one and only Grammy, that nobody can ever replace."

Emme

From the program distributed at Jan's Memorial Service on March 10, 2017 at the Cremation Society of Minnesota:

"Jan was born in Bagley, MN on July 28, 1941. She moved to Duluth at an early age and was raised in her beloved city on the shores of Lake Superior. She was a graduate of Central High School and completed her nurse's training in Duluth. As a high school senior, she was crowned Helen of Troy. Jan was a loving wife, mother, grandmother, aunt, friend, author, prayer associate and medical professional. She will be missed by everyone that experienced her gentle, loving and warm demeanor.

Jan was married to Rev. Allen C. Liles for the past 23 years. Together, they served as partners in ministry for Unity churches in Arizona and Minnesota.

During her medical career, Jan was a medical supervisor at the Park Nicollet Clinic in Saint Louis Park. Before that assignment, she was employed as a nurse at nearby Methodist Hospital in the pediatrics area.

Jan was a graduate of Coach University and practiced as a Life Coach while she and Allen were living in Lees Summit, MO. While in Missouri, she also served as an associate in the Silent Unity prayer ministry. Jan is the author of BECAUSE YOU MATTER, an anti-bullying book for elementary school students.

Jan is survived by her adoring husband Allen, daughters Danielle Miles (Darren) and Jamie Soland and son Shawn, and her three beloved grandchildren Jack Miles, Harry Miles, and Emme Miles.

From sympathy cards received after Jan's passing:

Dear Rev. Allen,

You're in my thoughts in the loss of your dear and beloved Jan. I was very sorry to hear of her passing and extend my deepest sympathy to you and your family. To me, you and Jan were the model of a devoted couple. I recall you spoke about being her caregiver. That is such sacred work and a true demonstration of love and commitment. It was a privilege to know both Jan and you.

Katherine R.

Rev. Liles,

I am forever grateful to Jan for her sharing you with our congregation. The beauty and light that showed brilliantly when you two were together is still an inspiration and blessing for me. I hope you take comfort in the magnificent memory of the love and joy you shared together.

Chris T.

Dear Al,

I don't have words strong enough or good enough to express my sadness on this day. I am comforted by many years and countless memories of my loving friendship with Jan. Her love for you and her family was a bright light for all. I am picturing her today dancing in eternity—in bright red heels.

Sharon V.

Dear Allen,

You and Jan, on her continued journey, are in my heart and prayers. I know that her spirit is still right where you are. I'm thankful that you and Jan have been in my life. The memory of you both will always be there.

Raymond T.

Allen: I know how much you and Jan meant to each other. She was such a radiant light. Jan will always be with us. I am crying with you.

Lindy L.

Thoughts From The Heart

A LETTER TO MY WIFE

Dearest Jannie,

I miss you so much. I can't believe you're gone. I keep expecting to hear you calling out "Babe! Babe!" from the next room. It's hard getting used to the silence in the apartment. I don't like it. I feel lost without you. I loved being your caregiver these past few years. It was the greatest honor of my entire life. I feel as though I've not only lost you but also my purpose—taking care of you. It truly deepened the love I have for you. I also think the caregiving strengthened what was already a great marriage. I know it made me a better man. Thank you for that. I hope I did a good job taking care of you.

I know you haven't felt well for the past few years. I've seen you struggling to get around with your walker, especially when we've had to go out for doctor's appointments and family gatherings. You've shown lots of courage despite your pain. I knew you were suffering. But I understand how much you still wanted to participate in everything, especially with the grandkids. They are going to really miss their "Grammy." As will I.

In my meditations each morning now, God tells me that you are pain free and moving around easily in Heaven. I hope that's the case. It makes losing you a tiny bit less painful, but only a little bit. I miss you most in the evening, after the sun goes down. It gets dark in my heart then and I feel the pain of your loss even more. It's hard climbing into our soft bed and not having you next to me. I miss our snuggling every night when I would put my arms around you and hold you close. Your pillow is having to substitute for you now. I press it tight against me. Sometimes when I wake up in the morning, I'm still clinging to it.

There will never be another you. I love you, My sweet Babe.

Your forever hubby.

Al

THE FOREVER PENNIES

At first, I hardly noticed them
My grieving mind was numb
from your unforeseen departure
This ancient brain, barely awake,
Plodded along in small half steps
Yet, soon I did start wondering
Where were these coins coming from?
Shiny pennies, tarnished pennies,
Old, scuffed and worn-out pennies
What angel or devil was strewing
This legion of pennies at my doorstep
Of course, I picked them up and
Tossed them into a drawer so that
They could commiserate together
Then I realized that these little
Pennies from Heaven
Were no accident at all, never were
They were your greeting to me
I'm still here, My Babe
I'm still here

Allen C. Liles

THE DAY WE MET

June 13, 1980

The first day we met was in a city by a river
No, not the mighty Mississippi
That was your river in Minnesota
I didn't really have a river in Texas
Instead we met near the Detroit River
Of all places. Can you believe it?
You were from Duluth, I was from Dallas
And we met in Detroit. Strange!
It was at a March of Dimes convention
You had chaired a successful Superwalk
And won a free trip to the Motor City
I was there on behalf of my company
Who was MOD's big corporate sponsor
I was also there to introduce a great man
Jonas Salk
He had discovered the Salk polio vaccine
Exactly 25 years before
What an honor for me!
Anyway, I met you for the first time
At the opening reception
I remember thinking how pretty you were
A blue-eyed beauty with a typical Norwegian look
But that's not what connected us
We started talking about our respective sons
They were both 18 and having the same challenges
That chat bonded us almost from the beginning
I had never met someone that shared so easily
 It was honest, open and refreshing
You began building your home in my heart then
And every day thereafter you added another touch
Was I lucky to meet you? Absolutely!
Did God bring us together? I think so
Were you the greatest thing that ever happened
In my life? Without a doubt!
Thank you, Babe
For winning that trip to Detroit

TO MY WONDERFUL WIFE

*It was in a city by the river
In shyness I approached you
And extended an invitation
That you accepted
To have a friendly lunch
With a stranger from Texas
It was the luckiest Friday 13th
In my life bar none
We dined, talked and
Then we parted
Well maybe not so fast
We met again by chance
That same evening
Fate? Could be
We ended up talking again
And then dancing
Magic? No doubt
It was the great beginning
That never ended*

—Your adoring hubby

WHAT YOU GAVE ME

You gave me so many gifts

You gave me permission, to express my feelings

You gave me loyalty, something I craved

You gave me warmth, when my world became chilled

You gave me understanding, when I didn't understand myself

You gave me strength, anytime my knees buckled

You gave me wisdom, from a higher perspective

You gave me spirituality, which awakened my spirit

You gave me love, whether I deserved it or not

You gave me compassion, what I cried out for

You gave me devotion, while teaching me its meaning

You gave me pride, in you and in myself

You gave me honesty, hard to accept but always crucial

You gave me forgiveness, the currency of love

You gave me fidelity, the only road you know

You gave me friendship, the love beyond love

You gave me God, the one thing I needed most

You gave me you, my dearest wife

THE HOPE OF GLORY

In wondrous view the sky above reveals a lustrous promise

That beyond our sight lies a broader world yet unseen

A timeless Kingdom graced by eternal beauty

Where our loved ones still play their unique melodies

If we strain forward in strong intent a sound does emerge

The hope of glory beckons through its heavenly voice

Rising now from within our soul's innermost repose

It bids us hear with sacred ear the closeness that awaits us

Despite an earthly separation so void of sight and form

If we but trust God's boundless Grace we find the face

Of those lost but awaiting us among the damp ashes of memory

"We're here!" they shout in unison hoping for our belief
that death cannot shut the steel door saying "nevermore"

"If you will but believe" they firmly plead in common thread

"The spiritual link from us to you remains ever strong"

"We are never gone from you in spirit," their caring words soar

"Reach out in love and we pour forth" they call once more

We extend our open hands and hearts while Heaven's link affirms

Their once proud glory retained, the bond of love again reclaimed

Photos

The Forever Penny

ABOUT THE AUTHOR

Rev. Allen C. Liles is a graduate of Baylor University in Waco, TX and the Unity School of Religious Studies in Unity Village, MO. Before being ordained as a non-denominational minister, he served as vice-president of public relations for the 7-Eleven Stores, and communications manager for the McLane Company. He was also Senior Director of Outreach for the Unity School of Christianity at Unity Village, as well as serving Unity Churches in Leavenworth KS, Sun City AZ, Minneapolis, MN, Bloomington, MN and Oakdale, MN.

Books by Allen C. Liles:

Oh Thank Heaven! The Story of the Southland Corporation
Sitting with God/Meditating for God's Divine Guidance

E-books:

The 12 Promises of Heaven/ http://smashwords.com/books/view/444920
Friends of Jesus/ http://smashwords.com/books/view/455617
E-Spiritual Rehab/ http://smashwords.com/books/view/481978
The Book of Celeste/ http://smashwords.com/books/view/593856
The Book of Floyd/ http://smashwords.com/books/view/615914
The Book of Ethan/ http://smashwords.com/books/view/647665

Audio/CD

The Peaceful Driver/Steering Clear of Road Rage/Unity

Op-Ed articles:

The New York Times—August 16, 1988
Barron's Financial Weekly—January, 1992
The Chicago Tribune—February, 1989
The Minneapolis Star Tribune-- July, 1993 and April, 2014
Unity Magazine—1995-2001

www.ingramcontent.com/pod-product-compliance
Lightning Source LLC
Chambersburg PA
CBHW060500240426
43661CB00006B/861